First Certificate
PASSKEY

Student's Book

NICK KENNY

MACMILLAN
HEINEMANN
English Language Teaching

Contents Map

Vocabulary	Language Focus	Help Sections	Exam Focus

UNIT SEVEN *Food for thought* 92

Vocabulary	Language Focus	Help Sections	Exam Focus

Food
Cooking verbs
Menus
	Gerund/Infinitive
	Too/Enough
	Zero/First conditionals
	Preferences
	If/Unless
	Future time 2: Intentions,
	  arrangements, decisions
	Relative clauses
	Comparisons
	Pronunciation: Vowel sounds
		Help with talking about a picture	**Paper 1:** Multiple choice; Reading for specific information;
			  Multiple matching
			Paper 2: Paragraph writing; Writing an article
			Paper 3: Cloze text; Error correction
			Paper 4: Multiple choice; Short extracts; Listening for specific
			  information; Multiple matching
			Paper 5: Talking about photographs; Expressing opinions;
			  Expressing preferences; Problem solving
			Exam practice

UNIT EIGHT *High-tech horizons* 109

Vocabulary	Language Focus	Help Sections	Exam Focus

Inventions and discoveries
Verbs to describe a process
Word formation – nouns
  from verbs
	Passive
	Agents
	Predictions – *Will/Going to*
	Agreeing and disagreeing: *So/Nor*
	Conditionals 2
	Pronunciation: /h/
		Help with gapped texts
		Help with word formation 2
		Help with writing – giving opinions
			Paper 1: Reading for specific information; Gapped text;
			  Multiple matching; Reading for main points
			Paper 2: Writing a report
			Paper 3: Key word transformations
			Paper 4: Matching information; Blank filling; Note-taking;
			  Multiple choice ; Short extracts
			Paper 5: Talking about photographs; Expressing opinions
			Exam practice

UNIT NINE *Working out* 132

Vocabulary	Language Focus	Help Sections	Exam Focus

Lifestyles
Electrical appliances
Word formation
Illness and health
Nouns/verbs from adjectives
	Present perfect continuous
	Regrets
	Conditionals 3
	Pronunciation: Word stress and
	  th sounds
		Help with speaking – giving opinions	**Paper 1:** Multiple matching; Reading for specific information;
			  Reading for main points; Multiple choice; Gapped text
			Paper 2: Writing a report
			Paper 3: Key word transformations; Cloze text
			Paper 4: Short extracts; Note-taking; Matching information;
			  Multiple matching
			Paper 5: Talking about photographs; Expressing opinions;
			  Expressing feelings
			Exam practice

UNIT TEN *It's a bargain* 151

Vocabulary	Language Focus	Help Sections	Exam Focus

Shopping
Words connected with money
  and trade
	Obligations
	Make, let, allow
	Wishes
	Complaints
	Pronunciation: Word linking
		Help with writing a transactional
		letter
			Paper 1: Multiple choice; Multiple matching; Gapped text
			Paper 2: Writing a transactional letter
			Paper 3: Key word transformations
			Paper 4: Note-taking; Short extracts; Multiple matching
			Paper 5: Talking about photographs; Solving a problem;
			  Expressing opinions
			Exam practice

UNIT ELEVEN *Our world* 168

Vocabulary	Language Focus	Help Sections	Exam Focus

Prepositions
Parts of a car
	Reported Speech
	Impersonal Passive
	Reporting verbs
	It's time
	Pronunciation: Shifting stress
	  and word stress
	Complaints
			Paper 1: Reading for specific information; Multiple choice;
			Paper 2: Writing a discursive composition; Writing a report
			Paper 3: Open cloze; Key word transformations
			Paper 4: Short extracts; Note-taking; Multiple matching;
			  Multiple choice
			Paper 5: Talking about photographs; Expressing opinions
			Exam practice

UNIT TWELVE *Finishing touches* 187

Vocabulary	Language Focus	Help Sections	Exam Focus

Word formation
Alone and *lonely*
Pets
Biographies
Relationships
	Review of tenses
	Question tags
	Future in the past
	Pronunciation: Contractions
	Uses of *do*
			Paper 1: Multiple matching; Reading for specific information;
			  Multiple choice
			Paper 2: Writing a transactional letter; Writing an article
			Paper 3: Word formation; Error correction; Open cloze
			Paper 4: Note-taking; Multiple matching; Short extracts;
			  Listening for specific information; Blank filling
			Paper 5: Giving personal information; Expressing opinions;
			  Talking about photographs
			Exam practice

Reference material
- Multi-word verb review
- Grammar Reference
- Wordlist

Macmillan Education
Between Towns Road, Oxford OX4 3PP
A division of Macmillan Publishers Limited
Companies and representatives throughout the world

ISBN-10 : 0 435 24489 2
ISBN-13 : 978 0 435 24489 7

ISBN-10 : 0 435 24498 1
ISBN-13 : 978 0 435 24498 9 (Greek Edition)

Text © Nick Kenny 1996
Design and illustration © Macmillan Publishers Limited
1998

Heinemann is a trademark of Harcourt Education, used under licence

Designed by Glynis Edwards

The author would like to thank all students and colleagues from the British Council, Milan, the International Language Academy, Cambridge, and the Cambridge Office, who have provided a source of inspiration over the years. Special thanks are due to Beth Weighill, Barbara Lewis, Margaret Twelves, and Jane Barnes for their help and advice, and particularly to my editors, Jill Florent and Xanthe Sturt Taylor.

The publishers would like to thank Emily Vivas, James Roy, Joanne Hazapi and Dave Briggs.

We would like to thank the following for permission to reproduce copyright material:
BBC Music magazine for 'When your discs start to slip' by Barry Fox, p110; Joyce Bond for 'Dogsbody' advertisement, p34; City Life for 'Christmas Presents' by Nayaba Aghedo and Aviva Dautch, p164; Nicky Dupays for 'Play It Safe' artwork in Radio Times, p136; Michele Elliott for 'Modern Manners' in Family Circle magazine, pp40/46; Emap Elan Limited for extract from 'Easy Ways to Beat a Cold' by Leon Chaitow in Here's Health magazine, p143; Esquire magazine for 'Drastic Plastic' by Joseph O'Connor, p160; Evening Standard for 'Head bans mobile phones in classroom' by David Taylor, p119; Ewan MacNaughton Associates for 'Jenga', p62; and 'Revolution that erupted from two volcanoes' by Adrian Berry, p178; 'Anti-fur group to bury 5,000 coats', p183; 'Gory Riddle of Wolfman' by Graham Bell, p54; 'High Heel Freak - Gloria Hunniford' by Jill Todd, p153; and 'Are you safe to go out without using a smog mask?' by Cathy Scott-Clark, p169; John Farley for 'The Marathon Man' in The Lady, p134; The Flora Project for text from their booklet 'Eating for a Healthy Heart', p93; Friends of the Earth for extracts from 'Help us stop this destruction', p174; The Guardian for 'Road to Freedom' by Berry Ritchie from Travel (World Tour) section, p82; and 'The Chips Are Down for Fast-food Wrappers' by Haydn Price, p180; Home Office for extracts from 'Practical Ways to Crack Crime - The Handbook', pp48 and 51; Independent Newspaper Publishing PLC for 'Keeping fit in private gains wider audience' by Roger Tredre, p136; 'Older Than Aztecs', p105; 'A long, lonely summer' by Mike Fielding, p205; and 'Where did you get that?' by Danny Worters, p191; IPC Magazines for 'Hands Down for Fingerprinting' by Lori Reid in Family Circle magazine, pp5/6; 'What can we do now, Mum?' by Judy Williams, p77; 'When you've been burgled' by Margaret Edwards, p50; 'When your body goes haywire' by Julie-Anne Ryan, p144; and 'Parachuting changed my life' by Su Woods in Living magazine, p197; Jo Knowsley for 'How henna gets under the skin' in The Sunday Telegraph, p9; Lamb Publishing for 'Horoscopes' by Jane Sunderland in Townswomen, p188; and 'Balloons Away!' by Margaret Drinkwater, p87; Money magazine for Trends article by Debbie Kent, p116; the National Magazine Company for 'Foreign Exchange' by Alison Bruce in House Beautiful, p29; Peters Fraser & Dunlop Group for extract from 'Long Live the Queen' by Ruth Rendell in Good Housekeeping magazine, p192; Radio Times for 'Fashion's Victim' by Nicki Household, p71; Redwood Publishing for extract from 'Chocolate tasting is like wine tasting - you don't swallow' interview with Sandy Collyer by Candida Crewe - Marks & Spencer Magazine, p17/18; Sainsbury's for extracts from 'Sainsbury's Living Today' leaflets, p96/124; JW Spear & Sons plc for photograph of 'Scrabble', p60; Sugar magazine for 'Models in the making' by Marina Gask, p23; and 'Is your friend hard work?' by Rosalyn Chissick, p198; Tesco for text from MultiSaver leaflet, p155; Mrs Margaret Twelves for 'Scrabble Activity', p61; UCLES for sample answer sheets © UCLES/K&J p209/210.

The author and publishers would like to thank the following for these illustrations:
Nancy Anderson, p101, p189; Kathy Baxendale, p4, p5, p7,.p19, p24, p26, p28, p33, p55, p70, p79, p114, p159, p200; Paul Beebee, p71, p77, p114, p120, p142, p191, p200; Joyce Bond, p34; Hardlines, p11, p26, p33, p47, p48, p52, p78, p84, p85, p86, p124, p157, p158, p159, p173; Rod Holt, p68, p117; Ed McLachlan, p141, p147, p166; Nicky Dupays, p136; Martin Sanders, p64, p109, p121, p133; Simon Stafford, p6, p22, p42; Rodney Sutton, p34, p56, p58, p133.

The author and publishers would like to thank the following for their kind permission to reproduce these photographs:
Ace Photo Agency p12, 171(t), 16, 25, 59, 109, 123, 128(r), 129(b,r), 132; The Anthony Blake Photo Library p92; Art Directors p29, 32, 151; Cephas p1(b), 12, 32, 59, 76, 97, 112, 129(t,l); Colorific p182(b); Karen Davies p9; Mary Evans Picture Library p 194; Express Newspapers p168, 169; Hutchison p 59, 170(t), 201(b,l); The Image Bank p16, 76, 175(b,m); Images Colour Library p25, 53(b,r),(t,r), 92, 97, 103, 129(b,l), 132; Impact p151 -Tom Webster p16 Peter Arkell p103(t,l) C Cormack p151, 175(b,l) Gary Parker p201(t,l); International Stock Exchange p 29; The Kobal Collection p195(l); Sue Mac Pherson/Oxford Games p 62; Madame Tussaud's p196; McCann Erickson p137; Network p 103; NHPA p 175(t),(b,r); Powerstock p 32, 82; Redwood Publishing p 17; Rex Features p23; Science Photo Library p 195(r); Tony Stone Images p12, 32, 43, 76, 80, 87, 109, 118, 128(l), 129(l), 132, 154, 170(m,b)(b), 171(m), 201(t,r),(b,r); Sygma p153; Telegraph Colour Library front cover, p32, 87, 97, 104, 171(b), 182(t); Unident p112; Viewfinder p1 (m), 32, 39, 53(b,l),(t,l), 87, 104, 109, 129(t,r), 132, 170(t,m).

Picture Research by Jane Taylor

Commissioned photography by Paul Freestone p1(t), 3, 8, 18, 19, 22, 39, 60, 77, 93, 94, 97, 120.

Printed in Thailand

2011 2010 2009 2008 2007 2006
27 26 25 24 23 22 21 20 19

Introduction

Dear Student

First Certificate PassKey is designed to help you prepare for all aspects of the First Certificate in English examination.

Each unit in the book includes a wide variety of exercises, which all develop the skills you need to pass the examination. You will also find a range of activities which help you revise the main grammar structures, increase your vocabulary, improve your reading and listening skills and develop confidence in listening, speaking and writing.

There are Help Sections throughout the book which give you advice on dealing with each type of question you find in the examination and tell you the best way to prepare.

At the end of each unit there are tests which give you practice in answering the type of questions included in the Use of English and Writing parts of the examination.

For further practice in multi-word verbs, unit summaries and extra practice exercises are provided at the end of the book.

You will also find a Reference Section at the end of the book with a summary of the important grammar points and lists of vocabulary including irregular verbs.

Below there is a more detailed description of the First Certificate examination.

I hope you enjoy using this book and are successful in the examination.

Good Luck!

The First Certificate in English Examination

More than 200,000 people take the First Certificate in English examination every year throughout the world. First Certificate assesses your general ability in English through tests of reading, writing, grammar, listening and speaking. The First Certificate in English examination was revised in December 1996.

What's in the revised FCE:

Paper 1 *Reading (1 hour and 15 minutes)*

- you answer 35 questions about four reading passages
- the passages are from authentic sources (e.g. from newspapers and magazines)
- there are matching and gap-fill exercises, as well as multiple choice questions
- the reading passages are quite long, and you need to use a range of reading skills to complete the tasks in the time allowed

Marking

For Paper 1 you have an answer sheet which you must mark with a pencil to show your answers. This is so that your answers can be checked by a computer. You can write on your question paper if you want to, but you must remember to copy all your answers onto the answer sheet before the end of the test – there is no extra time for this. There is an example of the answer sheet on page 209.

Paper 2 *Writing (1 hour and 30 minutes)*

- you write two answers, each of between 120 and 180 words
- there is one compulsory question where you are given some notes and are asked to write a letter

- you answer a second question from a choice of four, which can include an article or report as well as a story, letter, composition or an answer based on one of the background reading texts

Marking

After the examination your answer will be sent back to Cambridge and marked by an experienced examiner.

Paper 3 *Use of English (1 hour and 15 minutes)*

- there are five parts and you answer 65 questions about grammar and vocabulary

- the parts are: a gapped text with multiple choice questions, a gapped text where you write one word in each space, grammar transformation sentences, a text for error correction (find the extra word), a text with word formation exercises

Marking

For Paper 3, you have an answer sheet which you must mark with a pencil to show your answers. For some of the questions you must mark a letter (A, B, C or D), and for others you have to write a word or a short phrase. You can write on your question paper if you want to, but you must remember to copy all your answers onto the answer sheet before the end of the test – there is no extra time for this. There is an example of the answer sheet on pages 209–10.

Paper 4 *Listening (about 40 minutes)*

- there are four parts (each heard twice) and you answer 30 questions

- in Part 1 there are eight short listening passages, each with one multiple choice question. To help you, in this part only, the questions are recorded on the tape as well as printed on the question paper

- in Part 2 you must write notes to complete 10 questions based on a longer listening text

- in Part 3 you hear five short listening passages all about the same topic and complete matching questions

- in Part 4 there are seven multiple choice questions based on a longer listening passage

Marking

During the Listening test you must write down your answers on the question paper as you listen. At the end of the test you have five minutes to copy your answers onto an answer sheet. There is an example of the answer sheet on page 210.

Paper 5 *Speaking (about 15 minutes per pair of students)*

- the usual format is two students with two examiners – one examiner talks to the students, the other examiner just listens (in a few places there may be examinations with one student and one examiner, but you cannot choose to do the test in this way)

- you will be asked to talk about yourself and your everyday life, your family, hobbies, etc.; and also talk to your partner and discuss some photographs, solve a problem or give your opinions

Each of the five papers in the examination contributes a maximum of 40 marks to your final result. To pass the exam you need to score at least 120–125 marks out of a total of 200.

First impressions

Giving personal information

Louisa, Lars and Akemi have each written a short description of themselves as part of a pen-friend scheme organised by their teachers. Read the passages as quickly as possible and decide

1   who drives to work.

2   who has a long summer holiday.

3   who learns English at work.

4   who would make the most interesting pen-friend.

Tell your partner which one you chose and why.

My name's Louisa. I'm 19 years old and come from Bologna in Italy. I'm a student at the university, where I study Law. Most of my lectures are in the afternoon, so I usually get up late and study in the evenings. At weekends, I often go to the cinema with my friends in the winter, or to the seaside in the summer. My family has a house on the Adriatic coast, and we all go there every summer for two months. I'm very interested in environmental issues, and would like to meet students from other countries who share my views.

My name's Lars. I'm 26 years old and I come from Malmo in Sweden. I'm a trainee manager in a company which sells office equipment. I spend one week of each month in a different department so that I learn various aspects of the work. I generally spend at least one day per week out of the office as my job involves sales and marketing. My job's very interesting but rather tiring. I get up early each morning and drive ten miles to my office, but I still find the time to study English, because a teacher comes to the company twice a week. In my spare time I like to go skiing and I enjoy all water sports.

My name's Akemi. I'm 25 years old and I come from Tokyo in Japan. At the moment I'm living in Cambridge, where I'm a student of English at a language school. My interests are theatre, cinema and classical music, especially opera. In Japan I work in a large department store selling cosmetics. When I go home I hope to get a job using my English, maybe in a travel agency. My ambition is to travel all over Europe and learn another European language.

5 Now complete this table for each of them.

	Louisa	Lars	Akemi	You	Your partner
Age					
Nationality					
Occupation					
Interests					

SPEAKING 1
Exchanging personal information

1 Complete the information for you and your partner.

2 What questions did you ask your partner to get the information?
How _____ ? What _____ ?
Where _____ ? What _____ ?
Which grammatical tense did you use? Why?

3 Now ask the questions to as many people as possible in your group, and make a note of their replies. Compare with your partner.

4 Write a paragraph about yourself for the pen-friend scheme.

GRAMMAR 1
Present simple and continuous

Look at these examples of the use of the Present simple and continuous tenses. The two columns on the right tell you the grammatical tense used in the phrase and the time referred to.

	Tense	Time
States He is tall and thin He isn't American	Present simple	Always
Habits/routines She gets up early She's wearing jeans	Present simple Present continuous	Usually Now
Things which are always true The sun rises in the east The sun is rising	Present simple Present continuous	Always Now

Put a verb in these sentences in the correct tense.

1 Roland usually _____ a raincoat, but today he _____ an anorak instead.

2 Linda _____ at 8.00 am every day and _____ to work by car.

3 Frances never _____ high-heeled shoes, in fact she usually _____ sandals.

4 Matthew _____ in the centre of town but this week he _____ at his parents' house in the country.

5 Alex is a very reliable person, everybody _____ him.

6 Carol usually _____ to work on foot, but this morning it is raining so she _____ her car.

VOCABULARY 1
Clothes

1 Look around the room and make a list of all the articles of clothing that you can see.

2 Compare lists with a partner.

3 Add to the list some articles of clothing that you cannot see, but which people sometimes wear (maybe at another time of year).

4 Divide your list into 4 groups of words. You can decide how to divide them, but each group must have a title.

5 Show your groups to your partner and explain why you have grouped the articles in this way.

6 Look at these words. What type of words are they?

long	cotton
plain	thick
striped	high-heeled
leather	thin
woollen	short
long-sleeved	waterproof
tight-fitting	light
checked	heavy
short-sleeved	flat-heeled
silk	loose-fitting

7 Which of these words can be used to describe which clothes? Choose one article of clothing from your list to put after each adjective.

GRAMMAR 2
Order of adjectives

1 Look at these phrases:

a full-length red overcoat
a pair of red and white striped cotton socks
a loose-fitting black woollen pullover
a pair of brown leather shoes
a short-sleeved green cotton sweatshirt
a pair of white flat-heeled sandals
a plain blue cotton T-shirt

Now make similar phrases to describe articles of clothing that you can see.

2 What do you notice about the order of the adjectives?

3 Look at the four pictures below. Write one sentence describing the clothes worn by the person in each picture.

4 Link each of the expressions in the box to one of the pictures.

5 Write two more phrases to describe the people in the photographs.

a	in her early thirties	**f**	slim
b	in his late teens	**g**	heavily made-up
c	with short blond hair	**h**	well-dressed
d	with dark curly hair	**i**	casually-dressed
e	with short dark hair	**j**	of average height and build

▣ LISTENING 1
Describing people

1 Listen to the description of a woman the police would like to interview after a robbery. Is it one of the women in the pictures or not? Give your reasons.

2 Read this description of a woman the police would like to interview. Listen again and decide if it describes the same woman. Underline any parts which are different.

The woman is tall with short brown curly hair and brown eyes. She was wearing a long grey woollen overcoat and flat shoes, and was carrying a beige leather shoulder bag and an umbrella. She was described as being in her early thirties, and speaking with a Liverpool accent.

3 Write a similar description of another of the people in the photographs – or of one of your classmates.

4 Read your description to your partner or classmates. Can they identify the person?

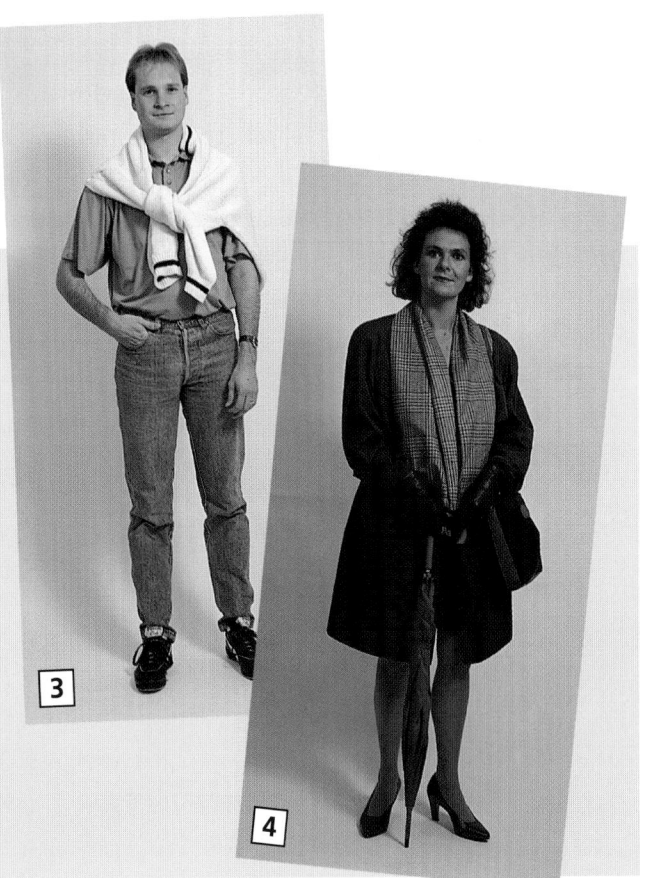

VOCABULARY 2
Wear/Dress

■ 1 Look at these examples.

> *How does he dress?*
> *What sort of clothes does she usually wear?*
> *What was he wearing yesterday?*
> *She usually wears a skirt and jumper.*
> *She usually wears a dress.*
> *Was she dressed in a skirt or trousers?*

1 What is the difference between *clothes* and *dresses*?

2 What is the difference between *to wear* and *to dress*?

■ 2 Using one word only, put the correct form of either *wear* or *dress* in each of the spaces.

1 He is _____ a blue jacket.

2 She was _____ a light summer dress.

3 He always _____ very well on these occasions.

4 This coat is very _____ . I need a new one.

5 That _____ is too short for her.

6 He got up, _____ and went to work.

7 She always _____ her son in blue.

8 I don't like that _____ you're _____ .

9 She went to the party _____ as a clown.

10 He has to _____ a jacket and tie in the office.

LISTENING 2
Note-taking

■ 1 Discuss these questions with your partner.

1 Can you judge a person's character from what they look like?

2 What about faces? What type of person do you associate with

- large/small eyes?
- thin/full lips?
- a round/square face?

■ 2 You will hear a radio discussion about faces. Complete the notes with a word or short phrase.

<u>Round Face</u>	– Lazy
	– [____1____] attitude
<u>Square Face</u>	– [____2____] and reliable
<u>Rectangular Face</u>	– Lucky
	– Good leaders
	– [____3____]
<u>Large Ears</u>	– [____4____] and enthusiastic
<u>Sticking-out Ears</u>	– [____5____] and
	[____6____]
	– Difficult to get on with
<u>Big Eyes</u>	– [____7____]
<u>Thick Eyebrows</u>	– Good leaders
	– Strong and [____8____]
<u>Full Lips &</u> <u>Wide Smile</u>	– [____9____] charming and popular
<u>Large Full Nose</u>	– [____10____], artistic and
	[____11____]

VOCABULARY 3
Describing personality

1 Look at these words which are used to describe a person's character and decide whether they are positive or negative.

sensible	dull	reliable
amusing	stupid	cold
boring	trustworthy	practical
strong	charming	helpful
selfish	foolish	observant
intelligent	bossy	lively
silly	responsible	fussy
patient	sensitive	friendly
entertaining	careful	honest
nasty	lazy	independent

2 Which of them would you use to describe yourself?

3 Can you add some more adjectives to describe your character?

4 Which words can be made into the opposite by adding a prefix?

> **Examples:** reliable – **un**reliable
> patient – **im**patient

READING 2
Reading for specific information

1 Answer these questions with a partner.

1 Why are fingerprints important to the police?

2 How can you take your fingerprints?

3 Now read the text quickly to check your answers. Why are fingerprints important to hand analysts?

4 Now read more carefully and match the words from the text on the left (line numbers in brackets) with the meanings on the right.

whodunnits (2)	of which there is only one
convicted (3)	parts of circles in fingerprints
unwary (3)	proved to be guilty
whorls (8)	murder stories
swirls (8)	not aware of danger
unique (9)	complete circles in fingerprints
irrefutable (12)	that cannot be doubted
ascribe (14)	work out the meaning
decipher (17)	link to
smudging (25)	making unclear

FINGER PRINTING

Hands down for clues to your personality

1 You don't need to be a follower of whodunnits to know that a careless fingerprint has convicted many an unwary villain. But fingerprints can also tell the
5 interested observer a great deal about your personality. Hand analyst Lori Reid explains how to take your own fingerprints – and what the whorls and swirls mean.

FINGERPRINTS are unique: no two people,
10 not even identical twins, possess the same pattern. They are our very own personal signatures, our calling cards, irrefutable marks of our identity. However, hand analysts have been able to ascribe particular
15 characteristics to the six basic types of pattern of fingerprints.

FINGER patterns are hard to decipher just by looking, but taking a print of them is easy and makes the patterns stand out
20 clearly. Either use the traditional ink pad, or try lipstick or shoe polish. Press the fingertip onto the pad, or rub lightly with lipstick or polish, then press firmly onto a sheet of paper, rolling the fingertip from one side to
25 the other to prevent smudging.

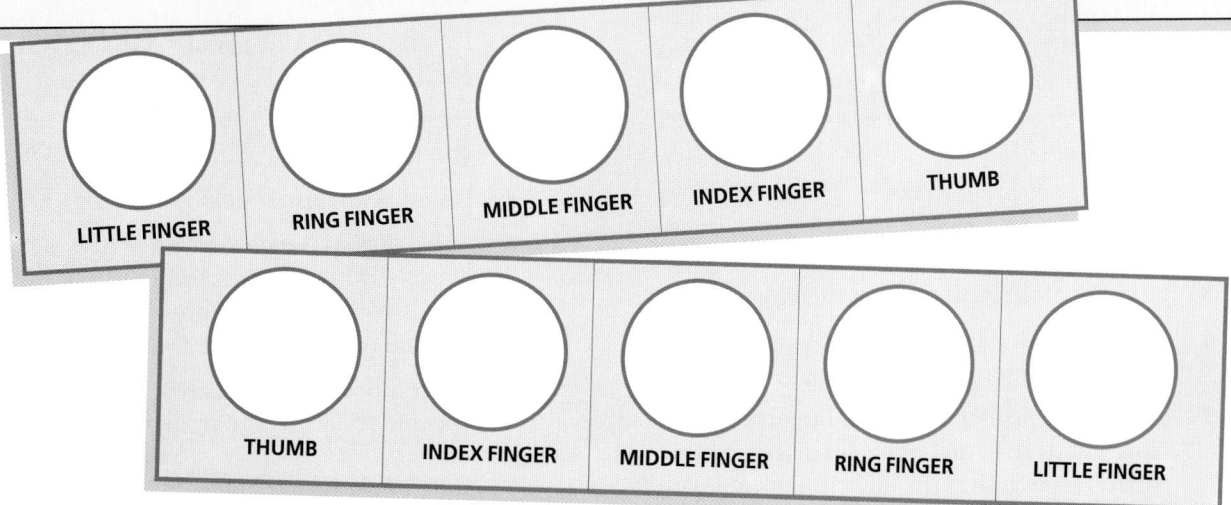

LITTLE FINGER RING FINGER MIDDLE FINGER INDEX FINGER THUMB

THUMB INDEX FINGER MIDDLE FINGER RING FINGER LITTLE FINGER

■**2** Decide who is student A and who is student B. Read your part of
the text and answer the questions below.

STUDENT A

THE WHORL

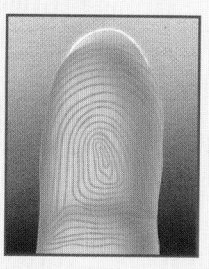

1 The whorl is the most individual of all
the patterns. It denotes a fixed, rather
inflexible attitude. Whorl owners hate
anyone telling them what to do. On the
5 ring finger it shows an artistic eye and
creative appreciation. On the little
finger it denotes quiet, deep thinkers.

People with a majority of whorls tend to
be slow to respond, and find it difficult to change their views and
10 opinions. This is because 'whorled' types need time to process
information; they need to think over and consider their answers.

THE COMPOSITE

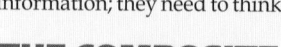

This shows an ability to appreciate all
points of view and in any occupation
where it is necessary to understand a
15 situation from all its angles – a judge,
lawyer, or teacher, for example – this
pattern is an advantage.

But when it comes to personal decision-
making, the composite can be a definite
20 drawback. Because people with this pattern spend so long
considering the alternatives, weighing up the pros and cons,
analysing their problems from every aspect, they tend to
complicate the matter and end up totally confused, unsure
which way to turn or which road to take.

STUDENT B

THE ARCH

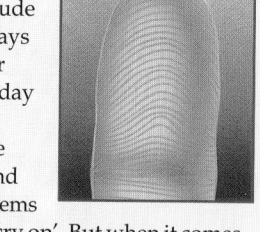

25 Arches denote a practical, sensible attitude
to life. People with this pattern are always
ready to help others. Firm realists, their
conversation is usually based on everyday
subjects or concrete, material topics.
30 They have plenty of common sense, are
thoroughly trustworthy and reliable and
as such tend to attract people with problems
who find them excellent 'shoulders to cry on'. But when it comes
to their own problems, they find it very difficult to put their
35 deeper feelings into words and are often in danger of repressing
their emotions.

THE LOOP

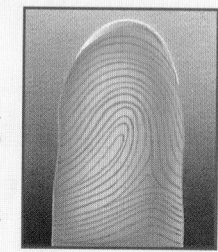

Loops represent flexible, adaptable and
versatile individuals. Loop owners are
open-minded and tolerant in character and
40 they need a large variety of interests to keep
them excited and stimulated throughout
their everyday lives. They need a constant
change of activities and they thrive on new
challenges and opportunities.

45 Loop owners make excellent communicators and are at their
best when they're working or dealing with other people. Any
environment where there is a free exchange of news, views and
ideas, suits them best. The loop is the mark of creativity. It indicates
an open, amenable approach and, above all, a love of new ideas.

---

1 Underline the words (adjectives and nouns) in
the text which best describe the personality of
the people with these fingerprints.

2 What other adjectives could you use to describe
such people? Choose from those in the box.

sociable	realistic	helpful
independent	reserved	religious
communicative	thoughtful	creative
unemotional	understanding	analytical
lucky	indecisive	adventurous
enthusiastic	imaginative	idealistic
lazy	fair	

3 Is it important which finger the patterns are on?

4 Now tell your partner(s) what you have found
out about fingerprints.

5 Look at (or print!) your own fingerprints. Decide
which patterns you have, and discuss with your
partner(s) whether the descriptions are true for
you.

🔊 PRONUNCIATION
Word stress

1 Look at the words in the box. How many
syllables are there in each word?

Example:
so/cia/ble

2 Listen to the words. Which syllable is stressed in
each word?

Example:
so/cia/ble

3 Listen again and repeat the words.

4 Look back at the part of the text which talks
about your own fingerprints. Underline all the
words with three or more syllables. Mark the
syllable which is stressed.

5 Remember when you are making lists of new
vocabulary always to mark the word stress.

🎧 LISTENING 3
Note-taking

You will hear someone giving a talk to a group of students about what to take with them on a walking holiday. Listen and complete these notes, made by one of the students, by putting a word or phrase in each of the numbered blanks.

Trip To Scotland

Travel:

To Scotland by ☐ 1

Travel in Scotland by ☐ 2

Accommodation: Staying in ☐ 3

Things to Take:

- Large rucksack for clothes.
- ☐ 4 *for lunch and study materials.*
- ☐ 5 *Waterproof coat with a* ☐ 6
- Plenty of ☐ 7
- Good thick ☐ 8
- Gloves - best type are ☐ 9
- Strong walking boots - ☐ 10 ones are best.
- ☐ 11 *- for the evenings.*
- Small ☐ 12
- Some glucose tablets or ☐ 13

GRAMMAR 3
In case

■1 Look at this phrase from the listening text.

Put your name and address inside and outside each piece of luggage in case it gets lost.

1 What time is referred to?
Which verb forms are used?

2 Compare these two sentences. What is the difference in meaning?

*Take a big anorak **in case** the weather is bad.*
*Take a big anorak **if** the weather is bad.*

3 Listen again and make a note of three phrases which include *in case*. Which tense follows *in case* in each example?

■2 Complete each of the following sentences in such a way that it means exactly the same as the sentence printed before it.

1 You should take a torch because the car might break down at night.
In case _____

2 Take an umbrella because it might rain.
In case _____

3 You should take a large bag because you might decide to do some shopping.
In case _____

4 Put some plasters in your bag because you might cut yourself.
In case _____

5 Pack an extra pair of warm socks because you might get cold.
In case _____

■3 Complete the second sentence so that it has a similar meaning to the first sentence. Use the word given and other words to complete each sentence. You must use between two and five words. Do not change the word given.

1 You should put a label on your luggage – it might get lost at the airport.
in
Put a label on your luggage _____ _____ at the airport.

2 Take an anorak in case the weather is bad.
because
You _____ the weather might be bad.

3 You should take a towel to the beach because you might want to go swimming.
in
Take a towel to the beach _____ _____ go swimming.

4 Take some bottled water with you in case you get thirsty.
because
You should take some bottled water with you _____ thirsty.

5 Take a book to read in case you have to wait a long time.
because
You should take a book to read _____ _____ wait a long time.

4 You are going on a day's walk across some rough hill country in Scotland in March. You are properly dressed for the trip and have a packed lunch with you.

1 Match the articles with the names in the box.

some rope	a water bottle
a box of matches	a tent
a first-aid kit	an umbrella
a sleeping bag	a penknife
a whistle	a rucksack
some chocolate	a map
an extra pullover	an extra pair of socks

2 You can only carry six of these articles with you. Decide which six are the most important to take and why. Discuss your choice with a partner.

3 Write six sentences using *in case* to justify your choice.

READING 3
Gapped text

1 Look at the photograph on page 9. Talk to your partner about what is happening and what you think about it.

2 Look through the article quickly and underline words which are:

- parts of the body
- parts of the world/nationalities
- names of people
- jobs

3 What do these times refer to in the article?

- three – six weeks
- an hour
- two days

4 Now read the article more carefully. As you read, decide which of the sentences or phrases **A–J** fits best in each of the spaces **1–9**. There is an example at the beginning (**0**).

A Aileen regularly travels around Britain for evening henna parties

B 'The growth in demand has been quite incredible' she says

C The initial effect is very dark and strange

D It is a reversal of henna's traditional role

E Suddenly the women have made up their minds

F The women gathered at Sarah's home agree

G It is 11 pm when everyone is dry enough to go home

H Aileen Marron set up Halawa Henna just over a year ago

I The specialist body painters have arrived

J They are paying to have their bodies painted with henna

1 **J**ANE has changed into her little black dress. She crosses and uncrosses her long legs nervously as she sips her Diet Coke. "Oh dear. I'm just not sure what I want to have done."

Karen, a photographer, and Lorraine, a financial consultant, sit
5 nearby on the sofa, looking through a book of curious and complicated Indian and Arabian designs. Sarah, who works for a Third World charity, studies the pictures as she opens a bottle of mineral water. "An Arabic armband," she says. "I don't know what my husband will think."

10 The women have gathered in Sarah's London home and are waiting for an evening of art with a difference to begin.
  0 **J** It will take between three and six weeks to wash off.

  1 They come from Halawa Henna in Manchester. It is time to make decisions. "I'm having a foot," says Jackie, a clothing
15 designer from Islington. "A whole foot?" Jane asks, surprised.
  2

Jane chooses a flowing Arabic pattern for one of her shoulders; Karen and Sarah choose floral armbands and Lynne selects Indian symbols above each ankle; Lorraine, soon to be married in church, selects an elaborate design of Indian hearts, choosing to
20 have them worked on her upper arm. "My wedding dress has three-quarter sleeves, so if my fiancé doesn't like it, at least it won't show."

  3 For centuries it has been used to decorate the hands and feet of Indian, Asian and Arabian women at festivals and
25 religious ceremonies. "The darker the henna, the more your mother-in-law likes you" is an old Eastern saying.

But it is only recently, with the arrival of body painting in Europe, that one of the world's oldest cosmetics has gained appeal in the West (henna has been found on the fingernails of Egyptian
30 mummies).

  4 She learnt the ancient art while growing up in Kuwait. When she came to live in Britain, she brought the craft with her and began experimenting on friends. She is surprised at the growing appeal of henna to British women.

35 **5** as she squeezes the dark green henna paste from a tube with a tip as fine as a needle. "We're getting requests from a broad range of people, it's no longer a specialist market."

  6 She is now also receiving invitations from throughout Europe to visit and share her skills. "We have a lot of interest
40 from people who are considering a tattoo and want to see how the design looks on the skin first," Aileen says. "Other people may have wanted a tattoo but then decide a temporary design is a lot better."

  7 The idea of a 'temporary tattoo' first appealed because
45 it seemed exotic and a little shocking. "I think most of us have secretly wanted to get a tattoo at some stage but simply didn't have the courage," says Jackie. Her toes have now been heavily

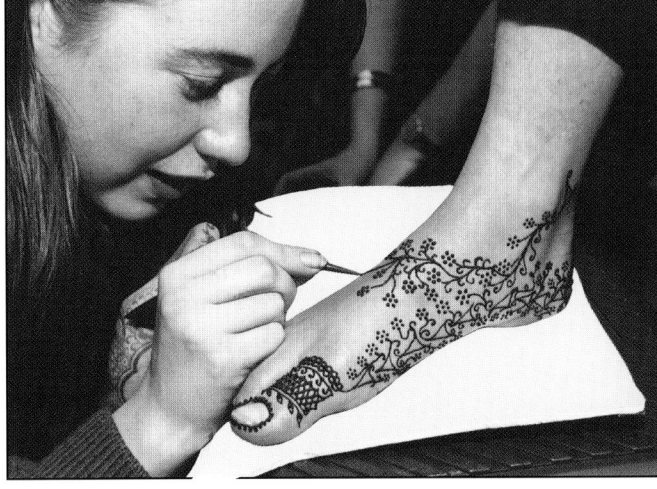

worked in Arabic patterns. Lorraine's armband is finished and Lynne is waiting for her ankle designs to dry. Jane is thrilled with
50 her shoulder decoration. "It's fabulous," she says, and chooses another pattern for her left arm.

  8 The patterns are applied in a thick greenish- black coloured henna paste which falls off as it dries, usually within an hour. At first, all that can be seen underneath on the skin is
55 a pale reddish pattern, but Aileen explains that the full colour takes two days to develop.

  9 But no one wants to risk spoiling their new artwork. Jackie walks into the sub-zero evening temperatures right foot shoeless; Karen has an exposed arm and Jane is still in her party
60 dress. "I'm definitely going to get my legs done in summer," she says.

5 Find words from the passage which mean:
  a come together in one place
  b detailed and complex
  c a big party or celebration
  d formal events
  e very old
  f trying something new
  g every part of
  h thinking about
  i lasting for a short time
  j not covered

6 Mark the stressed syllable in each of these words and practise saying them with your partner.

7 Underline other words in the article with three or more syllables. Mark the stressed syllable and practise saying each one with your partner.

HELP WITH WORD FORMATION 1

■1 Use one of the forms of the word *help* in the box to complete the gap in each sentence.

> ~~help~~   helper   helpless
> help   helpful   helpfully
> helped unhelpful

Example:
This exercise is rather difficult, can you *help* me please?

1 A new born baby is _____ and totally dependent on other people.

2 The shop assistant was very _____ . She didn't want to give me any advice.

3 Thank you very much for all the _____ you gave me when I was preparing for my exams.

4 She's a very _____ person, always there when you need a hand.

5 If you organise a party for very young children you need about one _____ for every five children.

6 John _____ Raquel to finish her homework yesterday.

7 'Shall I carry that heavy bag for you?' he said _____ .

■2 Look at this table for the base word *help*.

> **Verb:**
> infinitive   to help
> present   help/helps
> present participle   helping
> past   helped
> past participle   helped
>
> **Adjective:**
> helpful   unhelpful   helpless
>
> **Noun:**
> help   helper   helpfulness   helplessness
>
> **Adverbs:**
> helpfully   helplessly   unhelpfully

■3 Which form of the word *help* did you choose to complete the sentences 1–7? Fill in this grid.

Example:	*help*	*verb*
1		
2		
3		
4		
5		
6		
7		

■4 In Paper 3 (Use of English) Part 5 you have to change the base form of a word into another form, according to the context of the passage.

There are many ways in which words can change. Look at these examples.

1 Add a prefix:

build – **re**build   (verb)
happy – **un**happy   (adjective)
sense – **non**sense   (noun)
patiently – **im**patiently   (adverb)

2 Add a suffix:

speak – speak**er**   (verb – noun)
inform – inform**ation**   (verb – noun)
imagine – imagin**ative**   (verb – adjective)
careless – careless**ness**   (adjective – noun)
patient – patient**ly**   (adjective – adverb)
weak – weak**en**   (adjective – verb)
slow – slow**er**   (adjective – comparative)

3 Join two words together to make one new word:

finger + print – fingerprint
pen + knife – penknife
week + end – weekend
some + thing – something

4 Change the form of the word:

sell – sale   (verb – noun)
strong – strength   (adjective – noun)
teach – taught   (present – past form of verb)

Sometimes more than one change is possible:

profession – **un**profession**ally**
think – **thoughtless**

■5

1 Look at the words in the column on the right and the words in bold in this text. What type of change has been made?

Which two of these symbols are most attractive to you?

circle   squiggle   square   triangle

Psychologists think that the symbols which you **choose** can say a great deal about you. The first symbol you select shows the **strongest** part of your character; the part which you generally show off to **everyone** around you, while your second choice **uncovers** the qualities which you try to keep **hidden** below the surface.

PSYCHOLOGY
CHOICE
STRONG
ONE
COVER
HIDE

2 For these parts of the article write the new words in the spaces **1–10**. What type of change have you made for each one?

Circle ●

The circle is (1) _____ by people who are warm and sociable. You are popular and understand the (2) _____ of listening to other people's problems. You avoid (3) _____ because you can get other people's (4) _____ rather than fighting with them. You can easily see when people are not being (5) _____ honest with you.

CHOOSE
IMPORTANT
ARGUE
CO-OPERATE
COMPLETE

Squiggle

You enjoy life and it is (6) _____ for you to refuse the chance to try anything new. This (7) _____ means that you (8) _____ take on too many things at once and you never finish any of them. You usually have (9) _____ energy and most people are attracted towards your (10) _____ personality, but others might think you are a bit of a show-off!

USUAL
EAGER
TIMES
LIMIT
LIVE

3 Read the rest of the article and write in the missing words. Remember that the words which you put in the spaces must fit the sense of the whole passage, not just one line.

Square ■

If you choose this sign you are probably (1) _____ who spends hours thinking (2) _____ about problems. But sometimes people (3) _____ your practical nature and might confuse it with emotional coldness.

ONE
CARE
UNDERSTAND

Triangle ▲

You like to set a target and work towards it (4) _____ the cost. You probably know (5) _____ what you want in life and how to get it. However, (6) _____ is also very important to you and you have a good social life.

EVER
EXACT
FRIEND

WRITING 1
An article

■1 Look at these pictures. Describe the clothes that the students are wearing. Why are they wearing these clothes?

 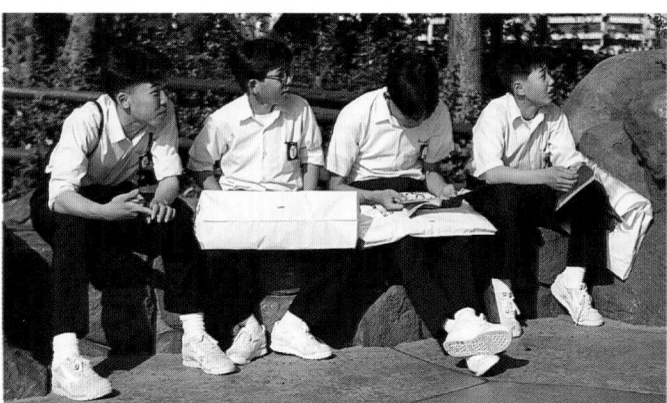

■2 In some countries it is quite common for school students to have to wear school uniform. Discuss the following with your partner:

1 Do you like the uniforms in the picture?

2 Are uniforms worn in your country? Do you like them?

3 What do you imagine the students in the picture think of their uniforms?

4 What are the advantages of wearing a school uniform?

5 Are there any disadvantages?

▭3 Five school students were asked for their opinions about uniforms. Listen and note down some of the advantages and disadvantages they mention.

Are their opinions the same or different from those you discussed with your partner?

The students were then asked to write an article for their school magazine about the advantages and disadvantages of school uniforms. Here is the best one for you to read. As you read, think about why it is a good article, and answer the questions which follow.

What are the arguments for and against compulsory school uniforms?

In many secondary schools in Britain the wearing of a school uniform is compulsory. Some schools argue that there are many advantages to this system, *but* students can often see some disadvantages too.

The main advantage of school uniforms is that they give a common identity to the school. Even when the students are on their way home, everyone knows which school they go to. This is important if the students misbehave, for example. *Another advantage* is that if all the students in a school wear the same type of clothes in matching colours and styles, then they tend to look smart when they are all together. *Finally,* students whose parents can't afford nice clothes look the same as everyone else and so don't feel inferior.

Most students don't agree with school uniforms, *however,* for a number of reasons. *Firstly,* when you have to wear the same clothes as everyone else you don't have a chance to develop personal taste in the way you dress. *Moreover,* people who look scruffy usually look scruffy in their uniforms too and you can always tell the people who come from poor homes because their uniforms are not as new or don't fit properly. *Lastly,* the main reason why most students don't like school uniforms is because most schools choose such horrible colours and styles, that don't suit young people at all.

It is clear, *therefore,* that there are arguments in favour of school uniforms and arguments against. *On balance,* most schools want them, but most students do not.

■**4** Match the words from the text on the left with the definitions on the right.

smart (para 2)	be the correct size
scruffy (3)	be the same colour or style
match (2)	of an untidy appearance
fit (3)	be the right colour or style for someone
suit (3)	tidy and attractive

HELP WITH WRITING ■
Planning and paragraphing

■**1** The article is divided into four paragraphs.

1 How do you recognise a paragraph?

2 How did the writer know when to end one paragraph and begin another?

3 Give each paragraph a title.

■**2** In the second and third paragraphs, a number of points are made. Here is part of the plan for the article.

Paragraph 1:	**Introduction**
Paragraph 2:	**Points in favour**
	a common identity
	b
	c
Paragraph 3:	**Points against**
	a no individuality
	b
	c
Paragraph 4:	**Conclusion**

1 Complete the plan by looking back at the article.

2 Look carefully at the introduction. What information does it contain?

3 Look carefully at the conclusion. What information does it contain?

4 Look carefully at the question. Does it ask for the writer's opinion?

5 What is the writer's opinion? When is it given? Why?

Many of the writing tasks in the First Certificate exam ask you to discuss a topic like the one in the example. One way of doing this is to present a balanced argument, as this author did, by dividing points for and against into two paragraphs.

■**3** Look at the words which are in italics. What contribution do they make to the article? Here are some other ways the writer could have made the same points:

1 *but* students can often see some disadvantages too.

On the other hand, students can often see some disadvantages.

2 *The main advantage* of school uniform is …
One advantage of school uniform is …
The first advantage of school uniform is …
One point in favour of school uniform is …
The greatest advantage of school uniform is …

3 *Another advantage* is …
A further advantage is …
One other advantage is …

4 *Finally,*
Lastly,

5 Most students don't agree, *however*.
Most students, however, don't agree.
Most students, on the other hand, disagree.

6 *Moreover,* people who look scruffy …
What's more, people who look scruffy …
Secondly, people who look scruffy …

7 *On balance,* most schools like them …
To sum up, most schools like them …
In conclusion, most schools like them …

Planning

■1 When you plan a piece of writing you need to think of three separate things:

1 The subject matter – what you want to say.

2 The layout – how this will be ordered and divided into paragraphs.

3 The language – finding the words in English to express what you want to say.

It is very difficult to do all three of these things at the same time. So it is important to think about your writing before you begin. You should decide what you want to say and plan the paragraphs before you begin to write. Then when you are writing you can concentrate on finding the right words and grammatical forms to express your ideas.

The following exercise will help you practise these skills.

■2 You have been asked to write an article for a school magazine.

With your partner or group choose one of these topics.

1 What can be said for and against a period of compulsory military service for young people?

2 Should sport be part of the school curriculum, or should it be left to the individual to organise?

3 What are the advantages and disadvantages of giving pets as presents?

■3 Now talk to your partner and list as many points as you can think of about the argument.

1 Divide the points into advantages and disadvantages.

2 Compare your list with the list of another pair or group who chose the same question. Add any new ideas to your list.

3 Now select the most important points – the ones you want to include in your article.

4 Think about your article – your plan will look like this:

Paragraph 1:	**Introductory sentence**
Paragraph 2:	**Points in favour** (advantages)
	a
	b
	c
Paragraph 3:	**Points against** (disadvantages)
	a
	b
	c
Paragraph 4:	**Conclusion**

Look again at the example article.

Read the introduction. Now write a similar introduction to your article, and plan the paragraphs.

■4 You are now ready to write the paragraphs of your article. Remember to use the expressions in italics above.

EXAM PRACTICE 1

1 Read the text below and think of the word which best fits each space.
Use only one word in each space.

When people are asked what they would most like (**1**) _____ change
about themselves, the two most (**2**) _____ responses are: losing weight
(**3**) _____ giving up smoking. At first glance (**4**) _____ of these
seem daunting enterprises. Researchers have found (**5**) _____ 97 per
cent of people who try to lose weight still weigh (**6**) _____ much if not
more a year later. This does (**7**) _____ mean that it is impossible to lose
weight. Most people (**8**) _____ go on a diet do not need to. They are
(**9**) _____ medically overweight and are often unrealistic in the targets
(**10**) _____ set themselves. More important, severe dieting is a very
inefficient (**11**) _____ to lose weight in anything more than the
short-term. So most dieters have chosen the (**12**) _____ thing to change,
and the wrong way to change it. As for smoking, a recent survey of
ex-smokers reveals that (**13**) _____ six per cent felt bad-tempered or
put on weight as a result (**14**) _____ giving up tobacco. More than half
of those questioned claimed they had been surprised (**15**) _____ how easy
the process had been.

2 An international magazine for young people is running a writing
competition. To enter the competition write an article (120–180 words)
on one of these topics.

1 What are the arguments for and against allowing children to
choose their own clothes?

2 What are the advantages and disadvantages of living in a place which
attracts lots of tourists?

3 Use the word given in capitals at the end of each line to form a word that
fits in the space.

How lucky are you?

Research has shown that the (**1**) _____ of people believe **MAJOR**
that luck plays an important part in their (**2**) _____ **DAY**
lives. About 60% of the people questioned thought
(**3**) _____ lucky in everything from health to personal **SELF**
(**4**) _____ to money. They also expected to be **RELATION**
(**5**) _____ in the future and thought that their luck was **FORTUNE**
connected to their own abilities.

The 20% of people who felt they were (**6**) _____ believed **LUCK**
their bad luck would continue. They were rather
(**7**) _____ and felt they were born unfortunate. **PESSIMIST**

It was very (**8**) _____ that the lucky people were outgoing **NOTICE**
while the unlucky ones often suffered from (**9**) _____ , **SHY**
and it may be that the lucky people are remembering
(**10**) _____ events, and putting to the back of their minds **SUCCESS**
those that did not work out well.

Work for a living

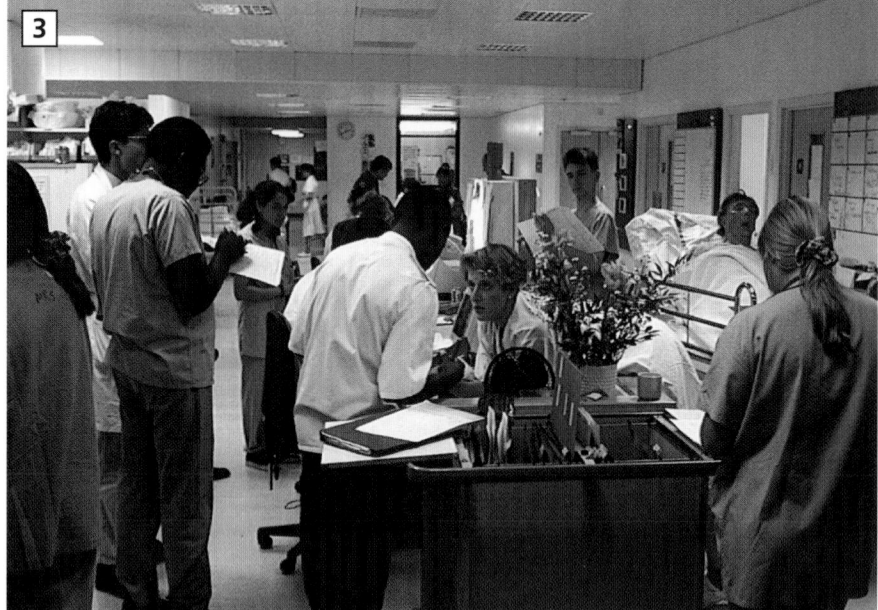

SPEAKING 1

Expressing opinions

Look at the three photographs and talk to your partner.

1 Which would be the best place to work? Why?
Which would be the worst place to work? Why?

2 Choose one of the places. Make a list of all the different jobs people do there.

3 Find someone who has chosen the same picture and compare your list. Add any new ideas.

4 Is there a job that you would be good at?

VOCABULARY 1

Skills and qualities

1 Look at the list of skills and qualities in the box. Which of them are necessary for the jobs on your list? Discuss this with your partner as in the example:

To be a _____ you need to have good _____ skills and to be _____ .

2 Can you think of some more skills and qualities needed for the jobs on your list?

Skills	Qualities
computer skills	patient
typing skills	physically
driving skills	strong
telephone skills	emotionally
interpersonal skills	strong
artistic skills	well-organised
language skills	intelligent
mathematical skills	caring
managerial skills	calm
financial skills	quick-thinking
	honest
	clean and tidy
	punctual

WRITING 1
Describing jobs

1 Read this paragraph and decide which job is being described.

To be a _____ you need to have a good general education and good interpersonal skills. You do not need a degree, but you have to do a special training course. Driving skills may be useful and you have to be honest, clean and tidy and very patient. A _____ needs to be calm in a crisis, quick thinking, and has to be emotionally strong. They are usually tall, well-built and physically strong, but they need to be caring people too.

2 Now choose one of the jobs on your list and write a paragraph about it like the one above.

3 Exchange paragraphs with a partner and decide which job their paragraph describes.

SPEAKING 2
Expressing opinions

Talk to your partner.

1 Which is the most interesting to work in: a restaurant, a food factory, or a supermarket?

2 Choose one of the places and make a list of the advantages and the disadvantages of working there.

READING 1
Reading for specific information

■ 1 Read the article quickly to find the answers to these questions:

1 Which company does Sandy work for?

2 What is her job called?

3 What does she have to do?

4 How long has she been in the food industry?

■ 2 Now read more carefully and find words which mean:

1 having too much of a good thing (line 5)

2 to try (line 9)

3 complete (line 12)

4 trying food (line 16)

5 well-ventilated (line 22)

6 too much (line 23)

■ 3 Are these statements true or false?

1 Sandy samples 10 kilos of chocolates every day.

2 She does not usually eat the chocolates she tastes.

3 She is the only chocolate taster at M&S.

4 She has not put on weight because of her job.

5 She has always wanted to work with food.

'Chocolate tasting is like wine tasting – you don't swallow'
SANDY COLLYER

Would working as a Confectionery Selector for Marks & Spencer be a dream come true for chocoholics? Candida Crewe finds out.

1 ONE DAY SANDY Collyer and a colleague of hers had to eat their way through almost 10 kilos of chocolates. It took them from 9am to 2pm. Afterwards they felt 'very, very unwell'. But their chocolate marathon was not a binge. It was all in
5 the course of duty. Sandy is one of the 11 people at Marks & Spencer who are responsible for chocolates and sweets. Her official title is Confectionery Selector. She has to sample
10 chocolates every day.

'That 10 kilos was unusual,' she said. 'The technologist and I had to try out an entire fresh cream range from one of our suppliers before it went off. It was a very hot day which made things worse.' Despite such excesses, Sandy is not overweight. 15 How come? 'Chocolate tasting is like wine tasting,' she told me, 'you don't swallow unless it's so good you can't resist. I think all of us in the office have become immune to chocolate. It no longer makes us put on weight.' Perhaps, after 15 years in 20 the business, Sandy has become immune to the temptations which, in her airy offices in the M&S headquarters in Baker Street, I found overwhelming. There were chocolates everywhere. 'When 25 I was little I, like every kid, wanted to work in the Mars Bar factory. When I began in confectionery I was just like a child in a sweet shop, eating everything. But that's worn off. I like chocolate, 30 but I'm not a chocoholic.'

4 What qualifications and training do you think Sandy needed to become a Confectionery Selector?

Read about Sandy's career and fill in the chart:

> Sandy was brought up in Essex. After A-levels she worked in banking for a year and hated it. Then, encouraged by a friend in retailing, she went to work at Harrods. 'I did my training there. I was a buyer for eight years – bread, patisserie, cakes – before moving into confectionery where I found my niche.'
>
> She enjoyed the challenge, the fast turn-over. In 1987 she moved to Marks & Spencer. Her basic responsibility is to develop new lines and she is in charge of both product and packaging. This involves a lot of travel in Britain and on the Continent, overseeing production, doing comparative shopping and visiting food fairs.

Sandy Collyer

Qualifications:

_____

Work experience:

_____ (1 year)

_____ (8 years)

_____ (since 1987)

Present responsibilities:

_____

_____

_____

GRAMMAR 1
To be/get used to + -ing

1 Look at these sentences about Sandy. What is the difference in meaning between **a** and **b**?

1 **a** She eats chocolate every day.
  b She's used to eating chocolate every day.

2 **a** In her job she travels a lot.
  b She's used to travelling a lot in her job.

3 **a** She didn't like working in a bank.
  b She couldn't get used to working in a bank.

When do we use the form *to be/get used to +-ing*?

2 Look at these comments made by foreign students living in Britain and answer the questions.

1 When I first arrived I didn't like the food, but now I'm used to eating potatoes every day and I quite like it.

What has changed for Dimitra? Why?

2 I'd studied the grammar, but I wasn't used to speaking and listening. At the beginning, you can't understand anything because it's all so strange, and then gradually you get used to hearing the language, and you begin to understand more.

What changed for Kunio?

3 A friend of mine couldn't stand the weather. He was here for four weeks, but never got used to feeling so cold and went back as soon as possible. I felt cold at first, but I'm used to it now and so I don't really notice.

Why was Ronaldo's friend unhappy? What didn't change for him? What changed for Ronaldo?

> You are used to + verb + -ing
> You get used to + verb + -ing
> You are used to + (the)noun
> You get used to + (the)noun

3 Use the forms in the box to discuss these questions:

1 What things do visitors to your country find it difficult to get used to?

2 Compare school life with working life.
What are students used to doing?
What do people starting their first job have to get used to?

4 Complete the second sentence so that it has a similar meaning to the first sentence. Use the word given and other words to complete each sentence. You must use between two and five words. Do not change the word given.

1 Juliet finds driving on the left very strange.
to
Juliet's not _____
on the left.

2 People in my country usually only have a sandwich at lunchtime.
not
They're _____
a big meal at lunchtime.

3 I always get up early, so it's not a problem for me.
to
I'm _____ up early.

4 Drinking a lot of tea is new for me.
not
I'm _____
a lot of tea.

5 After two or three days, you don't notice the cold weather so much.
get
In two or three days you _____
_____ the cold weather.

6 We've only had this computer for a couple of weeks.
getting
We're just _____
this computer.

7 In my country it's unusual to queue for the bus.
not
I'm _____ the bus.

8 Checking the meaning of words in an English-English dictionary is something new for me.
not
I'm _____
checking words in an English-English dictionary.

9 Tamara normally eats salad with every meal.
to
Tamara's _____
salad with every meal.

10 At John's new school he has to wear a uniform, which he didn't like at first.
getting
John is _____
a school uniform.

LISTENING 1
Note-taking

This is Carole, who is 22 and works for a large company. Carole has come back to her old school to talk about her experiences of work to students who are in their last year of school.

1 What job do you think she does?

2 What questions do you think the students will ask her? Make a list of possible questions. Listen to the talk and check if the students ask the same or similar questions to yours.

3 Listen again and complete the missing information about Carole.

> Her job: ....
>
> Her original ambition: ....
>
> Qualifications: ..'A' Levels in...............
> ..and Geography.......................
>
> Other languages: ....
>
> Training: ....
>
> Skills developed: ....
>
> Hours worked: ....
>
> Things which cause problems in her job:
> ..delays because of overbooking..
> ....
> ....
>
> Pay: ....

GRAMMAR 2
Present perfect/Past simple

1 Look at these phrases which Carole used to talk about her job, and answer the questions.

I've learned how to sort out those problems
The languages have been useful in my job
I've had lots of experience of dealing with people
I've had the chance to develop my interpersonal skills

1 When did these things happen?
2 Which tense did Carole use?
3 Why?

2 Look at these phrases which Carole used to talk about school, and answer the questions.

I never really liked school
I didn't work very hard
I liked the teachers in the sixth form
I enjoyed my A-level subjects

1 When did these things happen?

2 Which tense did Carole use?

3 Why?

Look at this diagram:

	'I liked the teachers'	'The languages have been useful'	
Past	Carole at school	Carole at work	Future
	Carole left school	Now	

Carole uses a different tense to talk about these two periods in her life because one has finished and one has not.

The **Present perfect** tense is used to talk about:		
	Tense	Time
Experiences		
I've been to London four times	Present perfect	in my life
I've seen that film already	Present perfect	in my life
Things that have happened in this period		
I've worked hard today	Present perfect	today
I've done lots of sport this week	Present perfect	this week
Things which have just or recently happened		
They've just arrived	Present perfect	this moment
I've seen him twice recently	Present perfect	recently

3 Look at the expressions in the box.

1 Divide them into those which talk about a present period and those which talk about a past period.

2 Choose four expressions from each list and write full sentences about your own educational or work experience.

at Easter · last Tuesday · in February · this century · in recent weeks · for the last 3 weeks · when I was a child · an hour ago · last week · this month · last month · two weeks ago · since I left school · since Christmas

4 Put the verb in brackets into the correct tense, Present perfect (*I have done*) or Past simple (*I did*).

Examples:
I *started* (start) working here last week.
I *have enjoyed* (enjoy) meeting you all today.

1 He _____ (pass) his exams last June.

2 She _____ (meet) her friend on Tuesday.

3 He _____ (learn) to type when he was at school.

4 She _____ (be) busy all this week.

5 Someone _____ (phone) you a few minutes ago.

6 He _____ (work) hard this term.

7 There _____ (be) a lot of work to do recently.

8 I _____ (have) any training on the word processor.

9 The twentieth century _____ (see) many technological advances.

10 Computers _____ (become) more important during the nineteen eighties.

PRONUNCIATION
Past tense endings

There are three ways of pronouncing the regular past tense ending -*ed*. Listen to the examples.

/d/	/ɪd/	/t/
enjoyed	wanted	liked

1 Add the words you hear to the correct column, /d/, /ɪd/ or /t/.

2 Practise saying the words with your partner.

3 To decide how to pronounce -*ed*, we have to look at the last sound in the verb. Look at your lists. What is the rule?

4 Add the words in the box to your three groups according to the pronunciation of the past tense ending. Now listen to the words in the box.

arrived	needed	listened	washed
helped	sounded	disappointed	trained
packed	discussed	educated	passed
tried	turned	skilled	

LISTENING 2
Selecting an answer

Listen to an interview at a job agency and complete the missing details on the form below.

Ace **JOB AGENCY**

Student/Temporary job application

Name: *Lucy* [_____1]
Address: [_____2] *Conway Street, Cambridge*
Subject(s) studied: [_____3]

Skills and experience. Please tick (✓).

	Yes	No	
Foreign Languages			4
Waiting at table			5
Cookery			6
Sports			7
Driving			8
Typing/WP skills			9

	Yes	No	
Shop assistant			10
Cashier			11
Music			12
Work with children			13
Office work			14

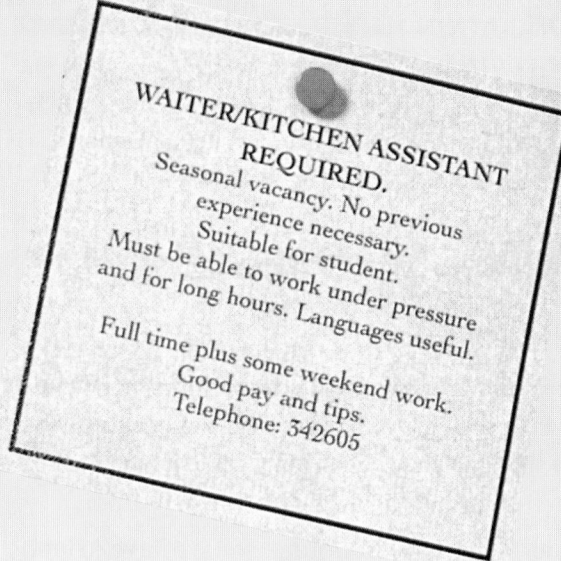

WAITER/KITCHEN ASSISTANT REQUIRED.
Seasonal vacancy. No previous experience necessary.
Suitable for student.
Must be able to work under pressure and for long hours. Languages useful.
Full time plus some weekend work.
Good pay and tips.
Telephone: 342605

Research Assistant

required by university professor writing book on Mozart.
Some musical knowledge desirable.
Must be able to type. Driver preferred.
4 month vacancy. Would suit student.
Office hours. **Tel: 342898**

Helper for friendly village hotel required.

Early mornings and lunchtimes only.
Reception work, answering the phone, dealing with enquiries, handling money.
Some typing. **Summer vacancy.**
Suitable for flexible student.
Pay plus breakfast & lunch.
TEL: 342411

Children's Nanny required for 2 months. Full time help for 4 lovely kids, includes a month with the family in a villa near Rome. Must be able to drive. No pay, but a great experience!
Tel: 342220

SPEAKING 3
Exchanging information

1 Using the information from the interview discuss which of the jobs on the left might be suitable for Lucy.

2 Write down the questions which Lucy will ask to get more information about the job you have chosen.

3 Decide who is Student A and who is Student B.
Student A should ask Lucy's questions.
Student B should answer them by inventing more information about the job.
Choose another job and change roles.

LISTENING 3
Matching information

You will hear five extracts from a radio programme where job vacancies are announced. For questions **1–5**, choose from the list **A–F** the person best suited to each job. Use the letters only once. There is one extra letter which you do not need to use.

A Janice Dalston (59 years) is a retired school-teacher with no family. She's looking for a job where she will meet people.

B Hayley Hawkes (20 years) has three years' experience of working in a food-processing factory and is now hoping to move into an office job although she has no training.

C Moll Jones (45 years) is returning to work now her family have grown up. She has just done a retraining course in secretarial/telephonist skills.

D Rosie Walters (25 years) lives in a village, but is willing to drive into town on her motorcycle. She has experience of working as a delivery driver for a pizza company.

E Susie Smythe (35 years) has two young children. She's looking for part-time work and used to be a dressmaker before she got married.

F Dawn Davies (17 years) has just left school where she got good exam results in English, maths and word-processing skills. She is looking for a first job that will give her commercial experience.

Job 1 _____

Job 2 _____

Job 3 _____

Job 4 _____

Job 5 _____

READING 2
Multiple matching

■**1** Discuss these questions with your partner.

1 What qualities do top models need?

2 How do models find work?

3 How do models start their careers?

4 Do you think modelling is a good choice of career?

■**2** Read the first part of the article and check the answers to questions 1–4.

models in the making

How do you get into modelling? Marina Gask visits Select model agency's New Faces photo shoot and meets some of the girls who've made it…

Part One

GETTING SORTED

So just how do Select find their models? Crissie Castagnetti, Director of Select, says:

'At least 50 per cent of our models get spotted when we're out and about. Wherever I go, I'm constantly looking at faces. I just do it unconsciously. One time I spotted a girl eating a hamburger in a motorway café, and gave her our number! Another girl, Samantha, was only 13 when she sent us a picture her aunt had taken of her. Within six weeks she'd done work for *The Face* magazine and the cover of French *Vogue.* Another girl got spotted whilst queuing in a bakery, and another whilst shopping in Miss Selfridge with her mum!'

WHAT IT TAKES

What exactly do Select look for ? Sarah Leon, New Faces booker, says:

'Lots of girls just come to see us (no appointment needed), or send pictures in. We can usually spot whether or not a girl's got potential within the first five seconds, but we have to meet her in person to be absolutely sure. Obviously, she has to be the right height (a minimum of 1 m 70 cm), with good skin and even features. But once she's got all that, we're looking for a special "something" that makes her individual. Lots of girls plaster themselves in make-up for the pictures they send in, but that's more of a hindrance than a help. Casual clothes and no make-up is best.'

Part Two

HOW THEY MADE THE BIG TIME

The time: One rainy Saturday afternoon.

The place: A posh studio in Farringdon, Central London.

The event: Shooting Select model agency's New Faces 'catalogue', which gets sent to advertising agencies and magazines (like *Sugar*), so that people know which models are available for fashion shoots, etc.

We thought we'd tag along and find out just exactly how you get to become one of modelling's new faces!

Emma, 17, *from Richmond, Surrey*

Emma thought she'd wait till she finished her 'A' levels before trying modelling, but fate stepped in when Select spotted her outside a nightclub!

'It's her sultry, exotic beauty that we noticed', says Crissie, director of Select. Since then, Emma's put her studies on hold for a year (she plans to be a lawyer), but she still finds time to continue training for the Olympic swimming trials, alongside the modelling!

Sam, 20, *from Wiltshire*

Sam was doing a degree in Computer Science when her sister persuaded her to enter a Levi's modelling competition with her. Sam got through to the finals, screened on TV, and although she didn't win, Select were so impressed that they offered her a modelling contract.

'Everyone was so shocked because I was always the quiet one!' laughs Sam. 'Five months on, things have been going so well that I've given up my course. Modelling's very rewarding, but I often get home too late and tired to go out.'

Jo, 19, *from Cambridgeshire*

'I'd gone to a fashion show in Glasgow with some friends, and got spotted by a talent scout who told me to find myself an agency in London,' says Jo. 'I had absolutely no plans to be a model – people always said I was too skinny!'

Jo's fresh prettiness and personality get her plenty of work, especially in *Sugar* magazine. Living mainly on burgers (tsk!), she'd give the whole modelling thing up tomorrow if she had to change her diet, and still plans to study psychology and French at university later. Sharing a flat with Sam makes the modelling life more bearable.

Hannah, 15, *from Islington*

When Hannah was 13, her mum's friend took some pictures of her and sent them to Select.

'She has beautiful hair and skin and a classic, timeless model look, ' says Crissie.

Life's been chaotic for Hannah, the star of Wella's Shaders and Toners ad, since she started modelling 18 months ago.

'It's difficult to fit the work in around school work, especially with my exams coming up. It's really weird to be on a shoot in Paris one day, then in a French class at school the next!'

3 Read about the four models and write a name in each space to show which model(s) each of the statements refers to.

She is a keen sportswoman	**0**	*Emma*
She was first seen on television	**1**	_____
She wants to study a language	**2**	_____
She was encouraged by a member of her family	**3**	_____
She had planned to try modelling later	**4**	_____
She has postponed her studies **5** _____	**6**	_____
She is combining work and study	**7**	_____
She was discovered by the Select Agency	**8**	_____
She hadn't thought of being a model	**9**	_____
She has appeared in a television commercial	**10**	_____

4 Match each of these multi-word verbs from the text with its equivalent. One has been done for you as an example.

1 to get into	to organise(yourself)
2 to make it	to postpone
3 to get sorted	to follow
4 to get spotted	to enter(a new career)
5 to be out and about	to pass(a test)
6 to tag along	to be noticed
7 to put on hold	to travel
8 to get through	to succeed(finally)

5 Find words in the text which mean:

1 person whose job is to find new models   (Part One)
2 something which makes things more difficult   (Part One)
3 photographic sessions   (Part Two)
4 which never looks old-fashioned   (Hannah)
5 very thin   (Jo)
6 very confused   (Hannah)
7 very strange   (Hannah)
8 something which makes things easier   (Jo)

▭ LISTENING 4 ▰

Note-taking

You will hear a discussion between two people who work in the personnel department of a large company in London. They have just finished interviewing three applicants for the job described in this advertisement.

1 Read the advertisement, then listen and complete the grid above with notes about the applicants.

Conference organiser

This is a great opportunity to use your organisational and interpersonal skills in an interesting and demanding role.

As Conference Organiser you will quickly take responsibility for organising part of our busy conference programme. The job requires a lot of common sense, good administrative and communication skills, and the ability to work as part of a team. Word-processing skills and a driving licence are essential, experience of computer graphics desirable.

	Strong points	Weak points
Terry		
Pattie		
Jack		

2 Listen again and complete these sentences with the names of the job applicants (Terry, Pattie or Jack) using information from the grid.

1 _____ isn't as smart as _____ or Jack.

2 _____ has got much more experience of computers than _____ .

3 _____ doesn't have as much experience of organising conferences as _____ or Terry.

4 I think _____ seemed more able to cope than _____ .

5 _____ was much smarter than _____ .

6 _____ and Jack have certainly got more experience of organising conferences than _____ .

GRAMMAR 3
Comparatives

■1 Divide the adjectives in the box into three groups according to how the comparative is formed.

enthusiastic	calm	old	tidy
responsible	able	nervous	reliable
smart	dirty	young	sensible

■2 Using adjectives from the box, write sentences about Terry, Pattie and Jack to show how each type of comparative adjective is formed.

Terry _____

Pattie _____

Jack _____

■3 Look at the information about Paul and Susie, two applicants for a job. Use the information to write six negative comparative sentences.

PAUL

Age:	26
Experience:	2 years
Attitude:	very enthusiastic
Personality:	excitable, sociable, talkative
Dress:	untidy – not very smart

SUSIE

Age:	24
Experience:	5 years
Attitude:	not very enthusiastic
Personality:	calm, serious, quiet, reserved
Dress:	very smart and tidy

Example:
Susie is not *as old as* Paul.

_____
_____
_____
_____
_____
_____

■4 Complete the second sentence so that it has a similar meaning to the first sentence. Use the word given and other words to complete each sentence. You must use between two and five words. Do not change the word given.

1 Mandy has more experience than Sally.
as
Sally doesn't _____ Mandy.

2 Patrick is certainly more punctual than David.
not
David _____ Patrick.

3 John isn't as well qualified as Sally.
than
Sally _____ John.

4 Jill's sister is more polite than Jill.
polite
Jill isn't _____ sister.

5 My interview lasted much longer than yours.
long
Your interview _____ mine.

6 Rod has got more experience than Sue.
much
Sue _____ experience as Rod.

7 Rachel was more nervous than Sarah.
not
Sarah _____ Rachel.

8 Steve's clothes weren't as smart as Mark's.
than
Mark's clothes _____ Steve's.

9 Lynda seemed more reliable than Liz.
as
Liz didn't _____ Lynda.

10 Sandra was more enthusiastic than Jeff.
not
Jeff _____ Sandra.

HELP WITH WRITING
Letters

■1 In Paper 2 Part 1 you have to write a letter. The type of letter will be either formal or informal.

Formal: To someone you do not know or to a company.

Informal: To a friend or to a member of your family.

With a partner:
Think of four reasons why you might write a formal letter.
Think of four reasons why you might write an informal letter.

■2 Read the job advertisement on page 24 again and look at this letter written as a reply.

> Dear Sir or Madam,
>
> I am writing to apply for the job of Conference Organiser as advertised in this week's newspaper.
>
> I left college two years ago, and since then I have worked as Personal Assistant to the Sales Manager of a large furniture company. The Sales Manager often travels abroad on business and I have to organise his travel arrangements and make sure everything runs smoothly in his absence. This involves talking to people in other departments in the company and answering telephone and fax enquiries from customers.
>
> I am used to operating a word processor and I would like to improve my skills in the area of computer graphics. I would be interested to know what type of computers you use and whether you would train me to use them. I enclose a copy of my cv for your information and I look forward to hearing from you.
>
> Yours faithfully
>
> *Collette Morris*
> Collette Morris

■3

1 Is this letter formal or informal?

2 What is the purpose of this letter?

3 What grammatical tenses does this letter contain? Underline some examples.

4 Find words or phrases in the letter which mean:

a for his job _____
b book his tickets _____
c when he's away _____
d using _____
e get better at _____
f tell me _____
g it's in the envelope _____
h answer me soon _____

5 Why did Collette choose these words and phrases?

■4 In the first question in the writing part of the examination, you are given instructions which tell you what you have to do and information which you should use when writing your answer. Look at this example:

You are interested in doing a part-time job to earn some extra money. You see this advertisement and you want some more information. You write to Health Action.

Read the advertisement carefully and the notes which you made. Then write your letter to Health Action, covering the points in your notes and adding any relevant information about yourself.

Write a letter of between 120–180 words in an appropriate style. You do not need to write addresses.

> ## Health Action Charity – Organiser
> **Health Action improves the health of young people by persuading them to do more sports and giving them information on healthy eating.**
>
> *when / how long?* — We need a (part-time) organiser for our busy office. You will be one of a dedicated team helping to raise money and plan publicity
> *travel??* — events (all over the world). You need to be
> *which??* — good at (languages), smart, confident on the telephone, and have lots of enthusiasm.
> Some weekend work. (Reasonable pay.) ???
> Start as soon as possible.
> **WRITE TO: Ms Janet Wallace.**

■5 Before you begin, talk to your partner.

1 What questions do you want to ask Health Action?

2 What type of information will you include in the letter?

3 Which grammatical tenses will you need to use?

4 Think of some useful words and phrases.

EXAM PRACTICE 2

■1 Complete the second sentence so that it has a similar meaning to the first sentence. Use the word given and other words to complete each sentence. You must use between two and five words. Do not change the word given.

1 I last went to Paris two years ago.
not
I _____ Paris for two years.

2 Mary is better paid than Neil.
as
Neil is _____ Mary.

3 Anne's wearing jeans and a T-shirt, which is unusual for her.
usually
Anne _____ jeans and a T-shirt.

4 Take a heavy sweater with you because it might get very cold this evening.
in
Take a heavy sweater _____ very cold this evening.

5 I usually only have some hot milk and a biscuit for breakfast.
not
I'm _____ a big breakfast.

6 You might have to carry your bag a long way, so don't take a big one.
in
Don't take a big bag _____ carry it a long way.

7 I haven't seen Greta since Thursday.
time
The _____ was on Thursday.

8 I always go to bed late, so it isn't a problem for me.
to
I'm _____ to bed late.

9 Look, Mick's a vegetarian, but he's eating roast beef.
usually
Mick _____ roast beef.

10 Jenny isn't as talkative as Simon.
talkative
Simon _____ Jenny.

■2 Here is a part of the reading text about Sandy Collyer. Fill in each of the numbered blanks with one word. When you have finished, turn to page 18 to check your answers.

Sandy was (**1**) _____ in Essex. (**2**) _____ A-levels, she worked (**3**) _____ banking and hated it. Then, encouraged (**4**) _____ a friend in retailing, she (**5**) _____ to work at Harrods. 'I did my training there. I was a buyer (**6**) _____ eight years – bread, patisserie, cakes – before moving (**7**) _____ confectionery where I found my niche.'

She enjoyed the challenge, the fast turn-over. In 1987 she (**8**) _____ to Marks & Spencer. Her basic responsibility is (**9**) _____ develop new lines and she is (**10**) _____ charge of both product (**11**) _____ packaging. This involves a (**12**) _____ of travel (**13**) _____ Britain and on (**14**) _____ Continent, overseeing production, doing comparative shopping and (**15**) _____ food fairs.

■3 Read this letter and look carefully at each line. Some of the lines are correct and some have a word which should not be there. If a line is correct put a tick (✓). If the line has a word which should not be there, write down the word. There are two example lines at the beginning.

Dear John

Thank you very much for your letter, which arrived this	0	✓
morning. It was lovely to hear you all about your	00	*you*
new job.		
I am now writing for to ask you a favour. A friend of	1	
mine, Melanie, she is living in England at the moment.	2	
Melanie is studying at a language school in London. Her	3	
course finishes only in two weeks, but she would like to	4	
stay on in England to do her First Certificate exam.	5	
Do you know anybody who might needs a babysitter or	6	
someone to help out with a housework? Melanie is free	7	
each day after lunch and at the every weekends too,	8	
and she really needs to earn some extra of money to pay	9	
for her new course.		
My friend Melanie is a very nice, nineteen-year-old girl	10	
from Holland. She has experience of looking after your	11	
children and has worked as an au pair in Canada. She	12	
has made her own flat so she certainly doesn't need	13	
help with finding some accommodation in London.	14	
I'm sure you can help because you can know so many	15	
people. Thanks a lot.		

Love,

Jill

Jill.

■4 A careers magazine for young people has asked you to write a short article on one of these topics (120–180 words).

1 What are the advantages and disadvantages of working in a place where food is either prepared, sold or served?

2 In what ways can working as a tour guide be enjoyable or difficult?

3 Teenagers dream of becoming top models, but what are the positive and negative aspects of a career in modelling?

■5 You see this advertisement in a local newspaper and you want some more information.

Read carefully the advertisement and the notes which you have made below. Then write your letter to Lion Films covering the points in your notes and adding any relevant information about your family.

Write a letter of between 120–180 words in an appropriate style. Do not write any addresses.

LION FILMS

Want to be in films?

We need people of all ages. Local families required next month as 'extras' to appear in crowd scenes with leading Hollywood stars in a major new film. Transport provided.

Write and tell us all about you and your family.

where to? ?
- When/how long?
- Hollywood stars?
- pay?

Out and about

Hotels and tourist trips don't always give you the freedom to enjoy a holiday the way you want it. Why not swap your home with another family and find out what life is really like in your dream destination?

A change may be as good as a rest, but when it comes to holidays, more and more people are discovering that home exchange – swapping your house with another family – is a good deal better than a package.

For a start, it's a financial winner. Compared with the daunting cost of even the most reasonable fortnight in the sun in a hotel or rented apartment, you will be paying literally nothing for accommodation.

There's also the pleasantly reassuring feel that both houses are therefore occupied and not an open invitation to burglars and vandals. And instead of a soulless hotel, you are part of a genuine community, probably with your host's friends and neighbours helping to make you welcome.

Foreign Exchange

If both families have children they will make local friends – and have the run of the resident toy cupboard. Experienced swappers agree that living as guests in someone else's house encourages mutual respect for each other's property – although it is probably sensible to pack away vulnerable treasures.

Some of the most successful home-swap holidays have made firm friends of the families involved – with the children becoming pen pals and even getting together to organise their combined holidays in subsequent years.

READING 1
Reading for main points

■ **1** What do you think are the advantages of swapping homes with another family from a different country as a holiday?

Are there any disadvantages or dangers?

1 Read the first part of the article and list the main advantages it mentions.

2 Are any disadvantages mentioned?

3 Decide who is Student A, B and C. This section of the article is divided into three parts: A, B and C. Each of you should read one part. Then follow your instructions below.

Student A

Read Part A and find this information:

- What two ways of making contact are mentioned?
- What do you give to the agency?
- What can the agency do for you?

Student B

Read Part B and find this information:

- What are some important things to do once you have found a family who want to swap?
- What information could be useful to the family?

PART A

Finding your match

How do you set about house swapping? Unless you can make your own arrangements privately through friends and contacts, the most practical way is to use one of the specialist agencies who put potential clients in touch with each other, either around the UK or worldwide. These companies differ in the services they offer, but in most cases you pay a registration fee (from £15 upwards) to be included in a directory which is then circulated to prospective swappers in the country of your choice.

In some cases you will be asked to fill in a comprehensive form, listing everything about your home from the number of beds and bathrooms to whether there are pets to look after or plants to water. There will usually be a photograph of your house in the directory – and perhaps also of your family – as well as the holiday dates you have in mind and your particular preferences as to location: town, country, seaside and so on.

Some agencies just put families in touch through their directories and thereafter leave all the arrangements to you; others will visit and vet individual properties, taking trouble to match each family's requirements, and some will also arrange air travel for you – and obviously charge accordingly.

PART B

Making contact

Once you've received your directory and settled on some 'possibles' you like the look of, it's sensible to write at once to several of them; all agencies stress the importance of getting your holiday arrangements made well in advance.

Having made initial contact with 'your' family, you should start to establish a relationship by post or, if practical, by telephone. You can then exchange photos and appropriate information.

When it comes to preparing for your guests, remember that they will be holidaying in a strange place, so it's worth spending time putting together an information folder with phone numbers for emergency services, doctor, police and so on, as well as details of local shops, restaurants, travel timetables and availability of baby-sitters. Include any instructions they may find useful for dealing with pets, houseplants or refuse collection. If you have a burglar alarm or complicated kitchen equipment, leave clear how-to-use details. It's also a good idea to contact your local tourist office for brochures on excursions, stately homes, theme parks and other local interests, so that you can leave your visitors with plenty of ideas for things to do and places to see.

Student C

Read Part C and find this information:

- What should you arrange or provide for the guest family before they arrive?
- What should the guest family do before they leave?

PART C

Changing places

Unless one family plans to arrive before the other has left, it's vital that you make failsafe arrangements for someone to meet the new arrivals, hand over the keys and make them welcome. In any case, do ask your neighbours to take a helpful interest. It's a nice idea to leave some basic provisions for the first couple of meals and perhaps a bottle of wine, but don't overcater by filling the freezer and inviting them to help themselves; part of the fun of a holiday is exploring local shops and cooking 'foreign' food, and although you may not think of your local Co-op as a treasure house of rare delicacies, it could well seem so to your guests.

Remember, too, if cars are included in the swap, to make sure that insurance arrangements cover everything, and that there is petrol in the tank. It's usual for services such as gas and electricity to be paid by the host family in each case, but any extra expenses such as long-distance telephoning should be settled up before the end of the holiday.

The departing family should also make sure they leave the house exactly as they found it, and replenish dwindling stocks of household goods such as loo paper or light bulbs. And a vase of flowers (not from the host's garden!) with a thank-you note will show your appreciation to the returning owner.

WRITING 1
Summary

1

1   Find some other people in the class who have read the same part of the article and compare your answers.

2   Now find partners who have each read different parts. Exchange information.

2   Complete these four paragraphs in your own words to summarise the article.

a   Exchanging houses is a good idea for holidays

because _____

_____

_____

_____

_____

b   The best way of contacting a family is _____

_____

because _____

_____

_____

_____

c   Once you've contacted a family you should

_____

_____

_____

_____

_____

d   Before your guest family arrives you should

_____

_____

_____

_____

_____

VOCABULARY 1
Housing

Imagine you work for a house-swapping agency and you are preparing the new brochure to send to possible clients.

1 Which of the descriptions **a–f** matches each picture **1–6**?

a There are fantastic views from this ~~one~~ modern, one-bedroomed, third-floor <u>flat</u>. The luxury block has a resident porter and private underground garage.

b For a larger family, or a gardening enthusiast, this detached house is ideal. It has five the bedrooms and is surrounded by a beautiful mature garden which also guarantees complete privacy.

c If you are looking for three good-sized bedrooms and an easy-to-maintain garden, this semi-detached house is perfect for you. It has recently been extensively modernised and has been a double garage attached.

d This delightful country cottage is the perfect place to escape from the stresses of city life at the weekends. The inside of the house has been completely rebuilt, while the outside has kept its traditional appearance.

e Few homes in the centre of the town are as much comfortable as this well-kept Victorian terraced house. There is a small garden at the front of the house and a sunny patio at the back.

f There are no stairs for to climb or clean in this suburban bungalow. It has a medium-sized garden and a garage, but needs some modernisation.

2 In each description underline the one or two words which give a name to the type of home described. Description **a** has been done as an example.

3 In each description there is a mistake – an extra word has been added. Cross out the extra word. Description **a** has been done as an example.

🔲 LISTENING 1

Part One

Selecting an answer

1   Listen to this telephone conversation and decide which of the four
    flats below, **A**, **B**, **C** or **D** is being described.

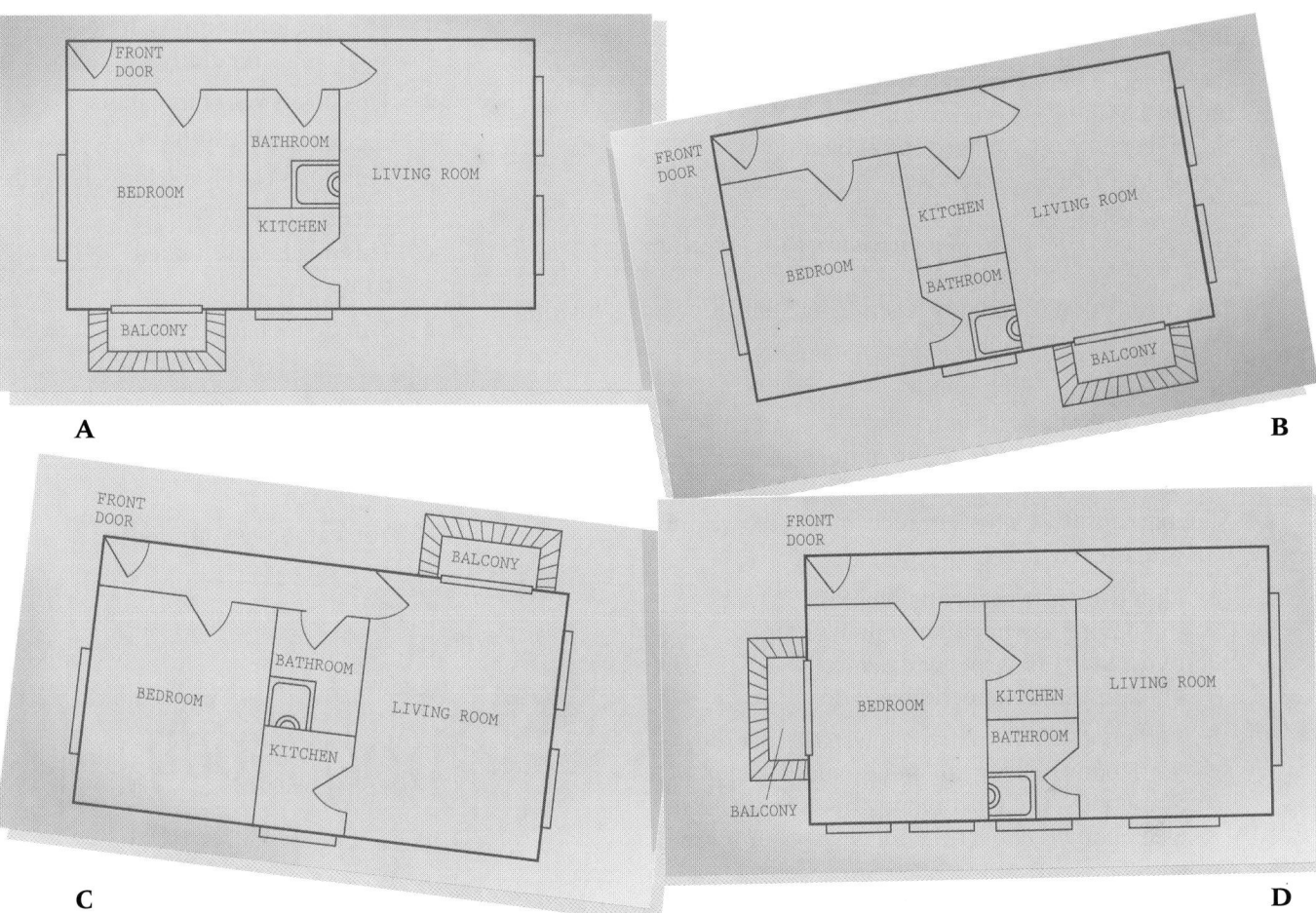

A

B

C

D

2   Listen again and tick (✓) the boxes to show
    which of these things the flat has got.

	yes	no	not mentioned
lift			
balcony			
phone			
shower			
bath			
garage			
cooker			
fridge			
central heating			

Part Two

Note-taking

Listen to the conversation and complete
Sharon's notepad.

Things that need doing	do it myself	have it done
bathroom needs cleaning		
windows need (1) _____	✓	
(2) _____ needs changing		
(3) _____ _____		
need repainting		
light switches need (4) _____		✓
(5) _____ _____		✓
needs (6) _____		
(7) _____ rail needs		
(8) _____ _____		

GRAMMAR 1
Causative have/Needs doing

■1 Look at these phrases from the listening text.

I'm having a new lock fitted
I'll have it done professionally

1 Who is going to do the work?
To have something done (causative *have*) is formed by:

the subject	= Sharon
the verb to have	= is having
the object	= her central heating
the past participle of the main verb	= serviced

● *Sharon is having her central heating serviced.*

This means that somebody is servicing Sharon's central heating for her.

Compare with:
Sharon is servicing her central heating.
This means that Sharon is doing the work herself.

2 Match a causative *have* sentence in **A** with its equivalent in **B** and the tense in **C**.

A 1 I have my newspaper delivered.
2 I'm having my newspaper delivered.
3 I've had my newspaper delivered.
4 I had my newspaper delivered.

B 5 Somebody delivered my newspaper for me.
6 Somebody delivers my newspaper for me.
7 Somebody has delivered my newspaper for me.
8 Somebody is delivering my newspaper for me.

C 9 Present continuous
10 Present perfect
11 Present simple
12 Past simple

Notice that in the causative it is the verb *to have* which tells us the tense.

■2 Match each verb in the box with one of the pictures.

feed	exercise
clip	groom
wash	train

■3 Use one of the verbs to complete each of the following sentences about the dog.

Example:
This dog is too thin, it needs *feeding* properly.

1 This dog looks untidy, it needs _____ regularly.

2 This dog is very dirty, it needs _____ thoroughly.

3 This dog's coat is too long, it needs _____ professionally.

4 This dog is lazy, it needs _____ daily.

5 This dog is badly behaved, it needs _____ properly.

■4 What can you have done to your dog at Dogsbody?

Example:
You can have your dog fed.

Dogsbody

CANINE BEAUTICIAN AND PET SERVICE

JOYCE BOND
WILLOWCROFT
LONGDROVE
WATT
CAR

Dogsbody

**Full Pet Service
By Qualified Person**

Anything from Hamsters to Horses.
Feeding, Exercise, Loving care and attention.

Dog clipping & grooming
(D.G. Diploma CSI)

All Breeds

Show ring training

Phone Joyce or Lesley on 0224 440921

5 With your partner discuss what you can have done at each of these places. Use the verbs in the box to help you.

a the hairdresser's
b the dentist's
c the garage

a	b	c
cut	fill	change
perm	take out	repair
shampoo	clean	check
dry	check	service
dye	X-ray	replace

6 Complete the second sentence so that it has a similar meaning to the first sentence. Use the word given and other words to complete each sentence. You must use between two and five words. Do not change the word given.

1 A shop mended my vacuum cleaner for me.
   had
   I _____ mended.

2 Last week, I took my car to a garage to be washed.
   had
   I _____ last week.

3 Someone is coming to repair the broken window in my house.
   am
   I _____ in my house repaired.

4 A famous designer made her clothes.
   had
   She _____ by a famous designer.

5 I'm having my photograph taken on Monday afternoon.
   is
   Someone _____ on Monday afternoon.

6 Her hairdresser has coloured her hair green!
   had
   She _____ green.

7 A cleaner is coming to clean my house thoroughly.
   am
   I _____ thoroughly cleaned.

8 The dentist has filled one of my back teeth.
   have
   I _____ back teeth filled.

9 Someone's painting my kitchen next week.
   am
   I _____ next week.

10 Emma's having her wedding dress made by her mother.
   making
   Her _____ wedding dress for her.

Expressing opinions

1 Discuss with your partner:

   Have you ever stayed as a guest in someone else's house?

   What are the good points and bad points about staying away from home?

   Have you ever had a guest staying in your house?

   What are the good points and bad points about having guests?

2 Decide with your partner who is Student A and who is Student B. Read the instructions below.

   Student A: Think of 5 things you should do when you are a guest in someone's house and 5 things you shouldn't do. Use the topics in the box to help you.

   Student B: Think of 5 things you should do when you have a guest in your house and 5 things you shouldn't do. Use the topics in the box to help you.

meals	television
sleeping	furniture
bathroom	kitchen
music	telephone

Now discuss the things with your partner.

READING 2
Multiple choice

1 Read this article about guests and hosts and choose the best alternative **A**, **B**, **C** or **D** for each question **1–4**.

Guests and Hosts

1 Visiting people one does not know very well is in many ways like visiting a foreign country. It means accepting others' customs and ways of doing things, and adapting to them in as agreeable a fashion as possible. Often, as with foreign visits, a certain amount of diplomacy is needed.

Children and animals

2 These have at least two things in common: the first is that they rarely behave well in company, or in someone else's home; and the second is that other people are unlikely to love them as much as their parents or owners and so are more likely to find their 'funny little ways' annoying rather than appealing.

Their children

3 Guests who genuinely like children, or at least genuinely like the children in question, have no problems, but those who do not must make an effort to take an interest, enquire into their progress and development, examine their new toys and so on.

4 As for courtesy towards children, there are rules:
■ Do not remind children of something silly they did when much younger, especially in front of siblings.

5 ■ Do not offend the dignity of children over six by talking to them only about childish things – they are just as likely to be interested in your trip to Marrakesh as are their parents.

6 ■ Do not cross-question shy children in order to get a response – include them in general conversation and assume that they will talk when they want to (and when they do, reply normally and don't say 'So you have got a tongue, then').

7 ■ Never discipline children in their own home unless they are actually interfering with your belongings or your person.

8 ■ In your own house you may ask them not to touch certain things, not to jump on the furniture and so on. Ask politely first (they may be allowed to do such things at home). If they persist, then you may be stern, but bear in mind that a child who likes you is far less likely to damage your possessions than one who does not.

9 ■ Do not expect children to sit quietly, keeping out of the way of conversation in a strange house unless you have provided them with something to do or look at.

10 ■ One very important point to be remembered about children, especially by those who are not used to them, is that silent children are listening hard. Anyone who says anything indiscreet in front of them must be prepared to take the consequences of hearing it repeated at a most inopportune moment.

1 What do children and animals have in common?

A When they behave badly people do not notice.
B People only really love their own.
C They often behave badly away from home.
D They can often be funny in company.

2 Guests who do not like children should

A talk to them about toys and childish things.
B ask them lots of questions if they are quiet.
C try to show some kind of interest in them.
D give them something to do to keep them quiet.

3 When can you discipline other people's children in their own home?

A When they jump on the furniture.
B When they interfere with your possessions.
C If they persist in doing something wrong.
D If you have already asked politely.

4 When children are very quiet it means that

A they are carefully following the conversation.
B they are bored and want something to do.
C they find conversation with adults strange.
D they are waiting for a chance to speak.

■ 2 Find words from the text that mean:

changing (paragraph 1)
pleasant (1)
not very often (2)
improbable (2)
makes you angry (2)
makes you feel pleased (2)
really (3)
ask (3)
look at (3)
being polite (4)
brothers and sisters (4)
answer – noun (6)
answer – verb (6)
things which you own (7)
things which you own (8)
given (9)
ready (10)
results (10)
inconvenient or embarrassing (10)

■ 3
Mark the stressed syllable on each of the words you found.

GRAMMAR 2
Genitive 's

■ 1
Look at these phrases from the text.

It means accepting others' customs

… in someone else's house.

■ 2
What are the rules for using the genitive 's? Think about singular and plural nouns. Which type of nouns take a genitive 's?

■ 3
Decide if each of the phrases **a–l** is correct, and if it is not, correct it.

a I am staying at my friends's house tonight.

b Don't discipline other people's children.

c Look at the childrens' new toys.

d This is Jeff and Sue's house.

e Is this anybody's seat?

f Rosies holiday sounded exciting.

g The dog has lost its bone.

h They went in their parents car.

i Are you going to Dave and Julie's party?

j She was wearing her's blue coat.

k Have you bought a cinema's ticket?

l Have you got yesterday's newspaper?

▭ LISTENING 2
Listening for specific information

1 Listen to this phone call between two friends who haven't heard from each other for a long time, and complete the details below.

New address _____

Type of house _____

Reason for moving _____

How long has Margaret lived there? _____

How long has Peter lived there? _____

How long has Margaret known Peter?

_____

2 Look at these phrases from the listening text.

I haven't heard from you for ages
No, we haven't talked since Christmas

When do we use *for* and when do we use *since*?

GRAMMAR 3
For/Since

■ 1
Put *for* or *since* in each of these sentences:

1 We haven't invited Auntie Joan _____ years.

2 I haven't seen him _____ his birthday.

3 I've lived here _____ I was a child.

4 I've had my new car _____ three months.

5 I've had this watch _____ longer than I can remember.

6 I've been to the gym six times _____ I came back from my holidays.

7 That car parked outside our house hasn't moved _____ last July.

8 John's been collecting stamps _____ he was at school.

9 No one has phoned me _____ weeks!

10 I haven't been swimming _____ they closed the old swimming pool.

■ 2
Look at these three sentences. Which one is different grammatically? In what way is it different?

1 I haven't seen him for ages.

2 It's ages since I saw him.

3 I haven't seen him since Christmas.

HELP WITH GRAMMAR
Key word transformations

■1 Part of the Use of English paper asks you to transform sentences from one grammatical structure to another. You are given a complete sentence. This is followed by a 'Key' word (printed in heavy type), and a new sentence which has a gap for you to complete. You must use the key word to complete the new sentence. You must also use no more than four other words. The new sentence must have a similar meaning to the first sentence. You cannot change the form of the key word.

Example:
I haven't had such fun for years.

This is followed by the 'key' word:
much
And the new sentence with a gap to complete:
It's years _____ fun.

The example is completed like this:
It's years <u>since I had so much</u> fun.

The meaning of the new sentence should be similar to the original, but it will have a different grammatical structure and sometimes different vocabulary.

Remember
- the new sentence must use the 'Key' word
- you must not change the 'Key' word
- you must write a maximum of five words in the gap (contractions like *isn't* count as two words)
- the new sentence will have a similar meaning to the original sentence

■2 Look at this transformation:

She left school five years ago.
since
It is <u>five years since</u> she left school.

1 What has changed? Why?
2 What has not changed? Why not?
3 What has been omitted?
4 What has been added?

■3 Is this an example of a good transformation?

Example:
He didn't arrive in time to meet her.
too
He <u>arrived too late</u> to meet her.

This is a good transformation because in the original sentence the meeting DID NOT take place.

The key word is used and there are a total of three words in the gap – the maximum is five words but in many transformations between three and five words will be necessary.

For questions 1– 6 decide if these are good transformations or not. If they are not good transformations, can they be improved?

1 I can't drive as well as my father.
than
My father <u>drives better than I am able to do</u>.

2 The water was so cold it was impossible for me to have a shower.
warm
The water <u>wasn't warm enough</u> for me to have a shower.

3 She liked London much more than Cambridge.
like
She <u>likes Cambridge</u> as much as London.

4 I always have breakfast before I leave the house.
until
I don't leave the house <u>until I have had</u> breakfast.

5 Let's go and have a swim.
we
Why <u>shouldn't we go and</u> have a swim?

6 John is the best footballer in the club.
well
No one in the club <u>plays football as well as</u> John.

■4 Complete the second sentence so that it has a similar meaning to the first sentence. Use the word given and other words to complete each sentence. You must use between two and five words. Do not change the word given.

1 It's three weeks since I received a letter.
not
I have _____ three weeks.

2 I haven't eaten in a restaurant for months.
since
It's _____ in a restaurant.

3 Dogsbody washed my dog for me.
had
I _____ Dogsbody:

4 The newspaper hasn't been delivered for ages.
was
It's _____ delivered.

5 Somebody cleaned Lidia's house before the guests arrived.
had
Lidia _____ before the guests arrived.

SPEAKING 2
Talking about photographs

Look at these wedding photographs. Talk to your partner about:

- the people and what they are doing
- their clothes
- what happened before the picture was taken

Could either of these be a wedding in your country? What would be the same or different?

🔊 LISTENING 3
Giving advice

■ **1** You will hear part of a radio phone-in programme where people ask an expert for advice on etiquette at weddings.

Listen to Part 1 and decide which of the problems **1–6** Mrs Romsey asks about. Write *Yes* or *No* in each box.

1 The best time of year for weddings. ☐
2 Who should make the guest list. ☐
3 Who should pay for the wedding. ☐
4 Whether to get married in church. ☐
5 How many guests to invite. ☐
6 Whether to invite her friends. ☐

■ **2** You will hear some more callers on the line to the same programme. For Parts 2, 3 and 4:

a Decide what the problem is.

b Discuss with your partner what advice would be appropriate in your country.

c Listen to see if the expert's advice is the same as yours or different.

SPEAKING 3
Asking for and giving advice

Think of some more questions about weddings or etiquette in other formal situations to ask the expert. Decide who is Student A and who is Student B.

Student A: You are the expert on etiquette. Give advice.

Student B: Ask the expert your questions. Then exchange ideas.

Look at these ways of asking for and giving advice from the listening.

> Should I make the ...?
> You should ask ...
> Ought I to ask for ...?
> You could ask ...
> Is it all right if I give them ...?
> You ought to ask ...
> What should I do about ...?
> Can I decide ...?

READING 3
Reading for specific information

1 Discuss with your partner:

1 How do you show your appreciation when someone gives you a gift?
What do you say?
What do you do?

2 What do you say if someone gives you a present you don't like?

3 Do you ever write letters to say thank you?

4 In what situation do you think a letter of thanks might be appropriate?

MODERN
MANNERS

by Michele Elliot

1 I remember, when I was about seven, agonising over how to thank my Aunt Pat for the excruciatingly awful jumper she'd sent me for my birthday. It was three sizes too big and a horrible mixture of brightly coloured wools. Needless to say I wasn't very happy about wearing it, still I was obliged to put pen to paper and be thankful in writing. But my parents had taught me not to lie and I was totally honest about what I was going to do with the present.

> Dear Aunt Pat
> thank you very much for the jumper. It is very big. there are many cold children in the world who do not get presents I will donate it to the oxfam shop
> love.
> Michele

2 My parents' philosophy of manners didn't extend to being that honest, so the note was altered before being posted:

> Dear Aunt Pat
> thank you for the jumper it is really very nice of you to knitid for me. It must have taken a very very long time thank you.
> Love
> Michele

3 But where do we stand on an old-fashioned concept like thank-you letters, when we live in a modern world of cordless phones and motorways that take us to Granny's and back in a day?

4 In any era, there should be good, solid reasons for asking our children to do things – and, for me, that's the hard bit – working out the reasons and explaining them.

5 Some 'traditions' make sense to me – like saying 'please' and 'thank you' because it makes other people feel good, or giving up your seat on the bus to someone less able because it's kind. Some don't make sense – like children not speaking until spoken to. It seems to me that we need to work things out as we go along.

6 So, what about those thank-you notes? In fact, I do usually make my boys write them when presents come by post. One reason is that receiving a thank-you note in a world of ever-ringing phones is special, and makes the recipient feel special; and because grandparents, especially, like to re-read notes, and show them to friends.

7 There's another reason, too, that's hard to define. I think it's because sitting down to write focuses your thoughts and the result is a little part of yourself that's unique (provided you didn't copy it from your sister).

8 Remembering my own struggles, I do try to make it easier on my children. It's hard to think kind thoughts when you're oppressed. So picture postcards make good thank-you notes. You can let the child choose one from some you have bought – and even address and stamp it for them. Older children can write a few lines; younger ones can just write 'thank you' and sign their name. Even little ones can draw a picture of themselves playing with the gift.

2   Read the article and find the answers to the following questions. Underline the parts of the text where you find the answers.

1   Why didn't Michele like the present from her auntie?

2   Why didn't her parents like her first letter?

3   Which other two traditions does she agree with and why?

4   When does she make her sons write thank-you letters?

5   What are the three reasons she gives for sending a note rather than using the phone?

6   What advice does she give parents about how to make letter-writing easier for young children?

Now compare your answers with your partner's. Do you both agree with Michele?

3   Look at the article again and find:

1   A word which means 'pullover'. (paragraph 1)

2   The material used to make pullovers. (1)

3   A phrase which means 'obviously'. (1)

4   A phrase which means 'to write'. (1)

5   A verb meaning 'changed'. (2)

6   The verb describing how pullovers are made. (2)

7   A phrase meaning 'what is our opinion?' (3)

8   A prefix meaning 'to do again'. (6)

PRONUNCIATION
Vowel sounds

1   Put these words into one of the boxes according to the main vowel sound.

could	first	groom	floor	don't
sure	sound	church	lock	off
ought	block	group	should	move
found	own	phone	though	cook
heard	house	choose	bought	only
door	would	work	now	

/ɜː/	/ʊ/	/ɒ/	/uː/	/aʊ/	/ɔː/	/əʊ/
girl	*good*	*got*	*room*	*how*	*more*	*know*

2   Now listen and check your answers.

WRITING 2
An informal letter

1 Look at the letter on page 28. This is an example of an informal letter.

How do you know it is an informal letter? Look at:

the first words of the letter (the greeting).
the content (the topics included in the letter).
the concluding words (the close).
the name at the end of the letter.

All of these things can help you decide if a letter is informal or formal.

2 Carol has been invited to spend the weekend with Tim. She is writing to refuse the invitation and make some other suggestions. The beginning and the end of the letter are complete. Put the middle paragraph into the right order.

You are invited to
attend my party on
Saturday
29th November

7.30pm
At the Oak Hotel

R.S.V.P

3 You are unable to go to the party, and you write a letter. Make sure your letter looks like an informal letter.

4 Write a letter to a friend you haven't seen for some time. Mention some recent news about yourself and people you both know.

```
                                    37 Castle Street
                                    Manchester
                                    M20 2BA

                                    4th May

Dear Tim,

Thank you very much for inviting me to come and stay with you for the weekend.
```

a would that be OK?
b as there isn't much traffic,
c I'd love to come and visit you,
d How about if I just came for the day on Sunday,
e and I can come home late in the evening.
f but I'm afraid I'm very busy at this time of year
g Getting to your house on a Sunday morning is easy
h and I don't think I can be away for a whole weekend.

```
Please let me know if this plan is all right. Maybe we can arrange a whole
weekend together later in the year. Then you can come and stay at my house –
we've got lots of room and my family are always very pleased to see you.

Best wishes,   Carol

P.S. Can you send me Erica's phone number? I think I've lost it.
```

READING 4
Multiple choice

1 Below is an article from a magazine about May Lin, a student from Hong Kong.

1 Apart from the English language, what subjects do foreign students go abroad to study?

2 Why do they do this?

3 What are the advantages and disadvantages of studying in a foreign country?

4 Read the article and find out:
- What subject May Lin is studying.
- How the course is organised.
- What her special interest is.

2 Match the words from the text on the left with the definitions on the right.

to take up (line 3)	therefore
arduous (line7)	gave up
dropped out (line 8)	difficult
hence (line 23)	accept
award (line 32)	prize

3 Answer these multiple-choice questions about the article.

1 Why did some people not complete the course?

  A They changed to another course.
  B There were too many students.
  C They did not pass the exams.
  D It was too difficult for them.

2 At the moment, May is

  A studying Cantonese at home.
  B working as part of her course.
  C looking for a job in Norfolk.
  D training to work in Hong Kong.

3 What will May do next year?

  A Learn another language.
  B Work as a furniture designer.
  C Complete her course.
  D Study marketing.

4 What advice does she give?

  A Speak as many languages as possible.
  B Learn English and another language.
  C It is not important which languages you speak.
  D Don't forget to practise your native language.

Name: May Lin, 20
Position: Industrial trainee
Qualifications (pending): BSc Hons Hotel and Catering Management
Company: Far East Enterprises
Institution: Norfolk University, UK
Entry requirements: Minimum 2 A levels

1 Currently in the third year of her Hotel and Catering Management course, May Lin was one of 70 young people to take up places in her year at Norfolk. She is
5 now one of a remaining 55. There is no doubt that training in hospitality management can be arduous, she says.

'Those who dropped out did so because it was too hard, too long or because
10 they no longer wanted to go into management.'

The Norfolk course consists of a four-year sandwich course; ie three years' study with a year's industrial placement
15 midway. May chose to return to Hong Kong for her training, in order to practise her Cantonese, and found her own placement with Far East Enterprises.

20 Although she is working on a similar programme, she is not on the Enterprises' trainee programme, and hence will not be offered a job at the end of it. But this suits her, as she has every
25 intention of returning to complete her course. 'I'm not sure yet where I want to work, and this way, I remain marketable in both Hong Kong and the UK.'

She's very interested in restaurant/kitchen
30 design, and has already won two major prizes for this in the UK. 'I won first prize in British Gas' Eastern Region award for kitchen design, and an award from Moderno Furniture for my restaurant
35 furniture designs.'

Her advice: 'Learn English, and possibly another language as well, as many customers speak languages other than their own. It doesn't really matter which
40 language – having another language could never be a disadvantage.'

HELP WITH MULTIPLE-CHOICE QUESTIONS ▬▬▬
Reading Texts

▬1 Look back at the previous exercise. Choose a question which you answered correctly. Now decide:

1 What is a multiple-choice question?

2 How did you choose the correct answer?

3 What is the purpose of the other three answers?

4 Why are they wrong?

5 Did you have any doubts? Why?

▬2 When answering multiple-choice questions these are important points to remember:

1 Read carefully and slowly to be sure you understand exactly what the passage says.

2 Look at the questions and try to answer them without looking at the alternatives. Try not to read all the alternatives until you have decided the answer in your own mind. Then find the alternative which is closest to your answer.

3 Some of the alternatives may seem logical or true, but be careful not to introduce your own ideas. Look back at the passage to find the exact place where you can find the answer and make sure it really says what you think it says.

4 When you have decided, look at the alternatives and decide why each one is wrong.

Listening Texts

▭3 Listen to this introduction to a radio programme. The first time you listen answer questions 1 and 2.

1 What is the main problem with office work?

2 What will the rest of the programme talk about?

▬4 Listen again and answer these multiple-choice questions.

1 What is the main problem with office work?

   A The regular hours
   B It's uninteresting work
   C You work very hard

2 What will the rest of the programme talk about?

   A Setting up your own business
   B Finding work to do at home
   C Re-organising your office

▬5 How are these multiple-choice questions different from those about the Reading text?

Multiple-choice questions seem more difficult with a listening text because you cannot go back and check your answers in your own time.

▬6 These are important points to remember:

1 Read the questions carefully before you listen.

2 The first time the text is played, listen for the answer to each question.

3 The second time the text is played, check that the other two alternatives are not correct.

4 Be careful not to introduce your own ideas, the questions refer to what the speaker says and means and nothing else. All three alternatives are equally possible – you cannot answer without listening and understanding.

5 Use the pauses between texts to read and be ready for the next question.

6 Don't panic! If you really do not understand anything, then guess. You still have a one-in-three chance of being right!

🔊 LISTENING 4
Short extracts

You will hear people talking in five different situations. Choose the best answer **A**, **B** or **C** for each question **1–5**.

1 You will hear an employee talking to a customer.

   Where are they?

   A at the dentist's
   B at the dressmaker's
   C at the hairdresser's

2 You will hear a man talking to someone who is going to do some work at his house.

   What are they discussing?

   A electrical work
   B decorating work
   C carpentry work

3 You will hear someone making enquiries at a garage.

   How does the customer feel?

   A disappointed
   B suspicious
   C angry

4 You will hear two people talking about a wedding.

   Who is the woman you hear talking?

   A the bride
   B the bride's mother
   C the bride's grandmother

5 You will hear someone talking toa new employee.

   Where is she working?

   A in a shop
   B in a restaurant
   C in someone's house

EXAM PRACTICE 3
■ 1

Complete the second sentence so that it has a similar meaning to the first sentence. Use the word given and other words to complete each sentence. You must use between two and five words. Do not change the word given.

1 Somebody repaired her bicycle last week.
   had
   She _____ last week.

2 He is not strong enough to do that job.
   too
   He is _____ that job.

3 Keith is not as well qualified as Sue.
   than
   Sue _____ Keith.

4 I haven't spoken to Mr Williams before.
   time
   This is the _____ to Mr Williams.

5 Somebody is repainting our house at the moment.
   are
   We _____ at the moment.

6 Linda hasn't got as much experience as Graham.
   than
   Graham _____ Linda.

7 The carpet still needs cleaning, doesn't it?
   not
   The carpet has _____ , has it?

8 One advantage of living in the country is clean air.
   favour
   One point _____ in the country is clean air.

9 I haven't been to the cinema for two months.
   since
   It's _____ to the cinema.

10 It's ages since I saw him last.
   for
   I _____ ages.

2 Use the word given in capitals at the end of each line to form a word that fits in the space.

If you have children, there are certain things	
to remember when you are visiting (**1**) _____	**BODY**
else's home. Children (**2**) _____ behave	**RARE**
well in company and other people are (**3**) _____	**LIKE**
to find them more (**4**) _____ than you do. It's	**ANNOY**
important that chidren are either (**5**) _____ in	**INCLUDE**
the conversation or given (**6**) _____ else to do.	**SOME**
If your children (**7**) _____ , you must	**BEHAVE**
discipline them (**8**) _____ as your hosts may	**IMMEDIATE**
have (**9**) _____ rules about behaviour than you	**STRICT**
do at home. (**10**) _____ , if your children damage	**FINAL**
any of your hosts' (**11**) _____ you must either	**POSSESS**
replace the damaged object or offer a (**12**) _____	**SUIT**
gift in its place. You must never offer your hosts	
money to replace the object.	

3 Read the text below and decide which word **A**, **B**, **C** or **D** best fits each space.

Once when I was a child, I (**1**) _____ with an aunt who served me cooked carrots – a huge portion. They were overcooked, yellow and disgusting. I (**2**) _____ one and then said 'No thank you'. In that house, (**3**) _____ manners dictated that you ate what was on your (**4**) _____ , even if you hadn't served yourself with it. There were starving children in Africa. Believe it or not, I was (**5**) _____ to sit at the table until bedtime. The next morning, the carrots were (**6**) _____ on my plate at breakfast. I was a stubborn little creature and never ate them nor stayed with that aunt (**7**) _____ . And I will not eat cooked carrots to this day. Since we want meal times to be a pleasure, I reckon the best way is to put the food in serving dishes and (**8**) _____ children help themselves. Have manner 'rules' that everyone (**9**) _____ to, but above all (**10**) _____ meal times fun. If we are too strict, too critical, meal times become tense.

1	**A** remained	**B** stayed	**C** visited	**D** rested
2	**A** attempted	**B** sipped	**C** tasted	**D** flavoured
3	**A** but	**B** even	**C** therefore	**D** though
4	**A** plate	**B** table	**C** menu	**D** helping
5	**A** powered	**B** pressured	**C** driven	**D** forced
6	**A** ever	**B** always	**C** yet	**D** still
7	**A** also	**B** after	**C** again	**D** more
8	**A** let	**B** permit	**C** allow	**D** leave
9	**A** accepts	**B** belongs	**C** admits	**D** agrees
10	**A** get	**B** cause	**C** make	**D** gain

Crime wave

SPEAKING 1
Exchanging information

1 What is a crime?
With your partner, match the crimes in the box with their definitions **1–10**.

burglary	shoplifting
murder	robbery
mugging	theft
minor offences	assault
forgery	kidnapping

1 stealing from shops while they are open

2 killing someone intentionally

3 stealing objects in general

4 breaking into buildings to steal things

5 attacking and hurting someone physically

6 making false documents

7 attacking someone and stealing from them in the street

8 stealing money from banks, etc.

9 taking someone prisoner and demanding money for their release

10 crimes such as illegal parking, speeding, etc.

2 Discuss with your partner:

Which is the most serious of these crimes?
Which is the most common in your country?
Which is the least common?

3 Look at this chart showing crime figures for a city in Britain for this year and last year.

Use the words in the box to talk to your partner about how these figures have changed.

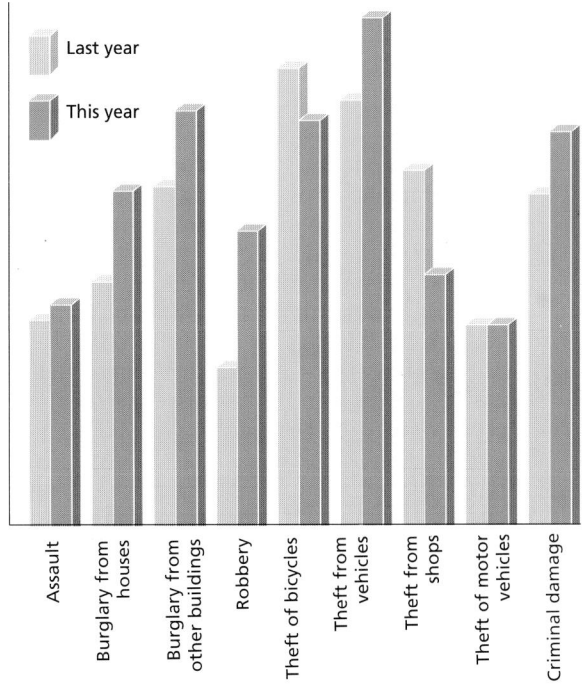

Crime figures for the last 12 months compared with those for the previous 12 months

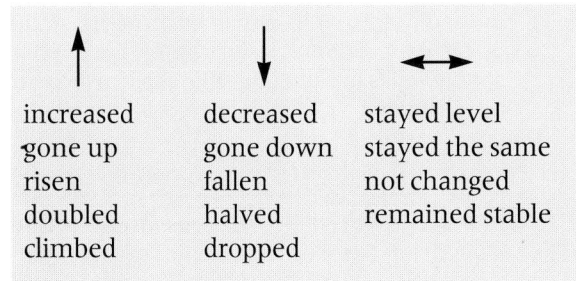

increased	decreased	stayed level
gone up	gone down	stayed the same
risen	fallen	not changed
doubled	halved	remained stable
climbed	dropped	

Example:
The number of burglaries from houses has gone up in the last year.

4 Talk to your partner about how we can prevent crime

- at home
- at school
- in other places

READING 1
Multiple matching

1

Crime, as we are all aware, has been a growing problem all over the world in the last 30 years. But we are not powerless against crime. Much is being done – and can be done – to reverse the trend. You can play a part in it.

2

The first step towards preventing crime is understanding its nature. Most crime is against property, not people. And most is not carried out by professionals; nor is it carefully planned. Property crimes thrive on the easy opportunity. They are often committed by adolescents and young men, the majority of whom stop offending as they grow older – the peak ages for offending are 15–18. Also, and not surprisingly, the risk of crime varies greatly depending on where you live.

3

This reliance by criminals on the easy opportunity is the key to much crime prevention. Motor cars, for example, are a sitting target for the criminal. Expensive, attractive and mobile, they are often left out on the streets for long periods at a time. The police estimate that 70–90 per cent of car crime results from easy opportunities. Surveys have shown that approximately one in five drivers do not always bother to secure their cars by locking all the doors and shutting all the windows. It's the same story with our homes. In approximately 30 per cent of domestic burglaries, the burglar simply walks in without needing to use force; the householder has left a door unlocked or window open.

4

If opportunities like these did not exist, criminals would have a much harder time. The chances are that many crimes would not be committed at all, which would in turn release more police time for tackling serious crime. Of course, the primary responsibility for coping with crime rests with the police and the courts. But there are many ways that you can help reverse the trend. So if you care about improving the quality of life for yourself, your family and your community, read on …

1 Look at these statements about crimes in Britain, and say whether **you** think they are true or false.

1 Most crimes involve our possessions and not ourselves.

2 Most criminals make enough money from crime to live on.

3 Most criminals follow careful plans.

4 Most criminals are young people.

5 Most criminals give up crime after a few years.

6 Most crimes are the result of carelessness.

7 20% of drivers never lock their cars.

8 70% of house burglaries are through open doors or windows.

Now read the extract about crime prevention and see if you were right.

2 Choose the sentences from the list **A–E** which best summarise each part of the text **1–4**. There is one extra sentence which you do not need to use.

A We make it easy for them.

B What to do to make your house safer.

C Let's work together against crime.

D How to reduce the number of crimes.

E Who steals what.

VOCABULARY 1
Crimes and criminals

1 Complete the following table:

Verb	Noun (crime)	Noun (person)
to steal		thief
to rob	robbery	
to	burglary	burglar
to commit an offence	offence	
to	mugging	mugger
to murder	murder	
to	forgery	forger
to shoplift		shoplifter
to kidnap		kidnapper

■2 Now put the correct form of one of the words into each of these sentences.

1 The police are looking for a gang which got away with £20,000 in a bank _____ .

2 She came home to find her house had been _____ and her car _____ .

3 A _____ broke into the school at night and took two video players.

4 Police are very concerned about the increase in _____ from parked cars.

5 The _____ knocked him to the ground and ran off with his briefcase.

6 I shouted 'Stop! _____ !' as the man ran off down the street with my bag.

7 When the bank _____ was arrested by the police, they found a shotgun in the back of his car.

8 Big stores in the city centre have reported a 25% increase in _____ this winter.

9 The bank checks all notes in a machine which can detect _____ .

10 She had committed a number of minor _____ before robbing the post office.

LISTENING 1
Blank filling

You will hear someone telling a police officer about a break-in at her home. Listen and complete the missing information on the form below.

DATE: *17th June*   TIME: *17.45*

NAME: _____ **1**

ADDRESS: _____
_____ **2**

Estimated time of offence: _____ **3**

Articles missing: Value: Identification:

_____ **4** _____ **5** _____ **6**

_____ **7** – _____ **8**

_____ **9** _____ **10**

Damage to property: _____ **11**

GRAMMAR 1
Sequence of tenses

■1 Look at these phrases from the listening text, and for each one decide:
- Which tenses are used
- Why each tense is used

1 I got home and found the door open.

2 As I was walking along the road to my house I noticed that the front door was open.

3 My neighbour was cleaning her windows, so before I went in I called to her.

4 They got in while I was out shopping.

5 Look at these examples of past tenses:

The **Past simple** is used to talk about:	Tense	Time
Events in the past		
I went to London in 1990.	Past simple	1990
Events that happened one after another		
I got home and made a cup of tea.	Past simple	one event, then another

The **Past continuous** is used to talk about:	Tense	Time
Events beginning in the past but not finished at a specific time in the past		
My neighbour was washing her car.	Past continuous	when I got home
What were you doing at 8.00 pm last night?	Past continuous	at 8.00 pm

The **Past continuous** and **Past simple** are used together:

a When one action is interrupted by another:
I was walking down the path when I noticed that the door was open.
While I was having a bath the phone rang.

b When one action takes place during a longer one:
When I was studying in Paris I visited the Louvre.
While I was living in London I went to the theatre regularly.

2 Change the verb in brackets into the Past simple or Past continuous.

1 I (phone) _____ my brother when the door bell (ring) _____ .

2 He (live) _____ in London when the accident (happen) _____ .

3 As it (rain) _____ we (decide) _____ to stay at home.

4 I (not hear) _____ the phone because I (sit) _____ in the garden.

5 They (break) _____ three plates while they (stay) _____ in my house.

6 They (do) _____ the washing up and then (go) _____ to the theatre.

7 During her visit to Milan she (go) _____ skiing every weekend.

8 When she (arrive) _____ Luke (play) _____ the guitar and Mary (read) _____ a book.

9 I (sit) _____ in the cinema when a thief (steal) _____ my handbag.

10 While she (watch) _____ television she (hear) _____ a loud crash.

READING 2
Gapped text

1 Read this magazine article about burglaries. Seven sentences have been removed from the article. Choose from the sentences **A–I** the one which fits each gap **1–7**. There is one extra sentence which you do not need to use. There is an example at the beginning (**0**).

Someone is burgled every two minutes in the UK

0 **D**

1 A burglar can enter your home, grab the most valuable portable items – and escape. Often these fast raids happen while the owner is at home,
5 perhaps in another part of the house or in the garden, leaving the front door or a window open. Or they may have just gone out to pick up the children from school and thought it
10 'wasn't worth' the trouble of shutting and locking the windows for that short time. The fact is that the majority of burglaries occur between 2 p.m. and 5.30 p.m. on a weekday.

1

15 Your call will show up on a screen at the local police station and an officer should be with you within minutes.

◆ If you see or hear obvious signs of entry (noises inside, jammed front
20 door, or the door locked from the inside), and suspect the burglar may still be in the building, don't enter. Make your emergency call from a phone box or from a neighbour's
25 house.

◆ If you are sure the burglar has gone, call your local police station rather than the emergency number. Ideally have the number readily to hand near
30 the phone.

◆ Don't destroy evidence. The police will take an impression of a damaged door, to check against records of tool

marks. They may also take finger
35 and footprints, in an attempt to link the crime with known burglars or suspects.

2

Walk around the edge of carpets as much as possible – dust impressions
40 of the burglar's shoe marks can be lifted and identified by special forensic techniques. The fingerprint powder the scene-of-crime officers will use can normally be removed
45 later from work tops and everyday glass and china by washing in warm, mild detergent.

3

Ask the officers not to dust any delicate furniture or possessions if you think
50 the powder may affect them in any way.

4

You will need this for the police and for any insurance claim. It will help you if you have already taken photographs
55 and written a description of your most valuable items – such as jewellery, video, CD player and CDs, hi-fi, camera, mobile phone and computer, including any detail of manufacturer
60 and model numbers. Items you have marked with your post code and house number will be easier for the police to return to you if they are found.

5

If you rent, the landlord should
65 arrange these for you. House-owners must make their own arrangements. Your insurance company may have emergency numbers for local tradesmen. Otherwise, contact
70 24-hour carpenters and locksmiths through recommendations or Yellow Pages. Your building insurance policy should cover the cost of repairs; remember to keep receipts.

6

75 Ideally, you'll have previously made and hidden a list of emergency numbers to ring with your bank account number and the numbers of the cards themselves.

7

80 The police may arrange for a Crime Prevention Officer to call who can give free advice on such measures as security locks, timing light switches and alarm systems, and may
85 recommend reliable firms who can install them. Remember that opportunist thieves are always on the lookout for signs that a property is vulnerable, so make sure you don't
90 advertise the fact that your house is empty. There's plenty of information available these days on how to prevent it happening to you – so make sure you take precautionary
95 steps now, before it's too late.

A Tell your bank or credit card company as soon as possible.

B Make a list of the stolen items.

C Avoid touching anything the burglar may have touched.

D Just 30 seconds can be all it takes.

E Prevent it happening again.

F Knowing what to do if you are a victim has become a necessity.

G Ring the police if you think the burglar is still around.

H Arrange for emergency repairs once the police give you the all clear.

I Most furniture can be cleaned with a good quality furniture polish.

2 Find words or phrases in the passage that mean:

take quickly (line 1)
easy to carry (2)
collect (8)
appear (15)
in a convenient place (29)
connect (35)
easily damaged (48)
things you own (49)
maker (59)
which you can trust (85)
put in (86)
easy to attack (89)

3 How many syllables are in each of the words or phrases you have found? Which is the stressed syllable in each word?

SPEAKING 2

Exchanging information and expressing opinions

Do you know anyone whose car has been stolen or broken into? Tell your partner what happened.

What can people do to protect their cars against this sort of crime?

Make a list of suggestions.
Compare with your partner.

READING 3

Reading for specific information

1 Read the passage quickly and find out what these numbers refer to:

- 460,000
- 20
- ¼

> **Apart from your home, your car is probably your most valuable possession. It's also your most vulnerable.**

KEEPING YOUR CAR SAFE

Car thefts and thefts from cars – typically of radios and cassette players – account for over a quarter of all recorded crime. Together they impose costs on everyone – the cost of the police time taken up in dealing with the offences, the cost of taking offenders through the criminal justice system, and the cost to motorists of increased insurance premiums.

Over 460,000 cars are reported missing in Britain each year and many of these are never recovered. Many of those which are found have been damaged by the thieves. A stolen car is also far more likely to be involved in an accident than the same car driven by its owner; car thieves are often young and sometimes drunk.

Yet car crime can be cut drastically if motorists follow a few simple rules to keep thieves out of their cars in the first place.

Most car thieves are opportunist unskilled petty criminals; many are under 20. So make your own car a less inviting target, to discourage thieves from trying.

2 Now read again and discuss the following questions with your partner. Underline the parts of the text where you find the answer.

1 How does car theft cost everyone money? (three things)

2 What often happens to cars that are stolen? (three things)

3 What sort of people are involved in this type of crime? (three answers)

⊡ LISTENING 2
Note-taking

Listen to two phone calls to a radio programme where a security expert is giving advice. Complete the missing information below.

First Caller:

Items stolen? _____ (1) and jewellery
Where from? _____ (2)
Expert's suggestions?

_____ (3)
_____ (4)

Second Caller:

Items stolen? _____ (5)
Where from? _____ (6)
Expert's suggestions?

_____ (7)
_____ (8)
_____ (9)

GRAMMAR 2
Making deductions

■**1** Look at these sentences from the listening text.

1 *It might have been one of the waiters.*
2 *It could have been the people at the next table.*
3 *It must have been a very brave thief.*
4 *The doors can't have been locked.*

What time do the sentences refer to?
What tense is used?

■**2** Decide if each of the sentences above means either: it's one possible explanation or: it's the only explanation.

■**3** Read this passage from a crime novel and find the three important facts which the inspector knows about the crime.

■**4** Look at Inspector Skea's notes on Agnes, Daphne, Marilyn and Derek on page 53 and decide if any of these people could have committed the murder, or not.

WRITING 1
Giving and justifying opinions

Write four paragraphs in your own words. Begin like this:

1 In my opinion, _____ can't have been the murderer because _____

_____
_____
_____

2 I think _____ might have been the murderer because _____

_____
_____
_____
_____

3 I think _____ could have been the murderer because _____

_____
_____
_____

4 But, I think _____ must have committed the murder because _____

_____
_____

So, who killed Keith Thurbold? All four suspects seemed to have good alibis for the evening, but one of them found time to kill Keith and dispose of the body.

Inspector Skea looked again at the report in front of her. The medical evidence seemed to confirm everything that she had been thinking. The body was found at nine p.m. in the woods twelve miles from Raybury town centre, but the medical report put the time of death at between six and seven p.m.

This was interesting. Each of the suspects had a car, and it would take about twenty minutes to drive those twelve miles along the small country roads on a normal day – but in the fog it may have taken longer.

She picked up her list of suspects again and quickly looked through her notes – ah, yes, there it was. The answer she was looking for! She just had a couple more questions to ask one of the suspects, then she would have the murderer.

1 Agnes Thurbold

Address:
4 Linton Terrace, Raybury.
Relationship:
sister
Motive:
family quarrel – they haven't
spoken for years
Alibi:

5.00	seen leaving the public library
5.10-6.15	alone at home, 'having dinner'
6.15	Mrs Jay (a friend) arrived
6.15-8.00	watched TV with Mrs Jay
8.00	took Mrs Jay home by car (10 mins)

2 Daphne Thurbold

Address
12 Dorchester Gdns, Raybury.
Relationship:
wife (separated)
Motive:
waiting for divorce, could
lose house and car
Alibi:

5.00	left work
5.30	seen arriving home by neighbour
5.30-6.15	alone at home
6.15-6.30	on phone to daughter in America
6.30-7.25	alone at home, getting ready and driving to the theatre (5 mins)
7.25	arrived at Raybury theatre looking calm and elegant
7.25-9.45	in theatre with friends

3 Marilyn Morecott

Address:
14 Alexandra Road, Raybury.
Relationship:
girlfriend
Motive:
she will inherit his money
and share in the business
Alibi:

5.00	left work
5.30	met friend in town centre
6.30-8.00	in cinema with friend
8.15-9.30	in pizzeria with friend

4 Derek Morecott

Address:
The Bungalow, Carter's Lane,
Raybury.
Relationship:
business partner, husband of
Marilyn (separated)
Motive:
jealousy, revenge?
Alibi:

5.45	left the office with Keith (secretary confirms)
6.30	arrived home alone (son confirms)
6.30-8.00	at home with son
8.00	son went out
8.00-8.40	at home alone
8.40-8.45	received phone call from London

HELP WITH GUESSING THE MEANING OF WORDS

When you are reading and you are not sure what words mean, it is possible to guess from the context. This is an important skill because in the exam you are not allowed to use a dictionary and you cannot ask anyone to explain vocabulary to you.

■ **1** In the following passage, the nonsense word 'spreg' has been used instead of some of the real words. Each time decide if 'spreg' is a noun, verb, adjective, adverb or another type of word.
What do you think 'spreg' means in each example?
Is there more than one possible answer?

We got up early this morning and as it was a (1) *spreggy* day we went to the zoo to see the (2) *spregs*. We've (3) *spregged* the zoo many times recently as we are (4) *spregly* interested in (5) *spregs* and so we went to the (6) *spreg* house first.

We were very lucky. We (7) *spregged* just in (8) *spreg* to see them (9) *spregged*. It was (10) *spreg*!

Example:
Word type – adjective
General meaning – describes the weather
Possible words – lovely, sunny, beautiful

■ **2** Compare with your partner. Have conversations like this:
Example: (1)
You: I think it must be an adjective.
Partner: Yes, and I think it describes the weather.
You: I think it might be 'lovely' or 'beautiful'.
Partner: Yes, or it could be 'sunny' or 'fine'.

READING 4
Dealing with difficult vocabulary

■ **1** Read this newspaper article quickly to understand the general sense. Ignore the words you do not know.

Are these statements about the article true or false?

1 A man arrived in Brampton covered in blood.

2 The blood may be human or animal.

3 Nobody is missing from the area.

4 The man may have killed somebody.

5 The police are looking for his jacket and trousers.

■ **2** Read again more carefully and choose the correct alternatives for these words in the text.

1 snowbound (line 3)
   is   **a** an adverb
          b an adjective
          c a noun

   It means **a** blocked by snow
          b snowing a lot
          c a thing for clearing snow

2 chin (line 4)
   is   **a** a noun
          b a verb
          c an adjective

   It means **a** a part of the body
          b a piece of clothing
          c a type of knife

3 frogmen (line 12)
   is   **a** a verb
          b a noun
          c an adjective

   It means **a** an animal
          b sub-aqua divers
          c a way of swimming

4 sheds (line 14)
   is   **a** a verb
          b a noun
          c an adverb

   It means **a** tools and equipment
          b digging holes
          c small wooden buildings

Gory riddle of 'wolfman'

BY GRAHAM BELL

1 **IT HAS ALL** the ingredients of what Sherlock Holmes would call "a three-pipe problem."

Out of the snowbound lanes walked a man, covered in blood from his chin to his knees, who announced to police: "I am a werewolf."

At first detectives thought the fresh blood caking his faded cream jacket belonged to an animal. But tests established it as human. Yesterday, with the man refusing to reveal any information, officers were trying
10 to account for all 6,000 residents of Brampton, near Carlisle, Cumbria.

Frogmen scoured lakes and the River Irthing which runs past the market town. Gardeners checked their sheds and families rang round sons, daughters, cousins and aunts.

So whose blood is it? "If only we knew," said James Shaw, owner of the Sands House Hotel, from whose car park the "werewolf" was picked up last Tuesday. "The police are being very thorough and are checking every
20 man, woman and child. They have been back to us five times."

The man, who lives near Brampton, has been questioned, but gives vague, enigmatic answers. Search parties have re-traced every footstep he is known to have made. Tracker dogs have combed woods and fields and people who spotted the strange, dishevelled figure have been interviewed at length.

Detective Chief Superintendent Stephen Reed said yesterday: "We are either looking for a body or someone
30 who is seriously injured. The amount of blood is consistent with one or the other. It is like a jigsaw puzzle you start from the wrong end. We have the centre piece and are now looking for bits to complete the picture."

Yesterday 30 uniformed officers and 12 detectives were cross-checking electoral rolls and picking their way over frozen fields near Hadrian's Wall. They are still searching for a black leather jacket which the man is believed to have discarded before his dramatic entrance into Brampton.
40 On Friday a man was remanded in custody by Carlisle magistrates, charged with burglary and assaulting a police officer.

3 Now make a table like this for the words shown below from the text.

Word	Line	Type of word	Meaning in text
Knees	*4*	*noun (pl)*	*joints half-way down leg*

faded (7)   footstep (24)   dishevelled (26)
scoured (12)   tracker (25)   jigsaw (31)
enigmatic (23) combed (25)   rolls (35)
re-traced (24)   spotted (26)   discarded (38)

Check your answers with your partner by practising as in exercise 2 on page 54.

4 Read the article again more carefully to answer these multiple-choice questions.

1 The man who walked into Brampton said

  a nothing that was helpful to the police.
  b that he had killed someone in the town.
  c that the blood was from a wolf.
  d that someone was seriously injured.

2 What have the police been trying to do?

  a Follow the man around Brampton.
  b Find out where the man lives.
  c Discover where the blood came from.
  d Make sure the blood is human and not animal.

3 What do the police think?

  a Someone could have been murdered.
  b Someone must have been killed.
  c Someone might have tried to kill the man.
  d The man may have been attacked by a wolf.

5 What do you think is the explanation for this mystery?

GRAMMAR 3
Relative pronouns

1 What is a werewolf?

1 A person who changes into a wild animal.
2 An animal which looks like a man.
3 A place where a murder is committed.

2 For each of these words from the passage, write a definition using *who, which* or *where*.

1 detectives (line 6)   6 sheds (14)
2 residents (10)   7 car park (18)
3 frogmen (12)   8 search parties (24)
4 lakes (12)   9 tracker dogs (25)
5 market town (13) 10 jigsaw puzzle (31)

3 Which of the words in exercise 2 are compounds – where two nouns are used together to describe one thing?

PRONUNCIATION
Compound nouns

1 Match the words in **A** with those in **B** to make compound nouns.

A	B
pass	man
pen	dresser
news	port
suit	knife
guide	cheques
first-aid	book
shop	kit
light	cleaner
hair	paper
vacuum	case
walk	lifter
travellers'	switch

2 Mark the stressed syllable on each compound noun.

3 Listen to check.

4 Write a definition for each of the compound nouns using *who, which* or *where*.

SPEAKING 3
Exchanging information

1 Student A: Read the instructions and look at the picture on the next page.
Student B: Read the instructions and look at the picture on page 58.

Student A

This is your hotel room as you left it when you went out this morning. Student B is telephoning you from the hotel to tell you that your room has been burgled. Describe to Student B where your possessions were, and find out what has been stolen.

HELP WITH WRITING
Reports

■1 You have been asked to write a report of the theft for the local police.

What information will be important? Decide which of these things to mention in your report: Are they necessary? Will they help the police?

- date and time of the theft
- list of the stolen items
- description of the stolen items
- who discovered the theft
- how long you have been on holiday
- what you think of the hotel
- who might have stolen the items
- whether the items were insured
- who you are and how you are involved
- the mess made by the thief

■2 You now have to write your report. Use these headings for your paragraphs. In which paragraph will you mention each of the points you chose from the list?

1	Personal information	**3**	What was stolen
2	What happened	**4**	Any other important information

■3 Compare reports with your partner. Look for any differences or contradictions and make any improvements before you give them to the police.

LISTENING 3
Blank filling

1 Look at these words connected with computers and discuss with your partner what they mean.

to log on   database   keyboard   network

2 What crimes are associated with computers?

3 You will hear part of a radio programme about a computer hacker, an amateur computer expert who breaks in to computer systems. As you listen, complete the sentences by writing a word or short phrase in each of the spaces **1–10**.

Neil didn't have (**1**) _____ when he left school.
He broke into computer systems using his (**2**) _____ .
He didn't intend (**3**) _____ the computer systems.
He was the first computer hacker to (**4**) _____ .
Some computer hackers work in (**5**) _____ .
Inspector James uses (**6**) _____ methods to catch hackers.
Neil used to leave joke messages for (**7**) _____ .
His messages became nasty when he thought he'd been (**8**) _____ . He didn't know that (**9**) _____ working alone got the messages.
Neil was surprised that he could beat such (**10**) _____ staff.

EXAM PRACTICE 4

1 Read the text below and think of the word which best fits each space. Use only one word in each space. There is an example at the beginning (0).

Quick as a Flash!

Some villagers (**0**) _____who_____ wanted to protect a rare bird's nest have finally solved (**1**) _____ mystery of the disappearing eggs. (**2**) _____ the last three years, a pair of rare birds has built a nest near the village of Sawton and every year the eggs (**3**) _____ vanished.

Last year, the villagers suspected thieves (**4**) _____ stealing the rare eggs and selling (**5**) _____ on the black market. This year, organised by local bird-watcher Margery Thisk, they (**6**) _____ weeks guarding the nest-site. They installed a burglar alarm and kept watch (**7**) _____ a powerful video camera.(**8**) _____ all their careful precautions, they found the eggs missing again.

However, the video recording has been (**9**) _____ to identify the thief, who is Mrs Thisk's black and white pet cat called Flash.

'We were watching the video playback (**10**) _____ Flash suddenly appeared and ran (**11**) _____ with one of the eggs' said a red-faced Mrs Thisk.

(**12**) _____ year, the villagers plan to fix a cat scarer to the tree (**13**) _____ the birds build their nest. This machine makes a very high-pitched noise (**14**) _____ birds and people cannot hear, but cats can and they do not like the noise (**15**) _____ all.

2 Read the text below and look carefully at each line. Some of the lines are correct, and some have a word which should not be there. If a line is correct put a tick(✓) . If a line has a word which should not be there, write the word in the space on the right. There are two examples at the beginning (**0**) and (**00**).

Car Crime

Apart from your home, your car is probably	**0**	✓
your most valuable with possession.	**00**	_with_
Over 460,000 of cars are reported missing in	**1**	_____
the Britain each year and many of those are	**2**	_____
never to recovered. Many of those which are found	**3**	_____
have been damaged by thieves. A stolen car	**4**	_____
which is also far more likely to be involved	**5**	_____
in an accident than the same a car driven	**6**	_____
by its owner; car thieves are often young and	**7**	_____
sometimes its drunk.	**8**	_____
Yet car crime can be to cut drastically if	**9**	_____
motorists follow a few by simple rules to keep	**10**	_____
thieves out of their cars in the first place.	**11**	_____
Most them car thieves are opportunist unskilled	**12**	_____
petty criminals; many are under twenty age. So,	**13**	_____
make your own car is a less inviting target,	**14**	_____
to discourage thieves from go trying.	**15**	_____

■3 Read the text below. Use the word given in capitals at the end of each line to form a word that fits in the space on the same line. There is an example at the beginning (**0**).

Technology and Crime

Modern (**0**) *technological* advances have led to great changes	**TECHNOLOGY**
in police work. Whilst computer (**1**) _____ are important	**NET**
in allowing the police to store efficiently the (**2**) _____	**INFORM**
they need, computer technology has also helped (**3**) _____ ,	**CRIME**
particularly those making (**4**) _____ of banknotes	**FORGE**
and other documents.	
The police can no longer rely on (**5**) _____ and	**FINGER**
other more traditional methods of (**6**) _____ . They	**DETECT**
have to keep up to date with (**7**) _____ in many	**DEVELOP**
fields. For example, the (**8**) _____ of the cordless	**INVENT**
electric drill left them (**9**) _____ against robbers of	**POWER**
telephone boxes.	
The police now devote more time to the (**10**) _____	**PREVENT**
of crime, by giving advice to motorists and householders	
about how to protect their possessions.	

■4 Write an answer of between 120–180 words to one of these questions in an appropriate style.

1 You have been asked to write an article for your class magazine on 'Some ways of protecting your home against burglars – the advantages and disadvantages of these methods'.

Write a short **article** for the magazine on this topic.

2 You recently saw an armed robbery.

Write a **letter** to a friend explaining what happened.

Student B
You are at the hotel. You telephone Student A to say that his/her hotel room has been burgled. Describe to Student A what you can see and find out what has been stolen.

Playing the game

SPEAKING 1

Expressing and justifying opinions

Talk to your partner:

1 Name the sport or game in each picture, and say:

What equipment is necessary.
What the aim is.
What skills are necessary.

2 What is the difference between a sport and a game?

3 Divide these activities into three groups:

a Sports.
b Games.
c Activities which are both sports and games.

squash	tennis	Scrabble
billiards	fishing	hockey
Trivial Pursuits	rollerskating	skiing
basketball	parachuting	chess
swimming	golf	rugby

🔊 LISTENING 1

Multiple matching

1 Talk to your partner about these things:

Do you enjoy playing board games?
Which games do you have at home?
How often do you play them?
When is the best time to play?

2 You will hear five different people talking about a new type of night club where people play board games. For questions 1–5, choose the phrase **A–H** which best summarises what each person is talking about.

A Games you don't find everywhere	Speaker 1 ☐
B Meals at the club	2 ☐
C How the club is organised	
D Bringing back childhood memories	3 ☐
E Games for different types of people	4 ☐
F How the club could be improved	
G Suitable for all the family	5 ☐
H A good late-night alternative	

GRAMMAR 1
Time linkers

■1 Below are some facts about the game of Scrabble.

Imagine that either you are playing the game of Scrabble for the first time, or, if you know Scrabble, you have to explain the rules to a friend.

Decide which of the following sentences contain important facts about how to play the game.

Compare with your partner.

> Scrabble can be played by two to four players.
>
> The board can be folded for storage.
>
> The first word must cover the star.
>
> Scrabble is played using small tiles.
>
> Scrabble is useful to practise spelling.
>
> Each tile has a number to indicate its value for scoring.
>
> You need a pencil and paper to keep the score.
>
> Each player must take seven tiles from the bag.
>
> The game was invented by an American.
>
> Covering the coloured squares on the board gives extra points.
>
> Scrabble can be played at any time of day.
>
> On each tile there is a letter of the alphabet.
>
> The game ends when the bag is empty and one player has used all his or her tiles.
>
> Each new word must use at least one letter from a word already on the board.
>
> As letters are used they must be replaced from the bag.
>
> Scrabble is not expensive to buy.
>
> Scrabble is very popular in the USA.
>
> Small Scrabble sets can be bought to use when travelling.

■2 In the instructions below fill each of the numbered blanks with one of the expressions from the box. Use each word or phrase once only.

during	as soon as	firstly	or	until
after that	then	to begin with	while	
so that	either	lastly		

(**1**) *To begin with* you need a Scrabble board, a set of letters and a pencil and paper to keep the score. You can play with two, three or four players.

(**2**) _____ each person takes one tile from the bag, and the person with the highest number on his or her tile will start the game. (**3**) _____ each person takes six more tiles from the bag so that everyone has seven letters.

The first player starts by making a word which covers the star in the centre of the board. (**4**) _____ the next player makes another word by (**5**) _____ creating a new word which crosses the original word (**6**) _____ by adding more letters to the original word.

(**7**) _____ players make a word they must take more letters from the bag (**8**) _____ they always have seven. All the players continue making words in this way (**9**) _____ there are no more letters in the bag and one person has used all his or her tiles.

(**10**) _____ playing try to cover the coloured squares as these increase the number of points on the tile. (**11**) _____ the game one person keeps the score by adding up all the numbers in each word played.

(**12**) _____ it should be remembered that Scrabble can take a very long time if the players are really keen and, of course, players get better with practice.

WRITING 1
Instructions

1 Think of a game or sport you know well. Make a list of the important facts or instructions people need to know in order to play the game.

2 Make sure the points are in a logical order.

3 Use your list to write some instructions for the game, using the passage above as an example.

You are going to read a magazine article. For questions **1–7**, choose the answer (**A**, **B**, **C** or **D**) which you think fits best according to the text.

A hit 20 years in the making

The building-brick game Jenga was no overnight success.

1 **T**AKE A HEAP of little wooden bricks. Make them into a tower. Pull out a brick at a time until the whole lot falls down.
5 Game over. Simple.

But brilliant. Jenga has sold in millions around the world. Yet Jenga is the success story which very nearly wasn't.

10 Flashback to the early 1970s. A teenage girl and her younger brother are playing on the terrace of their parents' house on a tea plantation in Africa.
15 They have borrowed a pile of small wooden bricks from a nearby saw mill which they stack in columns. The idea is to pull out loose bricks and replace
20 them on top. Eventually there is a thunderous and highly satisfactory crash.

For the girl, Leslie Scott, the game made a cheap and cheerful
25 Christmas present for relatives. She even had a local carpenter make little wooden boxes to store them in. She had no idea of the game's commercial possibilities.
30 "I thought that anyone who had bricks played with them the way we did."

Then she came back to England to work for a computer company
35 in Oxford. When Leslie went to dinner parties she took her game, which was very popular. So people suggested she should sell it.

40 Then a business contact suggested how the tiny imperfections which make it possible to remove the wooden bricks could be reproduced on a
45 commercial scale. Leslie decided to give it a try. In her innocence she went to her bank manager and asked for £15,000. He was nice and gave it to her.

50 So far so good. A local workshop agreed to make it and the game got a name, Jenga – Swahili for 'to build'. She booked a large stand at a major toy fair and set
55 off with several hundred sets in their smart plastic wrappings. It was here that she discovered the dreadful truth. Nobody wanted to know.

60 "I had taken a huge stand because I knew I was going to be up against the big companies. I stood there day after day and I didn't take a single order."

Leslie had discovered what every small games
65 inventor eventually finds out. Shops don't buy from companies who only make a single product.

By now she was heavily in debt. She got a few games into smaller shops but the money was
70 running out. Then her nice old bank manager left. The new nasty one suggested that the bank might want some return on its investment.

To carry on Leslie faced a hard decision. The loan had been guaranteed against her house.
75 She had also borrowed money from her mother. Mum was more important than the bank, but the house had to go. This is the point at which most small businesses fail. Leslie was saved by the brother of a friend who made a living
80 exporting to Canada.

In Canada the game was spotted by a representative of Irwin, a large games and toy company. It was the mid-1980s and another Canadian game, Trivial Pursuits, was taking North America by
85 storm. Irwin wanted an alternative and thought Jenga might be a big success.

Eventually a deal was signed, and gradually the game began to take off.

Last year Jenga sold three million games
90 world-wide. It is played in nearly 30 countries. There is even a pocket version in Japan made from plastic.

It made Leslie Scott a rich woman at 39. "I could live off the money, but I decided to set up my own
95 games company," she says. Oxford Games now specialises in designing up-market board games. But Leslie knows she is unlikely to invent anything quite so successful again: "In essence it is an incredibly simple game. I continue to enjoy
100 playing it."

---

1 The aim of Jenga is to

  A knock over a tower.
  B remove all the bricks from a tower.
  C change a tower into a box.
  D increase the height of a tower.

2 Leslie Scott originally invented the game

  A to amuse her children with it.
  B to play it with her family.
  C to make a lot of money from it.
  D to give it to her friends.

3 It is possible to remove the bricks in Jenga because

  A they are not a regular shape.
  B they are not all the same size.
  C they are made by hand.
  D they are made of wood.

4 What does 'it' in line 46 refer to?

  A Producing the special bricks.
  B Playing Jenga at parties.
  C Making Jenga commercially.
  D Visiting a bank manager.

5 Leslie Scott's first attempt to market Jenga was unsuccessful because

  A people thought her game was rather boring.
  B she didn't have any other games to sell.
  C nobody had heard of her game before.
  D there were lots of similar games on sale.

6 When Leslie Scott had financial problems she had to

  A sell her home to pay the bank.
  B borrow more money from the bank.
  C ask her mother to lend her more money.
  D let a friend's brother buy her invention.

7 What are 'up-market' board games (line 96)?

  A Games which are about making money.
  B Games which are very popular.
  C Games which are designed for adults.
  D Games which are rather expensive.

SPEAKING 2
Sports quiz

How much do you know about sport? In groups of three decide which are the correct answers to these questions. Use a dictionary to help you check your answers.

1 Which of these sports is not played with a racquet?
a squash
b badminton
c tennis
d cricket

2 Which of these sports uses an oval ball?
a soccer
b rugby
c water polo
d hockey

3 Which of these sports is not played over a net?
a volleyball
b tennis
c squash
d badminton

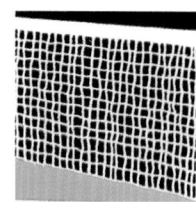

4 Which of these sports does not involve throwing something?
a javelin
b shotput
c pole vault
d discus

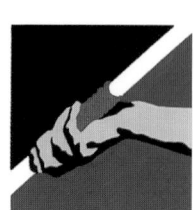

5 Which of these is not a swimming style?
a butterfly
b crawl
c breaststroke
d diving

6 Which of these is not a winter sport?
a tobogganing
b skating
c jogging
d skiing

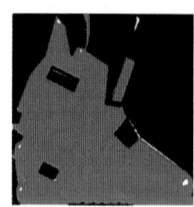

7 Which of these is not an Olympic sport?
a parachuting
b rowing
c shooting
d archery

8 Where was the 1994 World Cup final held?
a Los Angeles
b Chicago
c New York
d San Francisco

9 Which of these is not a martial art?
a judo
b karate
c croquet
d jujitsu

10 Which of these games is not played on a table?
a snooker
b dominoes
c darts
d billiards

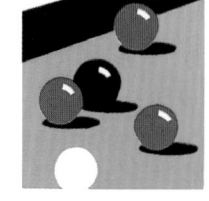

11 Which of these is not a water sport?
a windsurfing
b abseiling
c rowing
d snorkelling

12 Which of these games does not use goals?
a ice-hockey
b polo
c baseball
d lacrosse

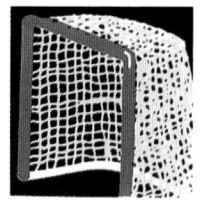

LISTENING 2
Selecting an answer

1 Before you listen look at this list of sports.

1 What do they all have in common?

2 Divide them into two groups, A and B, and give each group a title.

hockey	squash	baseball
rugby	badminton	tennis
soccer	golf	American football
volleyball	cricket	polo
table tennis	basketball	billiards

3 Now divide the same words into three groups and give each group a title.

4 Compare with other students. Did you make the same or different groups?

5 Listen to this radio interview and write down all the names of sports which you hear mentioned.

2 Now listen again and choose the best alternative **A**, **B**, or **C**.

1 We know that the ancient Egyptians played ball games because

    A it is mentioned in ancient stories.
    B ancient works of art show them.
    C sports equipment was found in tombs.

2 When were racquets invented?

    A In the fifteenth century.
    B In the sixteenth century.
    C In the nineteenth century.

3 Before the nineteenth century

    A the rules were different in different places.
    B the games had no rules at all.
    C nobody followed the rules.

4 In the nineteenth century

    A many new games were invented.
    B many old games were rediscovered.
    C old games were organised more formally.

5 Where were most modern rules set down?

    A In schools.
    B In villages.
    C In factories.

GRAMMAR 2
Used to

1 Look at these phrases from the listening text.

Each town or district used to have its own version of the same basic game.
People used to work out the rules over the years.

1 When did these things happen?

2 Did they happen at one specific point in time?

3 Do they happen now?

Look at these examples:

Our football team used to wear blue shirts.
Do they wear blue shirts now? (No)
Did they wear them often? (Yes)
When did they wear them? (In the past)

American football didn't use to be so popular.
Is it popular now? (Yes)
Was it popular in the past? (No)

Did you use to play table tennis at your old school?

NB *Used to* does not exist in the present.

2 Put the correct form of the verb (present, past or *used to* + infinitive) in these sentences.

1 When I was at school we _____ hockey twice a week. (play)

2 I _____ to the gym three times a week now that I have a car. (go)

3 Skiing _____ a sport for rich people only, but now many people can take part. (be)

4 I only _____ skiing twice during my holiday in Switzerland. (go)

5 My father _____ me to see football matches on Saturday afternoons before I was old enough to go alone. (take)

6 He _____ , but when he realised it affected his game he gave up. (smoke)

7 I _____ tennis and golf regularly when the weather is good. (play)

8 Before our local pool was built, I _____ six kilometres by bicycle to do my training every week. (travel)

9 My brother _____ to the stadium every week, but now he just sits at home and _____ football on the television. (go/watch)

10 I _____ a new tennis racquet for Christmas and I'm really looking forward to using it for the first time. (get)

SPEAKING 3
Exchanging information

Discuss these questions with your partner:

1 What sports do you play now? How often do you play?
2 What sports did you use to play?
3 Why did you give them up?
4 How has sport changed in recent years?

Talk about:
- equipment
- clothes
- number of spectators
- facilities in your area
- popularity
- sport on television

LISTENING 3
Selecting an answer

1 Fill each of the numbered blanks in the following passage. Use only one word in each space.

Skiing was originally invented because people in some areas needed to cross country (**1**) _____ was often covered in snow (**2**) _____ large parts of the year.

We know that men and women have (**3**) _____ skiing for at (**4**) _____ four thousand years. The remains (**5**) _____ ancient skis have been discovered dating from (**6**) _____ period, as well (**7**) _____ good examples of rock carvings showing early skiers. Old documents describe (**8**) _____ people used skis to follow animals, and (**9**) _____ type of hunting was common until the sixteenth century.

Today, skiing, which was originally (**10**) _____ a means of transport, has developed (**11**) _____ a leisure activity and an important part of the tourist industry in some countries. It is now enjoyed (**12**) _____ an increasing number of people each year.

2 Alice and Barry are talking about learning to ski. Listen and tick (✓) the problems which Barry had when he went skiing for the first time.

- ☐ expensive equipment
- ☐ too much snow
- ☐ too many people
- ☐ risk of accidents
- ☐ transport problems
- ☐ bad weather
- ☐ language difficulties
- ☐ bad teachers
- ☐ cost of lessons
- ☐ aches and pains

GRAMMAR 3
Past perfect

1 Look at these phrases from the listening text.

I'd never tried it before
They'd already had lots of practice
I'd never felt so miserable in my life

1 Which tense is used?
2 Why?

Barry uses the Past perfect tense to talk about things that happened before the story, which he is telling in the Past simple tense.

When we tell a story, we set a time in the past in which the narrative takes place. When we refer to times and periods before that, we indicate this by using the Past perfect.

Look at these examples:

	Tense	Time
I woke up early on Saturday morning.	Past simple	Saturday
It had been a very tiring week.	Past perfect	the week before Saturday
I'd never felt so tired until then.	Past perfect	in my life

Compare:

	Tense	Time
I arrived there late on Friday evening.	Past simple	Friday pm
It had been a very tiring journey.	Past perfect	before I arrived
I went to bed and fell asleep immediately.	Past simple	after I arrived

■ 2 Put the correct tense (Past simple or Past perfect) in each sentence.

1 I arrived late at the stadium and the match _____ . (start)

2 My legs ached after the match. I _____ tennis for over five years. (not play)

3 The team had a good season in 1995. They _____ nearly all their matches. (win)

4 Before the Olympic Games few people _____ of synchronised swimming. (hear)

5 We invited Geoff to our party but he _____ to go away that weekend. (arrange)

6 She started playing golf at the age of ten and soon _____ a regular player at the local club. (become)

7 John looked at the water below him and froze. He _____ from the top board before. (never dive)

8 As she _____ in a car rally before, she was able to give him some good advice. (take part)

9 He walked up to the rostrum with a smile. It was the sixth time he _____ a gold medal. (win)

10 There was a huge cheer from the crowd when at the end of the match the President _____ the gold cup to the winning team. (present)

WRITING 2
Narrative

■ **1** Look at the five pictures. With your partner decide the best order for the pictures to make a story.

■ **2** Read this account of the day. Is the story similar or different to yours? What about the order of the pictures?

A few years ago on a skiing holiday in the Dolomites I had one of the worst experiences of my life.

My friend and I had decided not to ski that day, the sun was shining and the snow was melting fast. We had decided, instead, to take the ski-lift to the top of the mountain and have a walk around, taking our picnic lunch with us.

As there was little snow left we met very few skiers and the bar at the top of the lift was empty. After drinking a quick cup of coffee we set out to explore the mountain top. We had lunch, sitting on a rock overlooking a deep wooded ravine. After finishing our sandwiches we decided to walk a little way further before turning back and following the path back to the bar.

The weather changed quite suddenly. We had been too busy talking to notice the approaching black clouds, but suddenly the sun disappeared and it became quite cold. We decided to turn back immediately and before long, reached our lunch spot. To our horror, however, we noticed that two paths led away from the spot through the trees. We hadn't noticed this before, and realised that we didn't know which path to take. Although we had a map with us, it wasn't helpful as it only showed one path through the woods. To make matters worse, it began to snow and we realised that soon we might not be able to find the path at all.

■ **3** What do you think will happen next? With your partner discuss some possible endings to the story.

Now read the end of the story. Is it the same as your story or different?

Despite all this, neither of us panicked and, after a brief discussion, we decided to choose the right-hand path. After about an hour of walking we realised that we hadn't recognised a single landmark and that the snow was falling faster and faster. What should we do? Should we turn back? It would take an hour just to reach the lunch spot. We would never get back to the ski-lift before it closed at 5.00 pm. There was no alternative but to carry on or to face a night on the mountain!

I was just beginning to get really frightened when I heard a shout in the distance. We stopped and, after a moment's silence, began to shout at the tops of our voices. We turned a corner of the path and saw ahead of us the ski-lift station. We had made it! However, it was not the top of the slope, but the bottom. Without realising it we had walked all the way down the mountain side.

Afterwards, in the safety of the hotel, I realised how lucky we had been and how close to disaster we had come.

4 The complete story is divided into five paragraphs, plus an introduction and conclusion.

1 How do we recognise a paragraph?

2 How did the writer know when to end one paragraph and begin another?

3 Can you give each paragraph a title?

4 What information is included in the introduction and conclusion?

5 Look at the verbs in the story.

1 Which tense is used for most of the story?

2 Which other tenses are used?

3 Read the story again. Underline the sentences in which other tenses are used and decide why. Compare with your partner.

6 Look at the words and phrases in **bold** type.

1 What contribution do they make to the composition?

2 Look at these phrases:

   a After that we went home.
   b After drinking our coffee we went home.
   c After coffee we went home.
   d Afterwards we went home.
   e After I had finished my coffee I went home.

What are the rules for using *after*?

3 Try writing some more phrases using *before*. Are the rules the same?

7 What is the difference between *although* and *despite*?

Finish each of the sentences in such a way that it means exactly the same as the sentence printed before it.

1 Despite feeling cold we kept walking.

Although _____

_____

_____

2 Although it was sunny I felt quite cold.

Despite_____

_____

_____

3 Despite the fact that it was snowing, I felt warm.

Although _____

_____

_____

4 Despite the large amount of snow, we had our picnic.

Although _____

_____

_____

5 Although we had a map we got lost.

Despite_____

_____

_____

NB *Although = Even though*
     Despite = In spite of

PRONUNCIATION
Intonation

1 Listen to a phrase read by two different people. How is the phrase different?

1 *although it was raining* ↗

2 *although it was raining* ↘

2 Listen to the phrases 1–10 and decide if the intonation is falling (it is the end of the sentence), or rising (the speaker means to continue).

1 despite the weather

2 although he had a map

3 after drinking our coffee

4 before leaving the bar

5 after finishing our sandwiches

6 a few years ago

7 after a moment's silence

8 after about an hour

9 to make matters worse

10 before it closed at five pm

3 Check with your partner. Practise saying the phrases to each other using falling and rising intonation. Can your partner hear the difference?

4 Complete each of the phrases **1–10** to make a whole sentence. Then read them to your partner with the correct intonation.

Examples:

Despite the weather, they ↗ had a picnic. ↘

They had a picnic, despite ↗ the weather. ↘

HELP WITH WRITING
Narrative

It is just as important to plan a narrative composition as it is to plan the type we looked at in Unit 1. It is difficult to concentrate on both writing the story and inventing the story at the same time, so you should:

1 Make notes of your ideas.

2 Make a plan of your paragraphs.

3 Write your introduction.

In the exam you have to write between 120 and 180 words in your story. If you choose to write a narrative, it will probably need to be about 180 words. The story you read on pages 68 and 69 is about twice that length, but it is a useful model of how to organise your writing.

To begin with, you might find it easier to write a longer story without a limit of words, and later to practise writing shorter stories within a time limit (45 minutes for each composition) as exam practice.

1 Choose one of the following titles:

1 Write a story about one of the happiest days of your life.

2 Write a story about a day when everything went wrong.

3 Write a story which begins 'It was an experience I will never forget'.

2 Make a list of the events in the narrative, and decide where you will divide the paragraphs. Don't forget that you will have a separate introduction and conclusion.

paragraph	model composition	your composition
1	• decided not to ski • went up ski-lift	
2	• long walk • lunch • walked a bit further	
3	• weather changed • turned back • two paths	
4	• long walk in snow – fear	
5	• home at last	

3 Now write your introduction. It should set the scene and the time.

4 You are now ready to write the paragraphs of your story. Remember to use *after, before, although* and *despite*.

READING 2
Reading for main points

■1 Discuss:

How important is it to have the right clothes and equipment when you play a sport?

Are there fashions in sports clothes in your country?

Do you think it is important to wear clothes with 'designer' labels?

■2 Read this magazine article about the TV programme 'Family Matters' and decide whether these statements are true or false. Ignore any words you do not understand.

1 The fashion for expensive designer trainers came to Britain from America.

2 Kelly's father is unemployed.

3 Kelly liked the trainers her mother bought her.

4 Kelly's classmates had always been nice to her before she started wearing the trainers.

5 In Kelly's old school the children hadn't been forced to wear their school uniform.

FASHION'S VICTIM

1 **TEENAGE TRAINER mania** has **swept** America, with reports of children being mugged and even murdered for their fashionable and
5 expensive footwear. As this week's Family Matters discovers, this obsession with designer labels has reached Britain. Recently a girl was **slashed** in the face because
10 she wouldn't 'give' another child her **trendy** new jacket.

But not having the right **gear** can also make children **targets**, like 14-year-old Kelly Parslow, from
15 Birmingham. Her parents can't afford to buy her the 'in' clothes, such as Reebok or Nike trainers and shell suits (her father is on indefinite sick leave and her mother,
20 Lynn, has two younger children as well). Last summer her mother did buy her some trainers, not a fashionable make, but ones which looked similar and cost only £7.99.

25 Kelly was happy with them, but when she wore them to school, her classmates weren't. 'They all started **taking the mickey** straight away,'

she **recalls**. 'They said "How much
30 did those things cost?", and they pushed me, called me a **pauper** and made up songs about them.' Then, after school, a group of seven or eight girls lay in wait for her, and
35 **scratched** and kicked her so badly that she ended up in casualty suffering from shock and contusions to her spine.

Her mother, Lynn Parslow, says:
40 'In my day, if you'd got the gear, you felt sorry for the ones who hadn't. You certainly didn't **taunt** them.' Kelly had been **picked on** before, because she was quiet, hardworking
45 and not interested in fashion – but not like this. She now goes to another school where the uniform rules are strictly observed. 'It's much nicer there,' says Kelly.
50 'Nobody minds about fashion. There are a lot of other children in my position, who can't afford things, and everyone leaves them alone.'

Dealing with difficult vocabulary

■3 Try to guess the meaning of these words in bold type in the text. Add to the list any other words which you do not know.

Word	Line	Type of word	Possible meaning
mania	(1)	noun	an obsession
swept	(2)	past participle	
slashed	(9)		
trendy	(11)		
gear	(12)		
targets	(13)		
taking the mickey	(28)		
recalls	(29)		
pauper	(31)		
scratched	(35)		
taunt	(42)		
picked on	(43)		

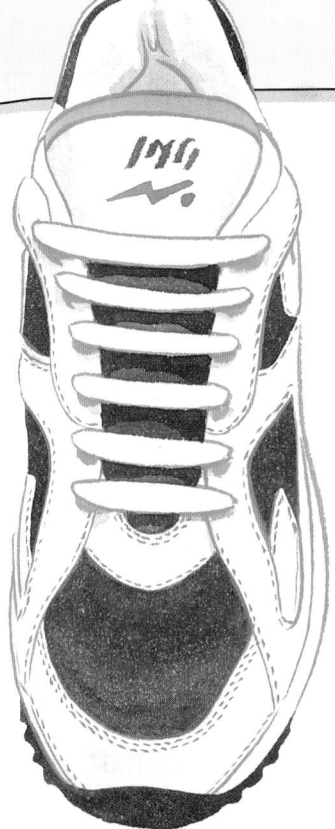

⊡ LISTENING 4
Short extracts

You will hear people talking in six different situations. Choose the best answer **A**, **B**, or **C** for each question **1–6**.

1 You will hear part of a lecture about the history of sport. How was sport commercialised in the past?

    A People had to pay to watch.
    B Players were paid for taking part.
    C Pubs provided large prizes.

2 You will hear part of a radio programme. What type of programme is it?

    A a sports commentary
    B a quiz programme
    C an interview

3 You will hear a man talking about an accident he had recently. How did he feel after the manager spoke to him?

    A angry
    B amused
    C disappointed

4 You will hear a woman giving some instructions to a group of children. What are the children going to do?

    A go fishing in a river
    B cook some fish for her
    C play a game at home

5 You will hear a public announcement. Where is the announcement being made?

    A at an airport
    B at a railway station
    C at a bus terminus

6 You will hear part of a music programme on the radio. What is the speaker talking about?

    A a compact disc
    B a concert
    C a video film

HELP WITH ERROR CORRECTION

In the First Certificate Paper 3 (Use of English) one of the exercises asks you to look at a passage where some of the lines are correct and some have an extra word added.

■1 Each of these sentences has an extra underlined word added which should not be there. What type of word (e.g. article, preposition, verb, etc.) has been added to each sentence?

1 You need a Scrabble board, a set of letters and a pencil and paper to keep <u>up</u> the score.

2 Next month I'm going on a course to learn <u>the</u> judo.

3 When I tried <u>and</u> to play golf, it was more difficult than I had expected.

4 I like <u>to</u> draughts but I don't really enjoy playing chess – it's boring!

5 Eric hurt his leg playing <u>in</u> football last week.

■2 In each of these sentences there is one extra word which should not be there. Cross out the extra word.

1 I want to work in the leisure industry when I will leave school.

2 My sister she likes to play tennis with her friends three times a week.

3 Some people who play sports insist that taking part in is sometimes more important than winning.

4 In the summer, I will be go swimming every morning.

5 Skis used to be made of the wood.

6 The referee's job in a game of football is to make sure of the rules of the game are observed.

7 Make sure you have all your valuables with you before to leaving the changing rooms.

8 Because he was not playing very well, Simon was yet left out of the team.

9 Without realising it, she had overtaken up most of the other competitors in the race.

10 Anne is looking forward much to going on a climbing trip next winter.

3 Look at this text. In each line there is one extra word added which should not be there. Cross out these words and decide what types of word they are.

Frisbee

	Type of word
The Frisbee was invented by students at the Yale	1 _____
University in the United States in1947. The first of	2 _____
games were played by with metal tins used to	3 _____
cook in cakes, and these were provided by a local	4 _____
baker named Joseph Frisbie, who had to a contract	5 _____
to supply much food regularly to the university. In	6 _____
1948, a young American man who had just left from the	7 _____
army produced a similar disc, but this a time made	8 _____
of the light plastic. Eventually he was able to sell	9 _____
up his invention to another company called Wham-o,	10 _____
which, after hearing about most the origins of the game,	11 _____
decided that to call their product Frisbee.	12 _____

- Although any type of word could be the extra wrong word in this type of exercise, the extra words are usually grammatical (eg prepositions, articles, pronouns, etc.) rather than information words (eg nouns, adjectives, etc.).

4 Read the text below and look carefully at each line. Some of the lines are correct, and some have a word which should not be there. If a line is correct put a tick (✓). If a line has a word which should not be there, write the word in the space on the right. There are two examples at the beginning (**0**) and (**00**).

Swimming

My favourite of sporting activity is swimming and I	**0**	*of*
try to go to my local swimming pool at least twice	**00**	✓
a week and swim it for half an hour or so. I like to	1	_____
go very early in the morning there because then the	2	_____
pool is quiet and the all other people who go at	3	_____
that time are serious swimmers just like me also.	4	_____
But I must to admit that it isn't always very easy	5	_____
to get up so early in the morning – especially in the	6	_____
winter or when it is going raining. Swimming is really	7	_____
a good exercise for the whole body and I find	8	_____
that it can helps me to relax. In fact, as I go	9	_____
up and down the swimming pool as fast as I can,	10	_____
anything else that I'm a bit worried about just goes	11	_____
straight out of my mind. The other good thing	12	_____
about going to the swimming pool regularly is that	13	_____
it's not expensive and you don't have got to buy	14	_____
lots of the special equipment before you start.	15	_____

EXAM PRACTICE 5

■ **1**   Read the text below and decide which word **A**, **B**, **C** or **D** best fits each space.
There is an example at the beginning (**0**).

Football in Brazil

The (**0**)*experience* of going to a football (**1**) _____ in Brazil is something which
even people who are not (**2**) _____ of the game will really enjoy. You
(**3**) _____ the big event together with thousands of screaming football
enthusiasts accompanied by the (**4**) _____ of drums and waving of flags. It's
not just that the football is great, there is a (**5**) _____ and genuine love for the
game which is (**6**) _____ from the way that rival fans (**7**) _____ peacefully
together. In addition to this Brazil has the most beautiful stadiums in the world.

There is (**8**) _____ rivalry between teams throughout Brazil and even smaller
provincial centres frequently have football (**9**) _____ which are well up to
international standards. It won't cost you a (**10**) _____ to get to see a game
and the stadiums are not usually (**11**) _____ , so it's quite easy to get a ticket
at the gate, instead of having to pay in (**12**) _____ .

Football is an almost year-round activity in much of Latin America and although
many of the (**13**) _____ teams in cities like Rio and Sao Paolo have some key
(**14**) _____ imported from Europe there are plenty of (**15**) _____ stars
and certainly enough to provide some very exciting football.

	A	**B**	**C**	**D**
0	event	happening	experience	evidence
1	play	match	contest	event
2	friends	leaders	experts	fans
3	watch	notice	regard	observe
4	ringing	blowing	beating	shouting
5	deep	low	extreme	far
6	seen	noted	obvious	open
7	mix	join	link	connect
8	powerful	severe	intense	near
9	grounds	places	courses	parks
10	sum	fee	treasure	fortune
11	entire	complete	full	occupied
12	total	advance	cash	future
13	larger	higher	upper	major
14	players	persons	performers	members
15	area	close	local	district

■ **2**   Complete the second sentence so that it has a similar meaning to the first
sentence. Use the word given and other words to complete each sentence.
You must use between two and five words. Do not change the word given.

1   Originally, tennis was an indoor game.
to
Tennis _____ an indoor game.

2   I haven't worn a tracksuit for years.
since
It's _____ a tracksuit.

3   Hang-gliding is not as frightening as free-fall parachuting.
than
Free-fall parachuting _____ hang-gliding.

4 Let's go skiing next weekend.
we
Why _____ skiing next weekend?

5 The sports shop is repairing my racquet at the moment.
am
I _____ at the moment.

6 I haven't played this game before.
time
It's the _____ this game.

7 Although it was raining, we played tennis.
that
We played tennis, despite _____ was raining.

8 They finished their game of cards and then they left.
had
They left _____ their game of cards.

9 When you are going mountain climbing, you should check the weather forecast first.
go
Check the weather forecast _____ mountain climbing!

10 Despite his injury, he continued to play.
he
Although _____ he continued to play.

∎**3** Read the text below. Use the word given in capitals at the end of each line to form a word that fits in the space on the same line. There is an example at the beginning (**0**).

Running

In ancient Greece running had a special (**0**) _importance_ at the opening   **IMPORTANT**
event of the Olympics and was part of all public games . (**1**) _____   **SUCCESS**
runners were held in great respect and received the (**2**) _____ rewards.   **HIGH**

Running is a natural (**3**) _____ , and as well as events like the   **ACTIVE**
marathon that require very special (**4**) _____ , it is also a   **PREPARE**
(**5**) _____ part of many other sports like football and tennis.   **CENTRE**
If athletes are (**6**) _____ , they can use opportunities to save   **SKILL**
vital seconds and increase their lead over other (**7**) _____ .   **COMPETE**
Regular running helps general health and (**8**) _____ , sharpening   **FIT**
the senses and improving the (**9**) _____ of the heart and lungs.   **EFFICIENT**
It can also improve stamina and general (**10**) _____ .   **STRONG**

∎**4** Write an answer to one of these questions. Write your answer in 120–180 words in an appropriate style.

1 You have been asked to write the story of a great sporting achievement for a sports newspaper.

Write an **article** for the newspaper about a recent sporting achievement or about an achievement from the past.

2 You want to enter a short-story competition. The rules say that the story must begin with the phrase: 'Finally the great day had arrived …'.

Write your **story** for the competition.

3 A magazine for young people is investigating the question: *How is your life today different from that of people of your parents' or grandparents' generation?*

Write a short **article** for the magazine based on your own experiences.

6

Travellers' tales

SPEAKING 1
Talking about photograph

1 Choose one of the pictures. Find a partner who has chosen a different picture. Compare your pictures.

Think about:
Where the people are   How they feel
Why they are travelling   How **you** like to travel

2 Talk to your partner. Imagine you are going on a long air, rail or road journey with your family, or with friends. What things would you take with you to make the time pass more quickly? Think about different types of journeys and holidays, with different people.

Make a list and then tell a new partner what you would take and why .

READING 1
Multiple matching

■ 1 Read this article about games to play to pass the time on journeys and holidays. For questions **1–12** decide which games are being described and write a letter **A–H** in each space. Some of the games can be chosen more than once. Where more than one answer is required, these may be given in any order.

For this game you need a good memory.   **1** ____

For this game you have to be fast.   **2** ____

This game involves drawing something.   **3** ____

This game is best played on the beach.   **4** ____

This game involves writing.   **5** ____   **6** ____

This game couldn't be played in a car.   **7** ____   **8** ____   **9** ____

This game needs someone to keep score. **10** ____   **11** ____   **12** ____

WHAT CAN WE DO NOW?

Don't panic if you hear this all too familiar cry. Here are eight simple games to pass the time on a long journey or when you're away from home.

A | Frogs in the Pond

The more frogs the better!

1 Fold a piece of paper into four, crease, unfold.

2 Fold corners into middle.

3 Fold the two side points into the centre fold.

4 Fold the triangle at the bottom up towards the top.

5 Fold each bottom corner into the centre fold.

6 Fold up the bottom portion.

7 Fold top half back down.

8 Fold the point of the top triangle over to make head.

9 Turn over. Put on eyes with a pencil.

Press your thumb on back of frog, let it slip off and the frog will jump. Put a shallow bowl on the floor, and see who can get their frogs into the 'pond'.

B | Clock Golf

Sink a bucket in the sand. Mark the clock numbers around it, about two metres away. Each player starts by standing at one o'clock and has to throw a ball into the bucket. When the ball is successfully sunk in the bucket, move on to the next number. The first person to reach twelve o'clock is the winner.

Although this game is normally played with balls, you could use stones if they are thrown carefully.

C | Beginning with

Everyone gets a piece of paper and a pencil. Fold the paper into four columns. In column one, write the list of ten categories – bird, country, food, clothing, girl's name, etc. In column two, next to each category write something which begins with a particular letter, say 'R' (robin, Rumania, roll, robe, Rita). Have a time limit; when time is up compare lists. Score one point if no one else has the same word in column two. Play again with different letters for columns three and four.

D | Knots

All players, except one, join hands in a circle. The one left out must turn his/her back while the rest tie themselves in knots, by stepping over, and ducking under, arms and legs. They must not let go of their hands. The player standing outside must now untie them without breaking the circle.

E | Thingumajig

One person thinks of an object and calls it a 'Thingumajig'. The others guess what it is by asking questions. 'Does it have legs?' etc. But the thinker can use 'Thingumajig' for other descriptive terms as well. 'Yes, and the 'Thingumajig' has 'Thingumajigs' in each corner!' After three guesses each, it is someone else's turn.

Alternatively, one person thinks of something and the others guess what it is by asking twenty questions (get someone to count). They can only expect a 'yes' or 'no' answer. Whoever guesses correctly has the next turn.

F | Fizzbuzz

This is a really tricky game and not suitable for young children. It is a counting game starting with one and counting in turn. But you must not say the numbers five and seven. Instead say 'Fizz' for five and 'Buzz' for seven. So 57 becoms 'FizzBuzz', and 72 becomes 'Buzz two', etc. Keep track of mistakes – the winner is the one who makes the fewest of them.

G | I packed my case ...

One person starts the game by saying, 'When I went on holiday I packed my suitcase with a ...' and they say something like 'a book', or yellow sunglasses. The next person has to start in the same way, repeat the first item, and add something else, and so on with the list getting longer. You're out if you forget an item.

H | Number plates

Everyone has to spot the numbers one to ten consecutively, on car number plates. See how high you can get!

Alternatively, write down a six-letter word. When you see the letters on car number plates, cross them off your list (one only per plate). The first person to cross off their entire word wins.

■2 Find words from paragraphs **A–H** that mean:

1 Two geometrical shapes (A/D)
2 Three words with their opposites (A/D)
3 The opposite of 'deep' (A)
4 Two parts of the body (A)
5 A multi-word verb meaning 'to stop holding hands' (D)
6 Two verbs with their irregular past forms (B)
7 A word meaning 'the person who' (E)
8 A word meaning 'difficult' (F)
9 A word meaning 'to see' or 'to notice' (H)
10 A multi-word verb meaning 'to put a line through' (H)
11 A word meaning 'complete' (H)

■3 Look at these words used in playing games. What do you say in your own language?

- It's my turn!
- You're out!
- Time's up!
- Score one point.

▣ LISTENING 1
Note taking

You will hear a recorded message about flights. As you listen, fill in the missing information with a few words.

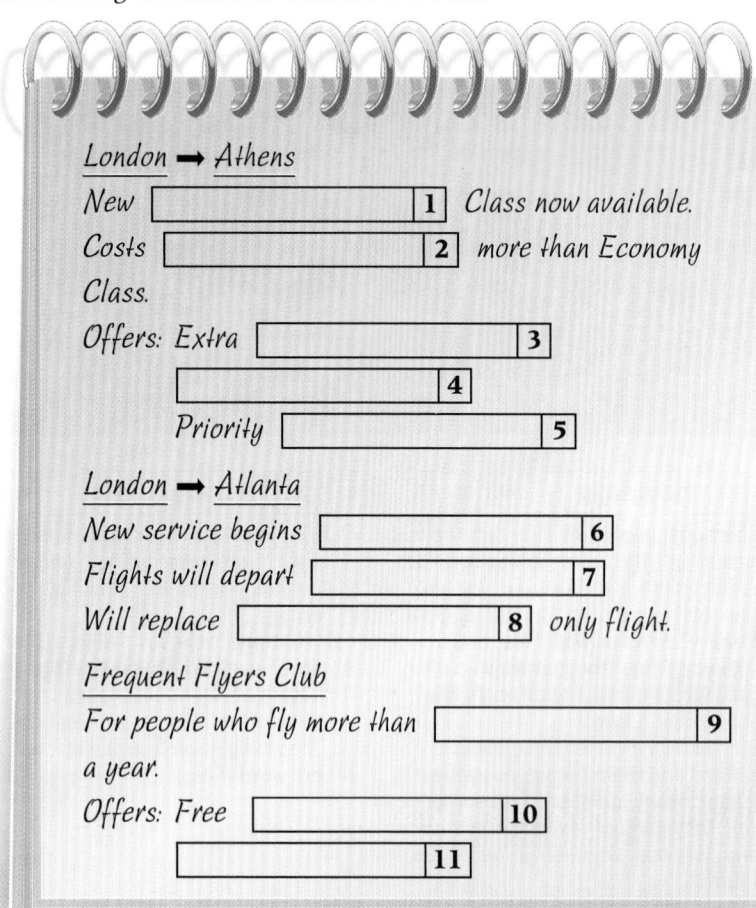

London ➡ Athens
New [　　　　　　1] Class now available.
Costs [　　　　2] more than Economy Class.
Offers: Extra [　　　3]
[　　　4]
Priority [　　　5]

London ➡ Atlanta
New service begins [　　6]
Flights will depart [　　7]
Will replace [　8] only flight.

Frequent Flyers Club
For people who fly more than [　　9] a year.
Offers: Free [　10]
[　11]

▣ PRONUNCIATION
Consonants

■1 Listen and decide which word is being said, A or B.

	A	B
1	fright	flight
2	fryer	flier
3	free	flee
4	wet	vet
5	fan	van
6	west	vest
7	leaf	leave
8	few	view
9	price	prize
10	jet	yet
11	train	drain
12	fright	fried
13	wrote	road
14	pack	back
15	sock	shock
16	joke	yolk
17	off	of
18	ice	eyes
19	loose	lose
20	rate	laid

■2 Now listen to all the words and repeat.

■3 Practise saying the pairs of words with your partner.

READING 2
Multiple choice

Read this newspaper article and for each of the questions choose the best answer, **A**, **B**, **C** or **D**.

FURY ON THE 22

YOU CAN IMAGINE how frustrated Tracy Lewis (24) of Linton felt after a seventy-five-minute wait for the delayed number 22 bus last Monday morning. Her frustration turned to anger, however, when she offered the driver a ten-pound note for her three-pound return fare to the city centre. 'Sorry,' he said, 'I'm not allowed to give change.'

The new rule, which came into force last week, means that passengers will have to have the correct money or buy a ticket before boarding the bus.

'I was furious,' said Tracy, 'none of the other passengers had change because they'd all been caught out in the same way. The bus company should have let us know about this in advance.' Tracy, in desperation, eventually gave the bus driver the ten-pound note, even though she got no change. 'I can't afford to do this every day!' she commented, 'but I have to go to work.'

The local bus company has now apologised for not giving due notice of the new policy but a spokesperson said: 'It's only like a vending machine – you just have to make sure you have the right money before you leave home. It should make it much easier for the buses to run on time if the drivers don't have to worry about giving change.'

1   Why was Tracy angry?
   A She paid more than the usual fare.
   B The fares had been increased without notice.
   C The bus was even later than usual.
   D None of the other passengers would help.

2   Why did the bus company apologise?
   A For not giving Tracy her change.
   B For the late running of the bus.
   C For not giving adequate notice.
   D For the attitude of the driver.

3   According to the bus company
   A Tracy should get her ticket from a machine.
   B people who argue make the buses late.
   C the new policy will improve punctuality.
   D you should buy a ticket before you board the bus.

GRAMMAR 1
Compound adjectives

■**1**   Look at these phrases from the article.

after a seventy-five-minute wait
      adjective   noun

This means a wait of seventy-five minutes.

a three-pound fare
   adjective noun

This means a fare of three pounds.

Notice that when the price or the time is used as an adjective it has no plural form.

■**2**   Finish each of these sentences so that it means the same as the sentence printed before it.

Example:
The holiday lasted two weeks.
It was *a two-week holiday*.

1   The walk only took five minutes.
   It was _____

2   It was a nine-month course.
   The course _____

3   The flight lasts twenty-four hours.
   It is _____

4   This contract is for two years.
   This is _____

5   The car cost five thousand pounds.
   It was _____

6   It is a three-hundred-pound holiday.
   The holiday _____

7   The ferry crossing to the island takes two hours.
   It is _____

8   It is a twelve-day coach tour.
   The _____

9   The train journey took three hours.
   It was _____

10   These tickets cost twenty dollars.
   These are _____

WRITING 1
Discursive composition

1 You have seen this travel quiz in a magazine. With your partner, decide which are the correct answers to questions 1–9.

2 Before you write the answer to question 10:
- make a list of points.
- decide how many paragraphs you will need.
- divide your points between the paragraphs.
- write an introduction.
- compare points with your partner. Add any new ideas.

3 Write your competition entry.

WIN THE DREAM HOLIDAY OF A LIFETIME!

Answer ten simple questions correctly and your name will be entered for the prize draw. First prize is a four-week round-the-world trip for two with a choice of itineraries.

1 Near which city would you find Heathrow Airport?
- **a** Miami ☐
- **b** London ☐
- **c** New York ☐
- **d** Edinburgh ☐

2 Which of these islands is not in the Caribbean?
- **a** Barbados ☐
- **b** Bermuda ☐
- **c** Jamaica ☐
- **d** Trinidad ☐

3 Which is the capital city of Canada?
- **a** Toronto ☐
- **b** Vancouver ☐
- **c** Quebec ☐
- **d** Ottawa ☐

4 Which of these countries does not have dollars as the unit of currency?
- **a** Canada ☐
- **b** Australia ☐
- **c** New Zealand ☐
- **d** Argentina ☐

5 In which country would you find the lost city of the Incas?
- **a** Peru ☐
- **b** Ecuador ☐
- **c** Mexico ☐
- **d** Brazil ☐

6 Which sea separates Great Britain and Ireland?
- **a** North Sea ☐
- **b** English Channel ☐
- **c** Irish Sea ☐
- **d** Atlantic Ocean ☐

7 Which of these countries has the largest number of islands?
- **a** Scotland ☐
- **b** Norway ☐
- **c** Greece ☐
- **d** The Philippines ☐

8 Which of these countries does not have English as an official language?
- **a** South Africa ☐
- **b** Jamaica ☐
- **c** Iceland ☐
- **d** India ☐

9 Which is the furthest from London?
- **a** Toronto ☐
- **b** Tokyo ☐
- **c** Buenos Aires ☐
- **d** Sydney ☐

10 In not more than 150 words say why you think a round-the-world trip would be a good experience for you – say who you would take with you and why.

VOCABULARY 1
Travel and holidays

1 Look at these words. When they are used to talk about holidays or transport, are they usually nouns or verbs, or both?

cruise	flight	fly	trip
travel	sight-seeing	journey	crossing

Put one of the words into the space in each of these sentences.

1 My _____ to the office each day takes me through some lovely countryside.

2 She's going to Madrid on a business _____ .

3 The _____ from London to Buenos Aires takes more than thirteen hours.

4 For their honeymoon they're going on a _____ around the Caribbean.

5 It has always been one of my ambitions to _____ overland to India.

6 We arrive in Rome at midday and after lunch there are two hours free for _____ .

7 The quickest sea _____ from England to France is by hovercraft.

8 You can either take the train or you can _____ , which is quicker but more expensive.

9 When I was in Paris I went on a day _____ to see the palace of Versailles.

10 _____ the Golden Gate Bridge was one of the most memorable parts of our visit to California.

2 Complete each of the following sentences with one word or expression formed from PACK.

Example:
They arrived at the hotel and immediately started <u>unpacking</u> their suitcases.

1 She went on a _____ tour where everything was included in the price.

2 The airport lounge was _____ with delayed holidaymakers.

3 A _____ lunch is included in the price of the day trip.

4 Before _____ your suitcase, it's a good idea to make a list of the things you want to take.

5 Don't forget _____ your new sunglasses before you leave.

3 Complete each of the following sentences by putting one word in each of the spaces.

Example:
He wanted to call _____*on*_____ an old friend while he was visiting the city.

1 The ship calls _____ several islands in the Aegean during the cruise.

2 The bad weather meant that the picnic lunch had to be called _____ .

3 We called _____ John in the car as no public transport goes to the village on Sundays.

4 In the middle of dinner the doctor was called _____ to an emergency.

5 It is a dangerous road and calls _____ extreme caution on the part of drivers.

SPEAKING 2
Expressing attitudes and opinions

Imagine you have received this fax.

> **Congratulations!!**
>
> **You have won First Prize!**
> **A four-week round-the-world trip for two in February of next year.**
>
> **More details to follow.**

Work with a partner.

1 Make a list of the countries you would most like to visit on your trip.

How would you like to travel?
- by air
- by sea
- by car
- by train
- on foot?

What information do you need about the countries on your list before you make your final decision?

2 Exchange ideas with another pair.

READING 3
Gapped text

■ 1 To really enjoy a round-the-world trip you need to spend quite a long time in each place. This probably means being away from home for much longer than one month.

What problems do you think you would have travelling away from home, for up to one year, for instance? Talk to your partner about the following things:

- clothes
- money
- health
- luggage
- family
- accommodation

■ 2 You are going to read a magazine article about a trip around the world. Six paragraphs have been removed from the article. Fill each gap **1–6** with the paragraph which you think fits best from the list **A–H**. There is one extra paragraph which you do not need to use. There is an example at the beginning (**0**).

A Another pressure point was accommodation. It is hard to say which is worse, a hotel room or one belonging to friends. The former lacks home comforts, the latter imposes behavioural constraints.

B One reason for our good health was that as our journey progressed we gradually became fitter. Neither of us was in very good shape when we left home. We hadn't had time to get fit, what with all the stresses and strains of preparing to go.

Road to Freedom

1 **Berry Ritchie and his wife, Carole, did it: they packed their bags, rented out their home and travelled the globe.**

5 *We fled our semi-detached nest in safe, suburban Richmond some 18 months ago. We bought round-the-world air tickets and left*
10 *London early in October.*

0   **H**

We visited some of the most exotic places in the world and some of the least. We stayed with friends in some places, and in hotels, motels and guest
15 houses. We travelled in taxis, buses, cars, vans, jeeps, rickshaws, trains and planes. We ate well and we ate badly. And all the time we were together. After more than twenty-five years. Just each
20 other. Alone at last.

I will pass over the day that we were supposed to fly to New York and didn't because my wife lost her passport. We discovered this on the way to the air-
25 port. Several hours passed before we found it, stored for safe keeping along with her diaries in my mother's attic. It was something that could have happened to anyone.

1

30 We were also consumed with misgivings about giving up our jobs, though the desire to make a break from routine had been one of the motives behind the trip. Our feelings came to a head one
35 morning in the rather shabby room we were renting in Brooklyn. We looked each other in the eye. 'Shall we go home?' we said together.

2

Less emotional and more predictable
40 was the problem of living out of suitcases. My theory that we could buy disposable clothes as we went along was wrong, at least from the perspective of a style-conscious Englishwoman.
45 The truth is that you get what you pay for, which in the Far East is often not much.

3

We learned that floor space, a view and a private bathroom were vital for a

C At the end of the first fortnight we felt desolate. We both missed our daughter. My wife, Carole, suffered from homesickness and missed her friends and colleagues.

D It couldn't last, of course. As months and continents passed, the pull of home and loved ones strengthened. Again there came a moment when we asked each other 'Shall we go home?'. This time, though, it was because we'd had enough, not because we were afraid.

E This back injury was not helped by having to carry our cases the length of the Sydney to Melbourne express train before finding a seat.

F We didn't miss television but books were a problem, solved by begging, borrowing and stealing. Books were also a major contribution to the weight of our luggage.

50 stay of any length. Usually we found all three, though sometimes not before a search. We wouldn't recommend you staying in the Transit Hotel in Jakarta.

4

Much of our reading was escapist, but we
55 did discover that books about their history and culture added to our appreciation of the countries we visited.
  We expected, of course, to be ill. Nothing serious, you understand, because we'd been
60 inoculated against everything. But we confidently feared food poisoning, snake bites, insect stings and a variety of alien fevers. In the event I caught a cold and Carole had to have a filling replaced in Melbourne, the home of
65 dentistry.

5

As the days turned into weeks the people we stayed with commented on how well we looked, and how young. We felt it. We also felt something else. We felt free.

6

70 We arrived back a year and a week after we left. After a month we recognised that being back home really had been hard!

G It was a rhetorical question, as we had let our house for the year and in any case the moment passed. It recurred, but with less and less intensity, though we never did stop missing our near and dear ones.

H Our journey took us in leisurely stages to New York and California, over the Pacific to Australia, through Hong Kong, Bali, Singapore, Thailand and Southern India and back through Europe.

3 Find words or expressions which mean

1 escaped (line 5)

2 slow and relaxing (H)

3 doubts and fears (30)

4 leave completely (32)

5 reached crisis point (34)

6 dirty and untidy (35)

7 point of view (43)

8 fashionable (44)

9 most important (49)

10 fit and healthy (B)

4 Make a note of other new words you have learned in the text which you think might be important to remember.

LISTENING 2
Selecting an answer

You will hear a customer in a travel agency asking about holiday insurance. For questions **1–6** decide whether the statements are true or false.

1 Insurance is not included in the price of the holiday.

2 He is staying in Madrid for less than 17 nights.

3 The insurance includes medical expenses but not an air ambulance.

4 If you miss your flight you get £1500.

5 If your plane is delayed for up to 12 hours, you get money from the insurance company.

6 You are insured for £1000 cash if your wallet is stolen.

GRAMMAR 2
Prepositions

1 Put one of these prepositions in each of the spaces.

on   by   in

1 I like to travel _____ train.

2 I've never been _____ an inter-city train.

3 I usually go to work _____ car.

4 I'll give you a lift _____ my car.

When do we use *by* and when do we use other prepositions?

2 Put a preposition in each sentence.

1 The fastest way from London to Glasgow is _____ air.

2 The cheapest way from London to Glasgow is _____ coach.

3 I'd love to go _____ a Mediterranean cruise.

4 We went to the USA _____ a jumbo jet.

5 He goes to school _____ his bike.

6 Travelling _____ train is more expensive than going _____ your car.

7 We decided not to fly _____ Ireland but to take the car _____ the ferry.

8 About sixty people can go _____ the coach. The rest will have to go _____ train.

9 If you go to the airport _____ underground you arrive _____ terminal three, but if you go _____ car you have to find the way _____ the car park _____ the terminal _____ foot.

10 The best way to reach the Scilly Isles is _____ helicopter _____ Penzance, but once there you should travel _____ the main islands _____ boat.

LISTENING 3
Directions

1 Joanne is new to London and has been invited to visit Derek in his flat in Walthamstow. She arrives at Walthamstow Station and can't find the way. She phones Derek. Listen to their conversation and draw the route on the map.

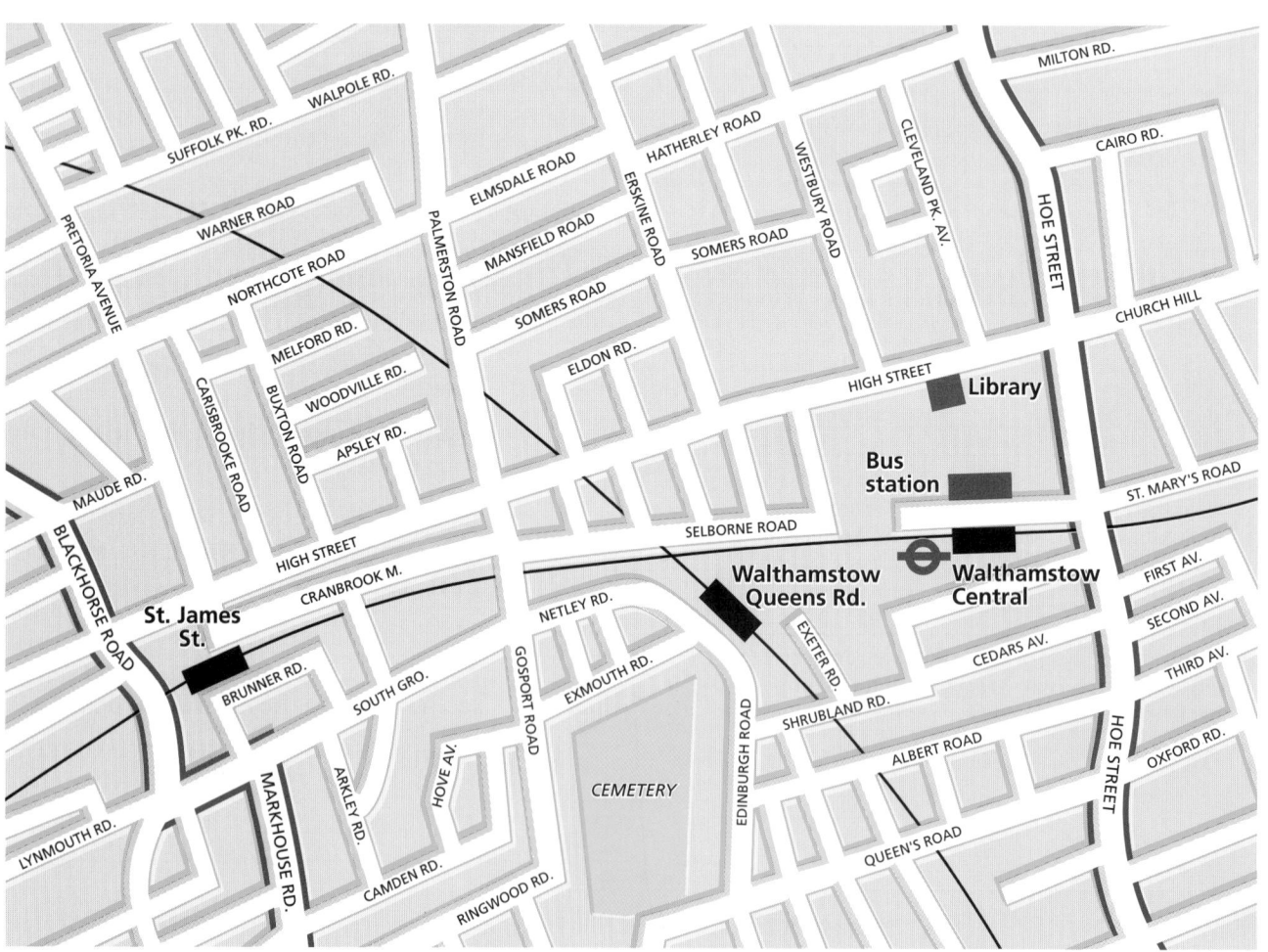

GRAMMAR 3
Giving directions

■1 The language of giving directions is quite complicated and many variations are possible. To avoid making mistakes you should follow these rules:

1 Use imperatives to tell people what to do.

   Examples:
   Turn left
   Turn right
   Go straight on
   Walk down the road

2 Use a preposition to tell people where things are.

   Examples:
   The bus station is on the right
   It's the third turning on the left
   It's opposite the station

3 Use *will* to tell people what to look for.

   Examples:
   You will see the library on your left
   You'll come to a large crossroads
   You'll find my house on the right

■2 Look at these sentences, and say which type they are – 1, 2 or 3 above.

1 When you come to the crossroads, go straight on.
2 Turn right as you come out of the station.
3 Turn left along Main Street.
4 Walk as far as the traffic lights.
5 You'll see the Bus Station, you can't miss it.
6 It's the third turning on the right.

■3 Put one preposition in each space if it is necessary.

1 Turn _____ right _____ the crossroads.
2 Walk _____ the road as far as the library.
3 Turn _____ left _____ Forest Road.
4 The shop is _____ the bus station.
5 My house is _____ Palmerston Road.
6 Go straight _____ at the traffic lights.
7 Turn _____ left and then _____ left again.
8 It's the third house _____ the left.
9 Take the third turning _____ the left.
10 At the roundabout, turn _____ right.

SPEAKING 3
Exchanging information

Look again at the map of Walthamstow. Ask your partner to give you the following directions:

1 From the library to Warner Road.
2 From Walthamstow Central station to Melford Road.

WRITING 2
Informal letters

Where do people arrive in your city, town or area? It could be at a railway station, bus station, harbour, airport or any other arrival point.

Write a letter to a friend who is coming to visit your home for the first time.

1 Apologise for not being able to meet your friend and explain why you are busy.
2 Give directions of how to get to your house from the arrival point.

LISTENING 4
Note-taking

You will hear Dave receive a telephone call from his friend Gianna in Italy.

As you listen complete these notes:

① Gianna arrives at _____ airport on flight number _____ from _____ at _____ on _____ .

② Angelo arrives at _____ airport on flight number _____ from _____ at _____ on _____ .

③ Gianna's fax number is _____ .

GRAMMAR 4
Future time 1

■1 Look at these phrases from the listening text.

We arrive at different airports
Angelo arrives at Heathrow Airport

Which tense is used and why?

We use the Present simple tense to refer to future time when we talk about timetables and other things which happen at fixed times and so cannot be changed.

Look at these examples of the Present simple:

	Tense	Time
The film begins at eight o'clock.	Present simple	tonight
The train leaves at five on Saturday morning.	Present simple	Saturday
Tomorrow is Sue's birthday.	Present simple	tomorrow

■2 Look at these sentences and decide if they are right or wrong.

Examples:
My plane leaves at 18.00.
(Right – It's the same time for everybody, and I can't change it)

I meet my sister at 2 pm tomorrow.
(Wrong – I can change the time because it only involves me and my sister)

1 Tomorrow is the first day of term.
2 I go to the theatre tomorrow.
3 Angelo starts English classes next week.
4 The party starts at 8 pm.
5 My exam is next Monday.
6 The restaurant closes at 6 pm.
7 I see my friend tomorrow evening.
8 Next year is a leap year.
9 The ferry leaves every half hour.
10 My family goes shopping next Saturday.

■3 Look at the sentences which you have decided are wrong in exercise 2. Which tense can you use instead of the Present simple to make them correct?

Example
I meet my sister at 2 pm. (wrong)

I'm meeting my sister at 2 pm.
I'm going to meet my sister at 2 pm.

Both of these corrections are possible but each means something different. In each case if you ask the question *when* the answer is the same – in the future/at 2 pm. So what is the difference?

■4 Look at these sentences and decide which sentences talk about an intention and which an arrangement.

1 I'm going to do lots of shopping while I'm in Paris.
2 They're meeting Angelo at 6 pm outside the station.
3 He's told me he's going to study much harder next year.
4 She's travelling to Athens with Rosa.
5 During my stay I'm going to look up lots of old friends.
6 We're getting a lift from a woman who lives in the same street.
7 Rod's flying to Australia at the end of the week.
8 My sister and I are going to see that new film at an open-air cinema tonight.
9 Cathy's going to retire and travel round the world when she's sixty.
10 I'm collecting my tickets and travellers' cheques on Wednesday.

■5 In this letter choose the best form of the verb.

Dear Bill,

Guess what! I (1) *come/am coming/am going to come* to Toronto for a couple of days next week.

My plane (2) *arrives/is arriving/is going to arrive* in Toronto at 16.30 on Wednesday. I (3) *stay/am staying/am going to stay* at the Hotel Metropole. My friend, Gill, (4) *meets/is meeting/is going to meet* me at the airport. We (5) *eat/are eating/are going to eat* with some friends of hers in the evening. While in Toronto, I (6) *visit/am visiting/am going to visit* as many of the sights as possible, so perhaps we could meet up one afternoon if you are free. Give me a ring at the hotel.

Best wishes,

Beth

READING 4
Gapped text

1 Have you ever taken part in one of these sports? Discuss with your partner

- why people do these things.
- what it must feel like.
- how you would feel doing these things for the first time.

2 You are going to read an article about a flight in a balloon. Seven sentences have been removed from the article. Choose from the sentences **A–I** the one which fits each gap. There is one extra sentence which you do not need to use. There is an example at the beginning (**0**).

Balloons Away!

0 I

1 I was told to be ready at 6.30 the next morning at the Black Horse pub wearing wellington boots and warm clothes.

1

I was going to fly in a hot air balloon.

5 The flight was supposed to have taken place at a summer balloon festival, but the weather had been so bad that no flying was possible. Now I was full of anticipation and keen to fly.

10 The three balloon pilots arrived, large cars pulling the trailers containing the baskets and all the equipment necessary for the flight. They began to unpack their balloons in an adjacent field.

15 At 7.15 a.m. we took off. **2**

It was so gentle that the only way I knew I must be going up was that the ground was going down away from us! Waving good-bye to my family, I did 20 not know which way to look out across the houses, gardens and fields, or down at the fields we had just left where the people and cars were rapidly beginning to look like toys.

3

25 Apart from the essential blasts of gas and flames which roared around my ears it was so quiet that I could hear dogs barking below. I could easily call out to the people in one of the other balloons 30 which happened to travel quite near us.

4

True, my feet were cold , but a rapid temperature gradient rose up my legs, ensuring my body and hands were warm and my head, nearest the burner, 35 was positively hot! **5**

As the pilot explained, we are the wind, we travel with it and there is no air resistance because we are not powered. Hence there is no feeling of movement 40 or progress as one is not being 'pushed'. Every sense was heightened in this magical environment. Once or twice I had black thoughts that there was only a basket between me and eight hundred 45 metres of nothing! **6**

One cannot fully give words to this unique experience. Aeroplanes and helicopters seem a noisy and dirty way to fly.

7

A Not with a jolt like in a lift as I had previously imagined, but with no feeling of movement whatsoever.

B I was surprised how incredibly peaceful it was up there.

C However, I soon put these panicky feelings away and concentrated on enjoying myself.

D It was not at all windy either.

E After weeks of uncertainty at last a life-long ambition was about to be fulfilled.

F It was rising gently up into the morning air.

G This was a peaceful and beautiful journey totally in tune with the environment.

H I had imagined it would be cold and breezy.

I It was ten o'clock in the morning when I received the telephone call.

3 Find the words that mean:

1 something you've always wanted to do

2 waiting with pleasure

3 next to

4 before

5 in any way at all

6 quickly

7 very necessary

8 made a loud noise

9 not like anything else

4 Look back at the completed text. Find and underline the expressions 1–4. Match each of the expressions with its meaning on the right (**A–D**).

1	about to	**A**	by chance
2	supposed to	**B**	should
3	keen to	**C**	going to (very soon)
4	happened to	**D**	want to very much

GRAMMAR 5
So/Such that

1 Look at these phrases from the text. What type of words have been underlined?

The weather had been so <u>bad</u> that …
It was so <u>gentle</u> that …
It was so <u>quiet</u> that …

2 Look at these phrases. How are they different from those in exercise 1?

It was such a cold day that …
It was such a gentle take off that …
It was such a quiet flight that …

3 When do we use *so ... that* and when do we use *such ... that*?

4 Complete the second sentence so that it has the same meaning as the first sentence. Use the word given and other words to complete each sentence. You must use between two and five words. Do not change the word given.

1 The plane was losing height ready for landing.
about
The plane was _____ land.

2 It was such a cold day that I wore an overcoat.
so
The day was _____ I wore an overcoat.

3 I met Nigel by chance in the supermarket.
happened
I _____ Nigel in the supermarket.

4 Her voice was so quiet that I couldn't hear her.
a
She had _____ that I couldn't hear her.

5 Daniela should arrive at five o'clock.
supposed
Daniela _____ at five o'clock.

6 That man was so rude that I didn't reply to him.
a
He was _____ that I didn't reply to him.

7 I would like to learn hang-gliding very much.
keen
I _____ learn hang-gliding.

8 We had such a dirty room that we checked out of the hotel.
so
Our room _____ that we checked out of the hotel.

9 I was just leaving when the phone rang.
about
I was just _____ when the phone rang.

10 I can't wait to go on holiday.
forward
I'm _____ on holiday.

HELP WITH GAP FILLING

1 When you have a passage with some words left out, how do you know which type of word is missing?

2 Look at the words in the box.

usually	happiness	whose	sleeps
the	into	behind	quick
green	an	slowly	such
walked	myself	and	pencil

Find an example of:

a verb _____

a noun _____

an adjective _____

an adverb _____

a preposition _____

an article _____

a pronoun _____

one other type of word _____

3 What is missing from each of these sentences?

			Type of word	Example answer
1	Roy jumped into his car and _____ away.	**1**	*verb (past tense)*	*drove*
2	Lois gave the keys to _____ mother.	**2**		
3	Dean got a black _____ for his birthday.	**3**		
4	There were five cars, a van _____ a motorbike.	**4**		
5	It was such _____ lovely day, I decided to walk.	**5**		
6	Nobody told _____ which road to take.	**6**		
7	He opened the package very _____ .	**7**		
8	I have _____ been to Paris.	**8**		
9	He walked _____ a ladder, which might be unlucky!	**9**		
10	Oh, thank you. What a _____ surprise.	**10**		

4 What type of word is missing in each gap in this passage?

Compare with your partner and together suggest words to complete the text.

	Type of word
It is remarkably easy (**1**) _____ reach Blackwell thanks to its excellent position at the crossroads of (**2**) _____ national motorway system. The area is also easily reached (**3**) _____ inter-city train or National Bus services.	**1** **2** **3**
Whatever your interests, you (**4**) _____ find Blackwell a surprising place to visit. It is situated (**5**) _____ the heart of the region known as Midshire. (**6**) _____ is a unique network of canals, a large country park and (**7**) _____ more to see and do in the region.	**4** **5** **6** **7**
The Blackwell area is varied and unpredictable with (**8**) _____ own strong local character, (**9**) _____ is reflected in the local inhabitants and in the abundance of pubs selling some of the (**10**) _____ pub food in Britain.	**8** **9** **10**

5 Remember that in Part 2 of the Use of English paper there are no multiple choice alternatives to choose from. You have to work out the words from the context. Most of the missing words will be grammatical words and not items of vocabulary (information words).

■**1** Read the text below and think of the word which best fits each space. Use only one word in each space. There is an example at the beginning (**0**).

Visiting Australia

Australia is quite (**0**) ____*an*____ easy place for tourists to visit. Australians travel widely within their (**1**) _____ country, so tourist facilities at the most popular destinations (**2**) _____ well-developed and information is simple (**3**) _____ obtain. Travelling with young children is especially easy (**4**) _____ Australia's population is young and big families are common, so children (**5**) _____ be taken almost everywhere. Australians are usually very willing to help visitors (**6**) _____ ask for advice, and are often generous with their hospitality.

Before organising a trip it is sensible to consider Australian school holidays. Throughout these periods, (**7**) _____ airline or hotel reservations at major tourist destinations can be difficult unless you plan a (**8**) _____ way in advance. Usually the holidays are (**9**) _____ December and January (the main summer break), a fortnight in May and about four weeks (**10**) _____ mid-August to mid-September.

During the Australian summer the tourist season is at (**11**) _____ peak. Most of the country slows to a complete stop just (**12**) _____ Christmas while many companies close in January for their (**13**) _____ summer holiday. Flights in and (**14**) _____ of the country as well as those between main Australian cities are usually booked (**15**) _____ .

■**2** Read the text below and look carefully at each line. Some of the lines are correct, and some have a word which should not be there. If a line is correct, put a tick (✓). If a line has a word which should not be there, write the word in the space on the right. There are two examples at the beginning (**0**) and (**00**).

I hate flying!

Flying is horrible. The first time I took to a plane I really	**0**	*to*
did not like it very much and now I find that every	**00**	✓
time I fly I get up to dislike it a bit more. The problems	**1**	_____
start from the moment you can arrive at the airport.	**2**	_____
You always seem to have to be there much hours too	**3**	_____
early for get your flight. Then you have to wait with	**4**	_____
lots of the other over-excited or rather tense people,	**5**	_____
and the only thing to do it is shop or sit around eating	**6**	_____
or drinking, whether you feel hungry or not so. After	**7**	_____
the usual delays, you are pushed onto a bus for a	**8**	_____
two-minute ride on across the airport to where your plane	**9**	_____
is waiting. You asked for a seat by the window, but you	**10**	_____
find you're sitting down in the middle of a row of three	**11**	_____
and no, you cannot change now your seat because	**12**	_____
the plane is full. Once you have recovered from that	**13**	_____
horrible feeling as the plane takes you off, a meal is	**14**	_____
served which includes things you've never seen before	**15**	_____
and which do not seem to have any flavour at all.		

3 Read the text below. Use the word given in capitals at the end of each line to form a word that fits in the space in the same line. There is an example at the beginning (**0**).

Holidays in Corsica

Knowing the island for over twenty years gives us an (**0**) *unrivalled*	**RIVAL**
advantage in (**1**) _____ to plan your Corsican holiday. And we certainly	**HELP**
don't abandon you once you've (**2**) _____ . Because we	**ARRIVE**
(**3**) _____ in holidays to Corsica we have a resident manager there.	**SPECIAL**
We also have two regional (**4**) _____ who are there to answer	**REPRESENT**
your questions and help to find a (**5**) _____ to any problems which .	**SOLVE**
might occur.	
Ideal for the independent (**6**) _____ , we offer a completely	**TRAVEL**
flexible (**7**) _____ : you can decide how to travel – either by	**PACK**
charter or scheduled (**8**) _____ , car, or train; it's also your	**FLY**
(**9**) _____ whether to hire a car for some or all of your holiday.	**CHOOSE**
Prices and other (**10**) _____ information are given in the enclosed	**ADD**
booklet.	

4 Write an answer to one of these questions. Write your answer in 120–180 words in an appropriate style.

1 You and your friends have decided to invite your teacher to a party at your home. Write a letter explaining how to get there from the school where you are studying.

2 Your English teacher has asked each student in your class to write a short story. The best story will be included in the school magazine. The title is 'An Unforgettable Journey'.

Write your story.

3 This is part of a letter you have received from a friend in another country.

> We're doing a project at school about how tourism has affected different countries and places. Please could you write me a short report on your country to include in the project?

Write about the changes caused by tourism and how people feel about them.

Food for thought

SPEAKING 1
Talking about photographs

■ 1 Look at these three pictures. With your partner, decide:

Where the people are.
What they are eating.
How they feel.
Which of the meals you would prefer and why.
If some types of meal are more suitable in certain situations than others.

■ 2

1 Work with a partner. Together make a list of the type of food you associate with the following:

Your country.
Great Britain.
The USA.
Another country you know about.

2 What is good or bad about the food of each of these countries? Are there any differences in the way people eat in these countries?

Talk about the following:

Times of meals.
Size of meals.
Eating out.
Eating at home.
The formality of meals.
Ways of preparing food.
Ways of buying and selling food.

READING 1

Reading for specific information

1 Look at this leaflet which advises British people about how to improve their diet. Read Part One and discuss with your partner whether each piece of advice would also apply to people in your country.

Part One

Eating for a HEALTHY HEART

Coronary heart disease is the greatest single cause of death in this country. It happens when cholesterol builds up on the inside walls of the arteries that supply blood to the heart. The blood vessels become narrower and eventually get blocked. This build-up of cholesterol can happen very slowly, and unnoticeably, over the years, and it can start at an early age.

There are several things which can affect your risk of developing coronary heart disease. One of these is the kind of food you eat. A healthy diet can lower the level of cholesterol in your blood and so reduce your risk of heart disease. Other things you can do to reduce the risk include:

♥ *NOT SMOKING*

♥ *TAKING REGULAR EXERCISE*

♥ *KEEPING TO A HEALTHY WEIGHT*

♥ *LEARNING TO RELAX, AND*

♥ *HAVING REGULAR BLOOD PRESSURE CHECKS*

A Well Balanced Diet

So how can we all change our diet for the better? The main messages to keep in mind are:

EAT LESS FAT
Especially saturated fat

EAT MORE FIBRE –
Fruit, vegetables, pulses and cereals.

EAT LESS SALT

EAT LESS SUGAR

This leaflet is all about eating an *enjoyable* healthy diet. It gives lots of ideas and recipes to help *you* eat for a healthy heart.

2 Find words or expressions in Part One of the leaflet which mean

1 one and only

2 provide

3 not so wide

4 in the end

5 obstructed

6 accumulation

7 without anyone realising

8 influence

9 reduce

3 How do you think it's possible to reduce the amount of salt and sugar in your diet? Make a list of suggestions with your partner.

Part Two

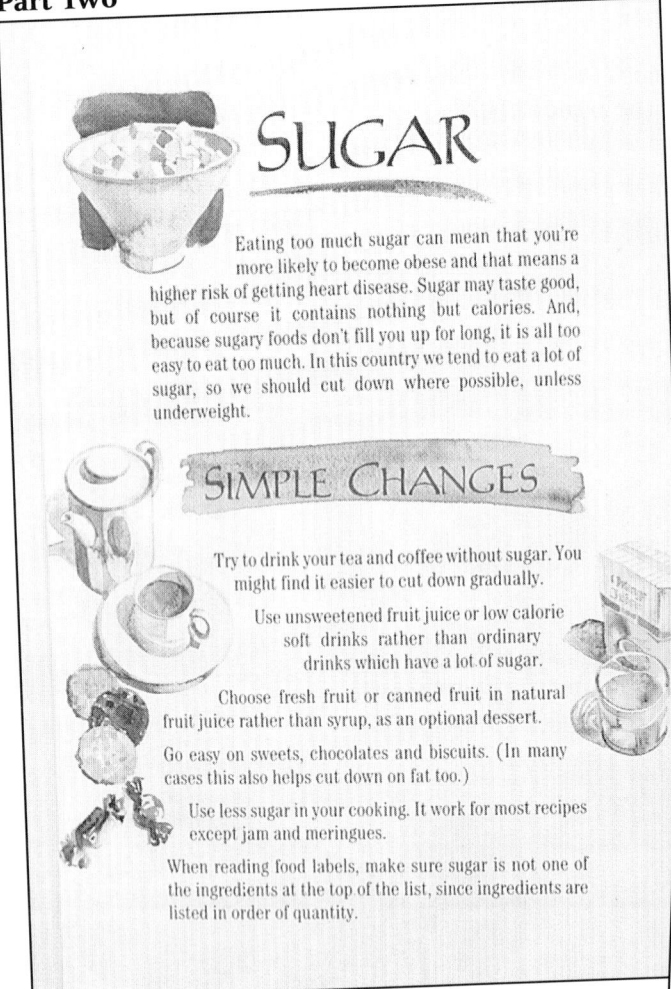

SUGAR

Eating too much sugar can mean that you're more likely to become obese and that means a higher risk of getting heart disease. Sugar may taste good, but of course it contains nothing but calories. And, because sugary foods don't fill you up for long, it is all too easy to eat too much. In this country we tend to eat a lot of sugar, so we should cut down where possible, unless underweight.

SIMPLE CHANGES

Try to drink your tea and coffee without sugar. You might find it easier to cut down gradually.

Use unsweetened fruit juice or low calorie soft drinks rather than ordinary drinks which have a lot of sugar.

Choose fresh fruit or canned fruit in natural fruit juice rather than syrup, as an optional dessert.

Go easy on sweets, chocolates and biscuits. (In many cases this also helps cut down on fat too.)

Use less sugar in your cooking. It work for most recipes except jam and meringues.

When reading food labels, make sure sugar is not one of the ingredients at the top of the list, since ingredients are listed in order of quantity.

Part Three

SALT

Everyone needs some salt but not nearly as much as many people actually eat. Too much salt has been linked with high blood pressure, which in turn can cause heart disease. So cut down on salt whenever you can.

SIMPLE CHANGES

Use less salt in cooking and measure the amount.

Try flavouring your food with lemon juice, herbs, spices or mustard, instead of salt.

Try to get out of the habit of adding salt at the table.

Cut down on salty snacks, such as salted crisps and nuts.

Try to avoid those canned and packet soups which are high in salt.

■ **4** Decide who is Student A and who is Student B.

Student A: Read Part Two of the leaflet.
Student B: Read Part Three of the leaflet.
Answer these questions:

1 Find two reasons for eating less sugar/salt.
2 What simple changes to your diet are suggested?
3 How relevant are these to your country?

Now tell your partner what you have found out.

■ **5** Without copying from the leaflet, complete each of the paragraphs which follow in your own words. Write about either salt or sugar.

1 It is a good idea to cut down on salt/sugar because _____

_____

2 One good way of doing this is to _____

_____

_____

3 Another good way is to _____

_____

_____

Gerund/Infinitive

You *risk getting* heart disease.
We *tend to eat* a lot of sugar.

■ **1** Notice that some verbs are followed by an infinitive (*to do*) and others by a gerund (*doing*).

In each of the following sentences choose which is best, gerund or infinitive.

Example:
Try to stop (<u>eating</u>/to eat) so many salty snacks.

1 I enjoy (reading/to read) books about nutrition.
2 I plan (going/to go) on a diet after the holiday.
3 I need (reducing/to reduce) the amount of fats in my diet.
4 I promise (cutting down/to cut down) on sugar in tea and coffee.

5 I suggest (changing/to change) your eating habits.

6 He postponed (going/to go) to the doctor although he often felt ill.

7 He was advised (going/to go) on a high fibre diet.

8 He refused (giving up/to give up) smoking.

9 You're more likely (becoming/to become) over-weight if you eat chocolates.

10 Avoid (buying/to buy) a lot of cream cakes.

LISTENING 1
Multiple choice

You will hear an interview with Dr Cooper, a prominent dietician, talking about the British diet.

Listen and choose the best answer **A**, **B**, or **C** for these questions.

1 The British have an unhealthy diet because they
   A don't know how to prepare simple foods.
   B don't have much time to cook proper meals.
   C don't understand what a healthy diet is.

2 What does the food industry say about junk food?
   A Nobody eats very much of it.
   B It's only one part of people's diet.
   C It's made from healthy ingredients.

3 What did the Glasgow research show?
   A People rarely eat processed foods.
   B Many people eat very little fresh food.
   C People don't eat at regular times.

4 Why is junk food bad for your health?
   A It doesn't contain important vitamins and fibre.
   B It isn't made from fruit and vegetables.
   C It doesn't provide enough sugar or fat.

5 What does Dr Cooper advise?
   A Give up eating junk food.
   B Avoid food which is advertised.
   C Eat a variety of different foods.

GRAMMAR 2
Too/Enough

1 Look at these sentences from the listening text:

*People eat **too** much junk food.*
*People don't eat **enough** fibre.*
*If your diet is varied **enough**, there's no problem.*
*We are **too** ready to be influenced by advertising.*

When do we use *too* and *enough* with nouns and adjectives?

2 Complete the second sentence so that it has a similar meaning to the first sentence. Use the word given and other words to complete each sentence. You must use between two and five words. Do not change the word given.

1 These vegetables are too hard; they're under-cooked.
have
These vegetables _____ enough.

2 This salad is too oily.
oil
There _____ this salad.

3 This cake is too stale to eat.
enough
This cake _____ to eat.

4 This hotel is too expensive for a large family.
much
This hotel _____ for a large family.

5 There's too little cheese for four people.
enough
There _____ for four people.

6 There are too few glasses for everyone to have a drink.
enough
We _____ for everyone to have a drink.

7 It's not warm enough to eat outside this evening.
too
It's _____ this evening.

8 Joanne doesn't speak loudly enough on the telephone.
too
Joanne speaks _____ on the telephone.

9 There's too little sugar in this coffee for me.
sweet
This coffee _____ for me.

10 This restaurant is too quiet. Let's try another one.
people
There are _____ restaurant. Let's try another one.

Multiple choice

Read this extract from a leaflet about food safety. Choose the
answer **A**, **B**, **C** or **D** which you think fits best according to the text.

The importance *of temperature*

■ How food poisoning is caused

1 Most food poisoning is caused by five
groups of bacteria – Campylobacter,
Salmonella, Clostridium, Listeria and
Staphylococcus. Even small numbers
5 of Salmonella cells can cause food
poisoning but other types of bacteria
have to be present in large numbers
before they make food dangerous. In
other words, they have been allowed
10 to grow and multiply for a sufficiently
long time to produce large numbers
of cells.

If Salmonella and Listeria are to
cause problems, living cells of the
15 bacteria have to be present in the food
when it is eaten. Normal, but thorough,
cooking should destroy these cells and
render them harmless.

Staphylococci are different because
20 they produce toxin (a poisonous
chemical) when they are growing.
Even though cooking may destroy the

bacterial cells, it is unlikely to inactivate
the toxin.
25 Food producers do their best to make
sure that food is not contaminated
with any food-poisoning organisms.
But if some should be in food, the
maintenance of a cold temperature
30 can do a lot to minimise growth and
therefore the risk of food poisoning.

The Food Hygiene (Amendment)
Regulations 1990 require that, from
April 1995, most short-life food must be
35 kept at 5°C or colder after manufacture
and throughout distribution and
display. Keeping such a cold temperature required many food companies to
buy better refrigeration equipment so,
40 until April 1995, a temperature of no
warmer than 8°C had to be maintained
for those foods.

Although there is no law governing
the performance of household
45 refrigerators, you should use a
thermometer to make sure your
refrigerator is operating at 5°C or

colder. Suitable thermometers are
available in Sainsbury's stores which
50 sell freezer accessories.

Once food has cooled to 5°C or colder,
if any food poisoning bacteria are
present most will grow only very
slowly and it would take a long time for
55 them to reach large enough numbers to
cause a problem. But, if Listeria should
be present, it will grow and multiply,
even at refrigerator temperatures. And
if the food is at 10°C, Listeria will grow
60 more rapidly than any other organism.

Frozen foods are stored at -18°C
throughout distribution and there is no
possibility of bacterial cells growing
and multiplying at that temperature.
65 But remember that neither chilling
nor freezing kills all bacteria, so it is
very important to keep chilled foods
chilled and frozen foods frozen until
they are used. Once they reach room
70 temperature, bacteria become active
again and food deterioration starts or
resumes from where it left off.

1 How is Salmonella different from other bacteria?

  A It multiplies more quickly.
  B A small amount can poison you.
  C Only living cells cause poisoning.
  D It causes other bacteria to grow.

2 How is Staphylococcus different from other bacteria?

  A The cells are destroyed by thorough cooking.
  B The cells take a long time to grow and multiply.
  C The poison is not destroyed by cooking.
  D A large number of cells are needed to poison you.

3 How does refrigeration help to reduce the risk of food poisoning?

  A It kills any bacteria that are in the food.
  B It stops the bacteria growing any more.
  C It prevents new bacteria entering the food.
  D It makes the bacteria grow more slowly.

4 How did the law change in 1995?

  A Once made, chilled food had to be kept colder.
  B Shops had to use new refrigeration equipment.
  C Chilled foods could not be contaminated with any food poisoning organisms.
  D All refrigerators had to have thermometers fitted.

5 What is it important to remember about chilled and frozen foods?

  A They are clear of bacteria and poisons whilst kept cold.
  B They should not be stored at room temperature as bacteria can grow rapidly.
  C Chilled foods should not be frozen completely.
  D They all contain Listeria which continues to grow in any case.

Instructions

1 Look at these verbs used to describe how food is prepared and cooked. Using your dictionary if necessary, divide the verbs in the box into those that talk about:

cutting mixing heating other

grill	knead	carve	roast
mince	fry	beat	dice
stir	slice	pour	bake
boil	chop	shred	simmer
add	peel	melt	grate

2 Look at the photographs and talk about the food in each one.

What ingredients does it contain?
How do you make it?
When would you eat it?
Do you like this kind of food?

3 These are some of the instructions for making the food in one of the pictures. They are in the wrong order. With your partner decide which food is being described.

Listen and put the instructions into the correct order by writing the numbers 1–14.

a pour the mixture into a square container
b decorate each piece with a nut
c beat the eggs into this mixture one at a time
d spread it all over the top
e take it out and leave it to cool
f melt some butter and pour it into a bowl
g put the pieces into a bowl
h cook it in the oven for forty minutes
i melt the chocolate over some warm water
j stir in the flour and cocoa and add some nuts
k cut the cake into twelve pieces
l break a bar of chocolate into pieces
m add the sugar and stir
n beat in one egg and some sugar

4 Use the verbs above to help you write the recipe for a dish from your country.

97

Conditionals 1

1 Look at these sentences from the listening text:

If you don't have any pecans, the other sort will be quite all right.
If you boil chocolate, you spoil the taste.

1 What tenses are used in these sentences?
2 What time is referred to?

Compare:

	Tense	Time
If it rains, I'll take an umbrella	**First conditional** If + present simple subject + will	I think it will probably rain (eg today)
If/When it rains, I take an umbrella	**Zero conditional** If + present simple subject + present	always (time not specific)
If I eat a lot of chocolate, I'll put on weight	First conditional	I have the chance to eat a lot of chocolate now
If I eat a lot of chocolate, I put on weight	Zero conditional	always/every time

2 In the following sentences change the main verb to either the present tense or *will* to show if it is what usually happens, or if it is related to real future time.

1 If I hear a noise in the night, I _____ (get up) to see what it is.

2 If I am on holiday, I usually _____ (eat) less.

3 If it rains tomorrow, I _____ (stay) at home.

4 If that letter doesn't arrive soon, I _____ (phone) them.

5 If pasta is cooked for too long, it _____ (become) uneatable.

6 If you cook that pasta for too long, it _____ (become) soft.

7 If you eat too much fruit, you _____ (get) stomachache.

8 If you eat all that fruit, you _____ (get) stomachache.

9 If you skip breakfast, you _____ (eat) more snacks.

10 If you leave ice cream out of the fridge, it _____ (melt).

11 If you leave that ice cream out of the fridge, it _____ (melt).

12 If you grow your own vegetables, you _____ (save) a lot of money.

3 Look back at sentences **1–12** and decide where both zero and first conditional sentences are possible.

4 Your class has decided to organise a meal out in a restaurant next week.

Look at the information below, and write some sentences about each of the restaurants using the first conditional.

Examples:
If we go to La Rustica we'll be able to have a pizza.
If we go to The Taverna, we'll get a 10% discount.

Pizzeria La Rustica eat with us or take away pizza, pasta and pudding, jazz nightly until 2am, young lively atmosphere no reservations – come early to get a good table – reductions for groups, open all day, every day.

The Jade Garden
authentic Cantonese and Indonesian dishes
vegetarian specialities small candle-lit tables.
Private room for groups (advance booking only).
Last orders 10.30. Indonesian music and dancing on Wednesdays. All major credit cards accepted.

The Taverna full range of traditional Greek food, a special vegetarian dish each day, tables outdoors for up to 10 people. 10% discount for parties of 6 or more. Good old-fashioned service. Open late on Friday and Saturday, we guarantee no loud music or entertainment – come and relax!

Yeoman of the Guard *best of British cooking – beef, lamb or turkey – serve yourself at the carvery, eat as much as you like for £12* (drinks and VAT extra). Choice of chips, roast potatoes or a green vegetable, large range of hot desserts with custard, perfect for wedding anniversaries & family occasions. 19.00–21.30, Mon–Sat.

Expressing opinions

Decide who is Student **A**, **B**, **C** and **D**. Discuss together which restaurant you would like to go to.

Look at the language in the box before you start.

Student A: You would like to try something different, and experience the food of another culture.

Student B: You are a vegetarian and would like a restaurant that has a choice of non-meat dishes.

Student C: You don't mind what you eat, but you would like some entertainment or live music.

Student D: You would like a quiet place with good service and a varied choice on the menu.

Preferences

I prefer eating Greek food to French food.

I'd prefer to go to a Greek restaurant.

I'd rather eat Greek food.

WRITING
Giving reasons

Write three paragraphs of 50 words each, explaining why you have made your choice. Begin each paragraph like this:

I don't think we should go to _____

_____

_____

_____

_____

Nor should we go to _____

_____

_____

_____

_____

I'd rather go _____

_____

_____

_____

_____

LISTENING 3
Multiple matching

You will hear a recorded information line which talks about five different restaurants in London. For each restaurant **1–5**, choose the comment **A–F** which best matches what is said about each restaurant. There is one extra letter which you do not need to use.

Restaurants

1 Gulliver's   _____

2 The Garden Room   _____

3 The Cenci   _____

4 Petals   _____

5 Walley's   _____

Comments

A You won't be kept waiting.
B There's not much choice.
C There may not be a free table.
D You can eat in the open air.
E The location is convenient.
F You may see famous people.

GRAMMAR 4
If/Unless

1 Look at these sentences from a discussion about restaurants.

If the owner is Spanish, they'll serve traditional Spanish food.

Unless the owner is Italian, they won't serve traditional Italian food.

What is the difference between *if* and *unless*?

2 Put *if* or *unless* into each of these sentences about the restaurants on page 99.

1 _____ we go to Yeoman of the Guard, we'll be able to eat British food.

2 _____ it doesn't rain, we'll be able to sit outside at The Taverna.

3 _____ we go to La Rustica early, we won't get a good table.

4 _____ we serve ourselves at the carvery, we can eat as much as we like.

5 _____ we go to The Jade Garden, we won't get to hear any jazz.

3 Complete the second sentence so that it has a similar meaning to the first sentence. Use the word given and other words to complete each sentence. You must use between two and five words. Do not change the word given.

1 Unless we book in advance, we won't get a table at that restaurant.
if
We won't get a table at that restaurant
_____ book in advance.

2 If he doesn't study harder, he won't pass the exam.
unless
He won't pass the exam _____ harder.

3 You'll only find the disco if you follow my directions exactly.
unless
You won't find the disco _____ my directions exactly.

4 Unless you've got a car, you won't be able to go to that restaurant in the country.
if
You won't be able to go to that restaurant in the country _____ a car.

5 Unless I have a glass of water, I'll faint.
if
I'll faint _____ a glass of water.

6 If it doesn't rain, we can have a picnic.
unless
We can have a picnic _____ rains.

LISTENING 4
Listening for specific information

1 Look at the menu for Simon's Restaurant. With your partner check that you understand all the vocabulary.

2 Listen to the conversation and circle on the menu the food and drink which the man and woman choose.

3 Listen again and write down the questions the waiter asks when he comes to take the order.

Simon's Restaurant

Starters
Soup of the day   £1.90
Egg & Prawn Mayonnaise   £2.80
Garlic Bread   £1.80
Fried Mushrooms with Garlic Sauce   £3.10
Chef's Prawn Cocktail   £2.90
Avocado Vinaigrette   £2.95

Main courses
Steaks served with French Fries & Fresh Vegetables
Peppered fillet steak   £8.70
Grilled T-Bone Steak   £8.20

Omelettes served with French Fries
Plain Omelette   £4.95
Mushroom or Ham   £4.20

Chicken served with French Fries or Jacket Potatoes
1/2 Roast Chicken   £6.60
Chicken Kiev   £6.85
Chicken Risotto   £4.75
Chicken Kebab   £5.65

Fish served with French Fries or Rice
Fried Cod   £3.95
Sole with Garlic & Cream Sauce   £5.75

Salads
Mixed Salad   £1.95
Special Californian Salad   £5.10
Chef's Unlimited Salad   £5.90
(Eat as much as you want)

Desserts
Apple Pie with Ice Cream   £2.10
Fresh Pineapple   £2.50
Chocolate Pudding with Hot Chocolate Sauce   £2.70
Fried Banana with Cream & Chocolate Sauce   £2.10
Black Forest Gateau   £2.35

Drinks
Malvern Sparkling Mineral Water (Bottle)   £1.35
Highland Still Mineral Water (Bottle)   £1.35
Orange Juice   £1.10
Sparkling Apple Juice   £1.10

Wines House Wine (Red or White)
Glass   £1.70
1/2 Carafe   £4.20
Carafe   £8.10

SPEAKING 3
Expressing attitudes and opinions

1 Look at the menu again and in groups of three act out the situation. Student A is the waiter and Students B and C are customers ordering a meal.

2 Look at the advertisement for Simon's Restaurant.

Your class has decided to go to Simon's Restaurant for a meal and you want to get the 12% discount. With your partners decide which dishes you think should be included in the 'Mini-menu' to provide a good choice for the whole group.

Simon's Restaurant

Fantastic group discount with our 'Mini-menu' offer!!

For groups of 12 or more we offer a special 'Mini-menu' scheme with a discount of 12%.

All you have to do is book your table at least three days in advance and at the time of booking tell us which of our dishes you want on your special 'Mini-menu'.

You can choose 2 starters, 3 main courses and 2 desserts from our main selection for your 'Mini-menu'.

Then, when you come to eat with us, your group must select their lunch or dinner only from among those dishes.

You all get a 12% discount!

Future time 2

■1 Look at these phrases from the listening text. Which tense is used and why?

I'll have an orange juice, please.
I'll have the Unlimited Salad.

We use *will* + infinitive when we make decisions, offers and promises at the time of speaking.

■2 Compare these phrases:

	Time of decision
1 a: I'm going to have an ice-cream. b: What flavour? a: Umm… I'm not sure, let's see the list… . …I know… I'll have raspberry.	I've already decided I decide now
2 a: I'm doing some shopping for Mary this morning. b: Oh, I'll take you in the car.	Already arranged Offer now
3 a: I'm leaving tomorrow. The train goes at 9.00 in the morning. b: Do keep in touch. a: Yes, I will. I'll write often.	Already arranged I promise now

■3 In each of these sentences decide which tense is most appropriate.

- Present simple – timetables and fixed times
- *Going to* + infinitive – intentions
- Present continuous – arrangements
- *Will* + infinitive – decisions, offers, promises

1 My friend _____ (come) to visit me this weekend.

2 'I'm so busy. I never get time to clean my car.'
'I _____ (do) it for you.'

3 John _____ (come) to clean my car for me tomorrow, as I never have time.

4 I _____ (look) around the shops. Do you want anything?

5 'Would you like to order now?'
'Yes, we _____ (have) steak and chips, please.'

6 'You still haven't tidied your room although I've been asking you for ages.'
'I _____ (do) it this weekend, honestly!'

7 'When _____ (leave)?'
'Next Sunday, I _____ (get) the train to London and then _____ (fly) to Paris.'
'What time _____ (be) your train?'
'It _____ (leave) at 9am and _____ (stop) at every station.
It _____ (take) two hours!'
'Oh, no! I _____ (give) you a lift to the airport in my car.'
'That's great, thank you.'

8 I can't come on Sunday. I _____ (give) Rose a lift to the airport.

9 'Don't forget to ring me and tell me what time to expect you.'
'Don't worry, I _____ (forget).'

HELP WITH TALKING ABOUT A PICTURE

■1 Look at photograph 1. Discuss the questions with your partner. Use the language in the box below to help you.

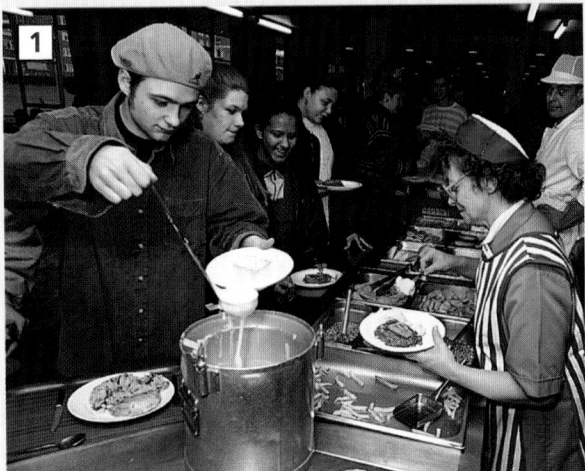

1   Who are these people?
young/old/middle-aged
man/woman/boy/girl
student/employed/customer/family member

2   Where are they? What are they doing?
smartly dressed/casually dressed
working/studying/relaxing/playing
sitting/standing
alone/with other people

3   How do they feel? What are they thinking?
happy/sad/bored/interested/lonely/nervous/
confident/tired, etc.

4   What else is happening in the picture?
What's in the background?
indoors/outdoors
furniture/buildings/objects/weather/decorations

5   What is your opinion of what is happening?
Would you like to be in this situation?
Could this happen in your country?

It looks as if they	He appears to be + verb + -ing
They look + adjective	I get the impression that he is
It looks like + (a) noun	Maybe they're
She seems to be + adjective	Perhaps they're
She seems to be + verb + -ing	They might be
He appears to be + adjective	They could be
	They may be
	They must/can't be

■2

1   Decide who is Student A and who is Student B.
Student A: Look at photograph 2.
Student B: Look at photograph 3.

This time, think about questions 1–5 and be ready to speak for one minute about your photograph.

2   **Student A:** Speak for one minute about your photograph.
Student B: At the end, say if you agree or disagree.

3   **Student B:** Speak for one minute about your photograph.
Student A: At the end, say if you agree or disagree.

◼3 In the exam you will each be given two photographs and asked to compare them. Look at these words and phrases used to compare things.

In this picture there are four people, **whereas** in this one there are five.

The first picture was taken at night **while** the **second one** was taken in the day.

While that woman looks happy, **this one** looks rather sad.

That picture was taken in a school. This one, **on the other hand**, was taken in an office.

◼4 Don't forget how to compare adjectives:

large	larger	largest
interesting	more interesting	most interesting

This photo isn't as <u>interesting</u> as that one.
<u>large</u>

◼5 Look at these pairs of pictures. Spend a few minutes thinking about what to say.

Student A: Compare pictures 4 and 5.
Student B: Listen and then say if you agree.

Selecting an answer

For each of the questions 1–7 listen and decide whether the statements are true or false.

1 The restaurants all have the same furniture.

2 The director's house is decorated in the same way as the restaurant.

3 Each restaurant serves some local specialities.

4 If the pictures were different prices would be higher.

5 Restaurant managers are not allowed to vary the standard of service.

6 The director thinks it would be bad to offer a special service.

7 The interviewer likes the restaurants as they are.

READING 3 ▮▮▮▮▮

Multiple matching

◼1 Discuss these questions with your partner.

1 Do you like chocolate?

2 How much chocolate do you eat?

3 What types of chocolate do you like?

4 When do you eat it?

5 What happens if you eat too much?

◼2 Read the article on page 105 quickly and underline the parts that answer these questions.

1 How much chocolate do British people eat per week on average?

2 Why do people become 'chocoholics'?

3 What are the aims of the Chocolate Society?

4 What will the society do?

5 According to Chantal Coady, what is the difference between real chocolate and commercial chocolate?

Discuss the answers to the questions with your partner.

3 Now read the article more carefully. Choose from the list **A–G** the heading which best summarises each part (**1–5**) of the article. There is an example at the beginning (**0**).

A The society's main belief
B Who should not join the society
C What the society will do
D Who should join the society
E What the society cannot do
F Chantal Coady gives an example
G Chantal Coady makes a decision

4 What is a chocolatier?

A A person who makes chocolate
B A place where chocolate is made
C A machine which makes chocolate

5 For each of these words from the passage, write a definition using *who* or *which*.

1 chocoholic (Part 1)
2 wrappers (1)
3 Mayans and Aztecs (2)
4 a newsletter (4)
5 gourmets (4)
6 powdered milk (4)
7 true chocolate (5)

Older than Aztecs

0	G

Chantal Coady has become so worried about the state of Britain's chocolate, she has decided that what the nation needs is a Chocolate Society. Considering that we eat an average 225 grams each per week, some would say that Britain is one huge chocolate society already. But Ms Coady, who runs Rococo Chocolates in London, the country's leading chocolatier, disagrees.

1

"Lots of people claim to be addicted to chocolate. The word 'chocoholics' is used as if everyone understands what it means. You see TV interviews with people who hide wrappers behind the furniture and obviously have quite serious eating problems, but to call them chocoholics is mistaken. They are talking about sugar addiction. It's the need for sugar they can't control, so they should join a sugar society, if such a thing exists!" Having taken the initiative in setting up a Chocolate Society, Ms Coady has absolutely no intention of setting up a support group for people with eating problems. She clearly disapproves of talking about chocolate in a language of sin, stolen pleasures and temptation, punctuated with lip-smacking oohs and uhmms.

2

Members will be enthusiasts of the real thing, proper chocolate – that dark and bitter substance which has exercised a powerful grip on civilisations throughout history, beginning with the Mayans and Aztecs.

3

The founding principles of this chocolate appreciation group are that the only necessary ingredients for good chocolate are pure cocoa solids, which have been mixed with a little cocoa butter, and a small amount of sugar. As a rough guide, the proportion of cocoa solids is the key; the higher the better and more bitter the chocolate. "We want to let more people understand what true chocolate is really about. Chocolate deserves much more status than most people would give it," says Ms Coady.

4

Starting with a programme of blind tastings, teach-ins, newsletter information and samples, the Chocolate Society's priority is to "draw the public's attention to the difference between the complex delicacy which the worlds great cooks and gourmets recognise as chocolate and the low grade, sweet confection which the British consume by the ton every week." Ms Coady points out that the principal ingredient of commercial 'chocolate' is not cocoa (on average a meagre 20 per cent) but sugar, solid vegetable fat and powdered milk. "These dietary villains are responsible for chocolate's undeserved reputation as fattening, tooth-rotting, and addictive," she says.

5

True chocolate is a far purer and healthier product according to Ms Coady, who illustrates her point through one of her own favourite chocolates – Valrhona's Carre de Guanaja, "A two-centimetre square contains 70 per cent cocoa solids but it has only a tenth of the calories of the typical so-called chocolate bar, and of course, you can always tell the quality of chocolate by listening for the brittle 'snap' which the genuine article makes when broken into pieces."

GRAMMAR 6
Relative clauses

1 What is the difference between these two sentences?

Ron is the boy who eats a lot of chocolate.
Ron, who eats a lot of chocolate, shops at Rococo.

2 Punctuate these sentences to show whether they include defining or non-defining relative clauses.

1 Chantal Coady is the person who runs Rococo Chocolate in London.

2 Commercial chocolate which the British eat in huge quantities is made with lots of sugar.

3 The Chocolate Society which is being launched next week aims to inform people about real chocolate.

4 Chocolate is a delicacy which has been known to civilisation since the Aztecs.

5 Rococo which is in central London is a shop which does not sell commercial chocolate.

6 Some people who eat too much chocolate call themselves chocoholics.

PRONUNCIATION
Vowel sounds 2

Put these words into one of the columns according to the main vowel sound. Then listen to check.

can	lack	thing	each
says	gap	need	real
dark	claim	any	can't
quite	heart	guide	young
them	might	love	much
plain	give	say	which
fat	week	past	

/eɪ/ state	/iː/ eat	/ɪ/ it	/aɪ/ hide	/e/ let	/ɑː/ are	/æ/ man	/ʌ/ but

1 Read the text below and think of the word which best fits each space. Use only one word in each space. There is an example (**0**) at the beginning.

Worcester Sauce

Fifty million bottles (**0**) ___of___ Lea and Perrins Worcestershire Sauce (**1**) _____ now sold every year in 130 different countries. The original recipe did not come (**2**) _____ Worcestershire, however, and at the beginning Mr Lea and Mr Perrins (**3**) _____ not even like it.

It was Lord Marcus Sandys (**4**) _____ , on his retirement as Governor of Bengal in India, brought the recipe (**5**) _____ Worcester in 1835. He asked the local chemist's shop, Lea and Perrins, to (**6**) _____ some up for him.

This they (**7**) _____ , also making (**8**) _____ for themselves. But, deciding it tasted horrible, they put it in the cellar and forgot (**9**) _____ it. Two years (**10**) _____ , when clearing (**11**) _____ the cellar they found the bottles, tasted the sauce and thought it was wonderful.

The sauce is (**12**) _____ made to the same secret recipe and the bottles you buy in the shops are about three years old. Even when one hundred years old, the sauce is said to (**13**) _____ not only safe, (**14**) _____ also still very good indeed, despite the (**15**) _____ that it contains only natural ingredients.

2 Complete the second sentence so that it has a similar meaning to the first sentence. Use the word given and other words to complete each sentence. You must use between two and five words. Do not change the word given.

1 I get a lot of pleasure from reading cookery books.
enjoy
I _____ cookery books.

2 Those chips were too cold to eat.
enough
Those chips _____ to eat.

3 It's the first time I've eaten Yorkshire Pudding.
never
I _____ Yorkshire Pudding before.

4 With luck, she will win the cookery competition.
lucky
If she _____ win the cookery competition.

5 How long have you been a vegetarian?
become
When _____ a vegetarian?

6 Try not to fry food which can be grilled.
avoid
You should _____ which can be grilled.

7 I'd prefer to go to a fast-food place.
rather
I _____ a fast food place.

8 Missing breakfast always gives me a headache.
get
If I _____ a headache.

9 Frozen peas are cheaper than fresh ones.
expensive
Frozen peas are _____ as
fresh ones.

10 If you don't boil the water the tea won't taste right.
unless
The tea won't taste right _____
water.

3 You have been asked to write an article for the school magazine. Choose
one of the following titles. Your article must be between 120 and 180
words.

1 Describe a meal that you enjoyed very much.

2 What are the advantages and disadvantages of eating out of doors?

4 Read the text below. Use the word given in capitals at the end of each
line to form a word that fits in the space in the same line. There is an
example at the beginning (**0**).

Fancy a Sandwich?

Harry Landin from Peterborough may be the owner	
of the world's (**0**) *oldest* sandwich. The ancient snack, with	**OLD**
just one bite taken out of it, was (**1**) _____ wrapped in	**FIND**
an old (**2**) _____ list, inside a worn-out nineteen-twenties	**SHOP**
sofa which Harry was (**3**) _____ up for his uncle. Harry	**BREAK**
says that the ancient sandwich was so well (**4**) _____	**HIDE**
that (**5**) _____ had ever noticed it. He thinks the	**BODY**
sandwich may have been (**6**) _____ by the person who	**LOSE**
built the sofa because people in those days used to eat their	
lunch as they worked.	
Peterborough museum's (**7**) _____ Director, Mrs Smith,	**ASSIST**
said that although the (**8**) _____ looked like meat, it was	**FILL**
most (**9**) _____ rather old cheese. Now Harry is looking	**PROBABLE**
for (**10**) _____ for what he can do with his sandwich as	**SUGGEST**
the museum has decided that it does not want to exhibit it .	

B **A**

C

D

High-tech horizons

Talking about photographs

1 Work with a partner. Choose one pair of pictures. Compare and contrast your pictures. Do you agree with the points your partner makes?

2 Talk to your partner about these topics. Use the boxes for ideas.

1 How you like to study.

> in class/in a library/at home
>
> with books/computers/TV
>
> in silence/with music
>
> alone/with a friend

2 How learning and studying is changing because of technological advances.

> changing job prospects
>
> computerisation
>
> interactive software
>
> the internet
>
> satellite TV

HELP WITH GAPPED TEXTS

■ **1** Look at these words and using your dictionary to help you, decide which refer to CDs and which to LP records.

> vinyl laser digital stylus
> pulses turntable lens

■ **2** Talk to your partner. What are the advantages of a CD system over cassette tapes and LP records?

■ **3** Look at these sentences taken from an article about CDs and LPs and answer the questions with your partner.

1 *This is because it is seldom worth repairing a cheap CD player, unless it is under guarantee.*

What does the word **this** refer to in the sentence? Where in the article will you look to find out what **this** is: before the sentence or after it?

2 *By following some clear instructions you can identify and reduce problems.*

Would you expect to find this sentence before or after a list of instructions?

3 *Worse, it may no longer keep the laser on track.*
What would you expect to find in the sentence before this one?

4 *But a fine hair can stop a disc playing if it blocks out too many pulses in a straight line.*

What do you expect to find before a sentence beginning with **but**?

5 *Unless they are handled and stored extremely carefully, LPs can become damaged and scratched.*

What does **they** refer to?

6 *They play on one player, but not on another, and sometimes they won't play again on the same player.*

Where must you look to find what **they** refers to?

In a text, what would you expect to find in the sentence before number 5?
And before number 6?

■ **4** Read the article. Eight sentences have been removed. Choose from sentences **A–I** the one which fits each gap. There is one extra sentence you do not need to use. There is an example at the beginning (**0**).

Why 'indestructible' CDs can sometimes misbehave

When your discs start to slip ...

Reports in the press recently have called the CD system 'less reliable than LPs'. This is clearly untrue, but why did the stories start? The fact is, there are moments when CDs seem to develop minds of their own. `0` `H`

The vinyl LP is a system where any imperfection in manufacture or damage to the surface is always picked up by the stylus and heard from any turntable. `1` ``

But the CD is a digital system. The player's laser reads a series of on/off pulses, without physically touching the disc's surface. Not every pulse must be read accurately – as long as the number of reading errors remains below a certain limit, the reconstruction of the music is complete. But if the number of errors rises above that level, the player loses the sound for a moment. `2` ``
So **it** repeats the same bit of music, like a stylus stuck on a record. All CD players contain electronics which perform 'error correction', filling or bridging gaps when pulses are missing or mis-read. The more expensive the player, the better the error correction.

CD players have a lens which focuses the laser on a tiny spot on the disc surface, and keeps it in focus even when the disc is slightly bent. `3` `` But in a dusty or smoky room, the lens may become dirty. Instruments exist (starting at about £10) for cleaning the laser lens.

Dust and surface scratches can prevent the laser reading a group of pulses. Lightly wiping the disc with a clean dry cloth will usually get rid of dust. Scratches can sometimes be polished away with special products. Only polish hard if the disc is unplayable.

Mysteriously, some scratches may have no effect at all, depending on the position, angle and size of the scratch. **4**☐ Just taking the disc out of a player and reloading it may make it play, because the player transport has centred it more accurately.

5☐

When a disc misbehaves, take it out, wipe it lightly, reload and try again. If **it** still doesn't play, try **it** on another player. If it plays, try a lens cleaner on your player. But if your player is old and was cheap, and consistently refuses to play discs that work on other players, the time has come to buy a new **one**. **6**☐

If a disc consistently refuses to play on more than one player, take it back to the shop and ask for a replacement. If **that** has the same fault, **it** is probably caused by a defect in the master disc used for pressing, and all copies will be the same. **7**☐ Some CD pressing plants do cut corners on quality, but record companies lose money on returned discs, and do eventually force the plants to improve their quality control.

If you do have problems, just think back twenty years and how difficult it was for people to buy a problem-free vinyl LP and then keep **it** in perfect condition!

A Expensive players have better lenses and are more likely to stay in line.

B Unless they are handled and stored extremely carefully, LPs can become damaged and scratched.

C This is because it is seldom worth repairing a cheap CD player unless it is under guarantee.

D By following some clear instructions, you can identify and reduce problems.

E Worse, it may no longer keep the laser on track.

F Again, we have to admit that cassette tapes are no better than LPs in this respect.

G But a fine hair can stop a disc playing if it blocks out too many pulses in a straight line.

H They play on one player but not on another, and sometimes they won't play again on the same player.

I Get your money back and wait for a reissue, or buy a copy abroad.

■**5** Compare your answers with your partner and tell your partner why you have chosen them.

■**6** With your partner, look back at the article and answer these questions. How did you know which was the extra sentence?

1 Find words in the passage that mean:
making things
correctly
read badly
very small
a little bit
cannot be played
strangely
loading again
behaves badly
making a disc

2 Which of the words you have found include a prefix? What do these prefixes mean? Find some more examples of these prefixes in the text.

3 What do the words in **bold** refer to in each of these extracts from the article?
a so **it** repeats the same bit of music
b if **it** still doesn't play, try **it** on another player
c the time has come to buy a new **one**
d if **that** has the same fault, **it** is probably caused by a defect
e and then keep **it** in perfect condition

⊟ LISTENING 1 ▌▌▌
Part One

The passive

▬ 1 Listen to Part One of this conversation with the manager of Britain's largest pizza factory and put one word in each space in this passage.

The factory makes (1) _____ pizzas per week. Most are immediately (2) _____ but some are (3) _____ and then sold fresh. The most popular type is the (4) _____ -sized pizza, which accounts for about (5) _____ % of the pizzas bought in shops. This is because they are seen as (6) _____ and (7) _____ .

▬ 2 Look at this sentence from the text.

Pizzas are made at the factory.

What verb form is used and why?

▬ 3 Complete this grid:

The Passive

	Active	Passive
Present simple	someone makes the pizza	the pizza is made
Present continuous		the pizza is being made
		the pizza has been made
Past simple	someone made the pizza	
	someone was making the pizza	
Past perfect		the pizza had been made
Going to		
Will	someone will make the pizza	
Must		the pizza must be made
Have to		

Part Two

1 Look at the pictures of the pizza factory on page 112 and label them with the words in the box.

dough	base	topping
oven	delivery	lorry

2 Listen to Part Two of the conversation and put one of the verbs from the box in each of the spaces **A–I** to show the process of pizza-making in the factory.

cooked	wrapped	frozen
coated	delivered	assembled
rolled	mixed	stamped

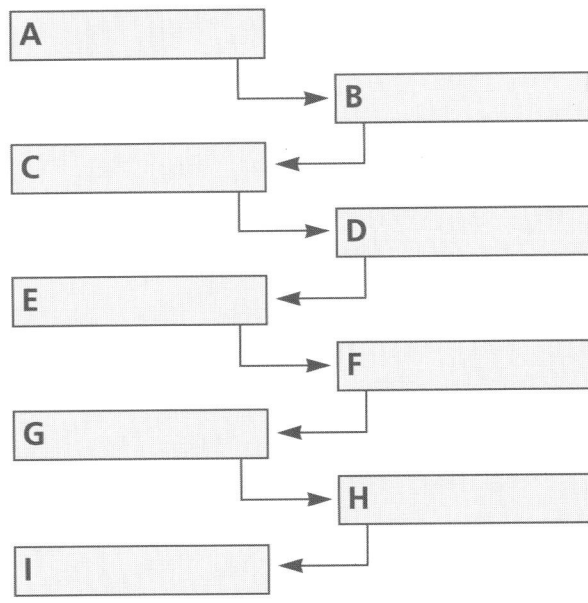

3 Which of the stages mentioned is shown in each of the four pictures opposite?

4 Listen again to check your answers and then write a sentence using the passive form of each of the verbs in the box to describe how pizzas are made in the factory.

5 Complete the second sentence so that it has a similar meaning to the first sentence. Use the word given and other words to complete each sentence. You must use between two and five words. Do not change the word given.

1 They are designing a new machine.
is
A new machine _____ designed.

2 They have to switch on the photocopier ten minutes before using it.
be
The photocopier _____ ten minutes before use.

3 A mechanical breakdown caused the delay.
by
The delay _____ a mechanical breakdown.

4 Someone will meet you at the airport.
be
You _____ at the airport.

5 Personal computers are changing our working lives.
by
Our working lives _____ computers.

6 We must keep the ovens at a constant temperature.
be
The ovens _____ a constant temperature.

7 They freeze the pizzas in batches of twelve.
are
The pizzas _____ batches of twelve.

8 Children are going to eat most of our pizzas.
be
Most of our pizzas _____ by children.

9 We put the pizzas in boxes for delivery.
are
Our pizzas _____ for delivery.

10 You can buy either frozen or chilled pizzas in most shops.
be
Either frozen or chilled pizzas _____ in most shops.

113

SPEAKING 2

Expressing and justifying opinions

Work with your partner. Match the beginning of each sentence
1–16 with the end of a sentence **a–p** to make complete statements
about inventions and discoveries. Use the phrases in the box in
your discussion.

> it can't have been
> it must have been
> it may have been
> it would/might have been

1	The telephone	**a**	was opened in Pasadena in 1948
2	The first flight	**b**	was devised by Sony in 1978
3	The first breakfast cereal	**c**	was developed by Pemberton in 1886
4	The first McDonald's	**d**	was calculated by Ptolemy in 2nd Century AD
5	The first travellers' cheque	**e**	was invented by Bell in 1876
6	The Walkman	**f**	was transmitted by Marconi in 1895
7	The first radio message	**g**	was made by Wright in 1903
8	The laws of the pendulum	**h**	was first marketed in Denmark in 1955
9	Coca-Cola	**i**	was produced by Penguin in 1935
10	Acupuncture	**j**	was invented by Heinz in 1876
11	The value of pi – (π)(3.1416)	**k**	was discovered by Columbus in 1492
12	The first heart transplant	**l**	were established by Galileo in 1591
13	Lego	**m**	has been practised in China since 2000 BC
14	The first paperback book	**n**	was performed by Barnard in 1967
15	The American continent	**o**	was produced by Kellogg in 1893
16	Tomato ketchup	**p**	was countersigned in the USA in 1891

GRAMMAR 1
Agents

1 **Discuss with your partner:**

1 In what situations do we use the passive in English?

2 When is it necessary to use an agent (eg *by* someone)?
Look at these examples:

a Espresso machines were developed in Italy at the end of the last century.

b The answer sheets are checked by a computer.

c The telephone was invented by Bell in 1876.

d My friend was bitten by a dog.

e My car has been stolen.

3 Change these sentences into the active form.
Did you find some easier to change than others? Why?

2 Match each of the examples above to one of these three situations in which the passive is used:

1 When the action is more important than the agent.

2 When we do not know (or do not want to say) who the agent is.

3 When we are describing a process.

3 Look at each of these active sentences. Change them to the passive, and decide whether to include the agent or not.

1 The postman has delivered a lot of letters this morning.
A _____

2 Someone has stolen some money from my bag.
Some _____

3 People are drinking more coffee than tea these days.
More _____

4 Pizarro first brought potatoes to Europe in 1554.
Potatoes _____

5 You have to return all videos to the shop before 6 p.m.
All videos _____

6 You are not permitted to smoke in the cinema.
Smoking _____

7 An electric element in the boiler heats the water.
The water _____

8 The company employs forty-five technicians.
Forty-five technicians _____

9 Someone invented the Espresso machine in Italy.
The Espresso machine _____

10 Some people have not returned books to the library.
Some books _____

4 Compare with your partner. In each case decide which sounds better – the active, the passive, or does it make no difference?

SPEAKING 3
Expressing attitudes and opinions

1 With your partner make a list of:

a Ten objects which you think will soon be out of date (e.g. LP records, which are being replaced by CDs).

b Ten objects you think will be important in the future.

Compare with other students.

2 Discuss with your partner which of these things will change a lot in the next ten years, and how:

- shopping and money
- working and leisure
- family life
- communications

READING 1

Reading for specific information

1 Read the article quickly, and answer the questions below.

1 Which of the things you talked about in Speaking 3 are mentioned in the article?

2 The article is about Britain. Which of the predictions are also true for your country?

Trends

1 **H**ow will society change in the next century? *Debbie Kent* looks at some future changes.

Forecasting the future is a risky
5 business. But that doesn't mean we can't say anything about the next decade. In fact one trend is almost completely predictable: population growth. The population of the UK,
10 currently just over 57 million, **is expected to** keep rising to hit 59 million in the next ten years. Most significant is how the structure of that 59 million will change. The
15 number of 16 to 19 year-olds has been falling since the baby boom generation reached adolescence in the early 1980s, and it will stay low through the 90s and into the next
20 century. On the other hand, the proportion of older people will grow. In the next ten years more than 45% of us **will be over 50**.

Some implications are clear.
25 Fewer school leavers and a workforce that is growing only slowly will have an impact on the labour market. Employers **may have to**
30 **look** elsewhere to fill vacancies – to women with children and older people.

At the other end of the scale, the growth in the number of elderly people means a fresh look at the
35 idea of retirement. For the first time **most of us can expect to have** 30 years of retirement to look forward to.

Although society will still be
40 made up largely of conventional families, **there is a growing trend** for fewer stereotypical households: more homes will consist of single adults. Then there will be house-
45 holds split by divorce, mixed households of second marriages, and three generations living under one roof. The average household size **is predicted to fall from** 2.7
50 people to 2.4 people in the next ten years.

Finance is one of the areas that **is likely to** undergo fundamental change in the next few years. If full
55 European monetary union takes place, we **could routinely be using** a 'hard ECU' or some other denomination of Euro-wide currency even for our spending at home.

60 Will we be using hard currency at all? The answer is almost certainly yes, for low-value transactions and for that small but intractable section of the population that does
65 not have a bank account. But the cheque **should be** pretty much on the way out in the next ten years. According to Roger Taylor of Midland Payment Transmission Services,
70 developers of payment card systems: "Transactions will be primarily plastic-based but people won't carry as many cards."

So the walletful of plastic is
75 likely to be replaced by a single multi-function card that will act as cheque book, credit card, cash dispenser and debit card. Haven't we got that (or almost) already?
80 The difference is that the future version will be a 'smart card' with a built-in memory. It will carry as much information about you as a personal organiser – details of bank
85 accounts, credit ratings, insurance, salary – and will be able to pass that information on to anyone you choose to do business with.

2 Now read more carefully and decide whether these statements are true or false.

1 There will be an increase in population.

2 The proportion of young people is going to increase.

3 The number of working women is likely to increase.

4 There will be fewer jobs for older people.

5 There will be more people living in each house.

6 Coins and banknotes will no longer exist.

7 Everybody will have a bank account.

8 Most people will use cards to do their shopping.

9 There will be more types of card in use.

10 The smart card is like a small computer.

3 Look at the phrases in the article which are in **bold** type and decide which of them expresses

1 Something that will definitely happen.

2 Something that is probably going to happen.

3 Something that is possibly going to happen.

SPEAKING 4

Expressing opinions

Make predictions about the next decade using the pictures and phrases in the box below.

is expected to	will be
may have to	most of us can expect to
is predicted to	there is a growing trend
could be using	is likely to

Talk to your partner about some of the following:

sport	the family
holidays	money
your life	the economy
social problems	food
international relations	music

WRITING

A report

In what ways do you think life will change in your country in the next ten years? How much will this affect you personally? Write a report of between 120 and 180 words.

LISTENING 2

Blank filling

1 Before you listen, discuss with your partner the meanings of these words. What you think the listening will be about?

screen   credit card   keyboard   microchip   telephone card   satellite

2 Listen to this radio interview and as you listen complete the sentences by writing a word or short phrase in each of the spaces **1–10**.

Smart cards have been successfully used by banks in [_____ **1**] .

The microchips inside the smart card represent [_____ **2**] of its thickness.

The smart card is similar in size to [_____ **3**] .

The smart cards are a good way of [_____ **4**] safely.

Club owners like the cards because they make people [_____ **5**] .

The machines which read the cards are sometimes slow and [_____ **6**] .

The machines are similar in size to [_____ **7**] .

Smart cards are also useful for carrying your [_____ **8**] .

You need [_____ **9**] to get access to confidential information.

Mick says that successful tests have been carried out in [_____ **10**] .

GRAMMAR 2
Will/Going to

1 Look at these phrases from the listening text.

I think everyone will have them ten years from now.
From tests that have been carried out in France, we can see that they're going to be very popular.

I think people will use them here too.
It's not going to be long before…

When do we use *will* and when do we use *going to* for predictions?

	When?	Why?
From the bookings we've received we can see the show is going to be popular.	future	we can see from the bookings
I'm sure the show will be a great success.	future	this is my opinion
Look at the clouds. It's going to rain.	future	we can see from the clouds
I think it will be fine this weekend.	future	it's only my opinion

2 Complete these sentences using *will* or *going to*.

1 Do you think smart cards _____ become popular?

2 Hurry up, the train is already in the station. We _____ miss it.

3 Look, Clive's gone a strange colour. Do you think he _____ be sick?

4 I think Greece _____ win the next World Cup.

5 Looking at our statistics, we can predict that crime rates _____ increase in the next few years.

6 I believe there _____ be a complete change in attitudes towards money in the next decade.

7 The fortune teller who reads my palm tells me I _____ have four children.

8 Do you think Anna _____ accept the new job she has been offered?

READING 2
Gapped text

1 What is the person in the photograph doing?
Why are these things popular?
Who usually uses them?
What are the advantages and disadvantages of using them
  – for the user?
  – for other people?

2 You are going to read a newspaper article about mobile phones. Eight sentences have been removed from the article. Choose from the sentences **A–J** the one which fits each gap. There is one extra sentence you do not need to use. There is an example at the beginning (**0**).

A Mr Hudson has now written to parents.

B 'It's a fashion really, people like posing with them.'

C However, other pupils said dozens of 15-year-olds had them.

D It's clear that we'll all soon be using them in exactly this type of situation.

E He works for his dad at weekends and pays the bill himself.

F Matthew Johnson,15, caused a disturbance in his maths class when his phone went off.

G I can see there are good reasons for people giving them to their children.

H His phone even rang in an English exam.

I 'It's a sign of the times we live in, I suppose, but it tries my patience.'

J A price war has caused the cost of mobile phones to fall.

3 Complete each of these sentences about the article.

1 Students are allowed

_____

_____ .

2 But they are not allowed

_____

_____ .

3 If students use phones in class,

_____

_____ .

4 Discuss with your partner:

Do you think Mr Hudson has made the right decision? How do you think the students feel about it?

Head bans mobile phones in classroom

WHEN a 15-year-old boy answered his mobile phone in class, head teacher Peter Hudson knew he had to stop the invasion of this great necessity of modern life. **0** **J** This has started a fashion which has swept through the school in north London. 'I decided enough was enough when two 15-year-old boys started ringing each other from different classrooms,' said Mr Hudson. **1**

'I have now banned students from taking their mobiles into class. **2** They are a good security device if youngsters are wanting a lift home in the dark and because some of them have free calls in the evening, it's a good way of freeing up the family telephone.' **3** He has explained that students are allowed to take their phones into

school but warned that they will be confiscated if they are used in class.

4 'It was a present to myself before Christmas. Only a couple of people knew I had it, but when it started ringing, everyone knew. You could say the teacher was a bit annoyed, she took it straight off me and confiscated it.'

Matthew paid £70 for his phone and pays the monthly bills of about £20 with earnings from his job at a local restaurant. He does not always take it to school but says he could not do without it. 'People from work can contact me and friends can get in touch when I'm out. It's changed my life.' Matthew estimates that about 20 of the 300 students in his year now have their own phones. **5**

Mustafa Hassan, 16, took a mobile out of his school bag. He said: 'I got it as a birthday present from my parents – it cost £300 and the bills are about £40 a month because I use it a lot to call my friends.' **6**

He admitted that he had used his phone in class and once received a call during a geography lesson. **7** 'It went off in my pocket and the whole place just turned around. I switched it off quickly before the teacher realised where the ringing had come from.'

Kyri Demetriou, 15, also has a mobile phone. 'Loads of people got them for Christmas, everyone wanted them,' she said. **8**

LISTENING 3

Note-taking

1 Ruth and Michael are discussing the best way to reorganise their office. Listen to Part 1 and mark on the diagram the new position of the pieces of equipment below. Write the letters A–E on the diagram.

2 Listen to Part 2. Michael is talking to his boss about buying new office equipment. Write down the advantages of buying the new fax and laser printer which they mention.

Advantages of new fax :

Advantages of laser printer:

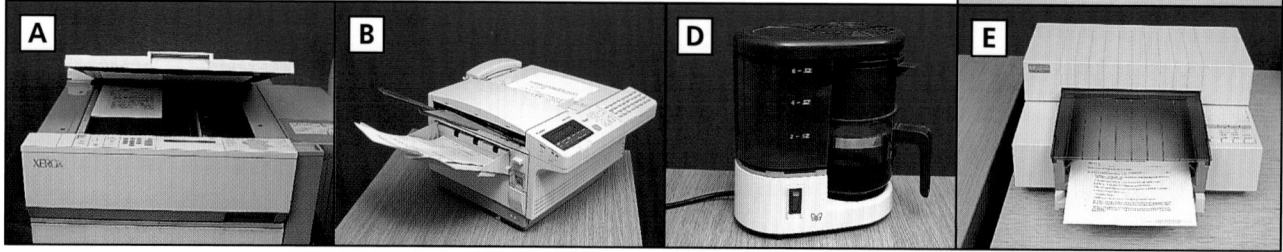

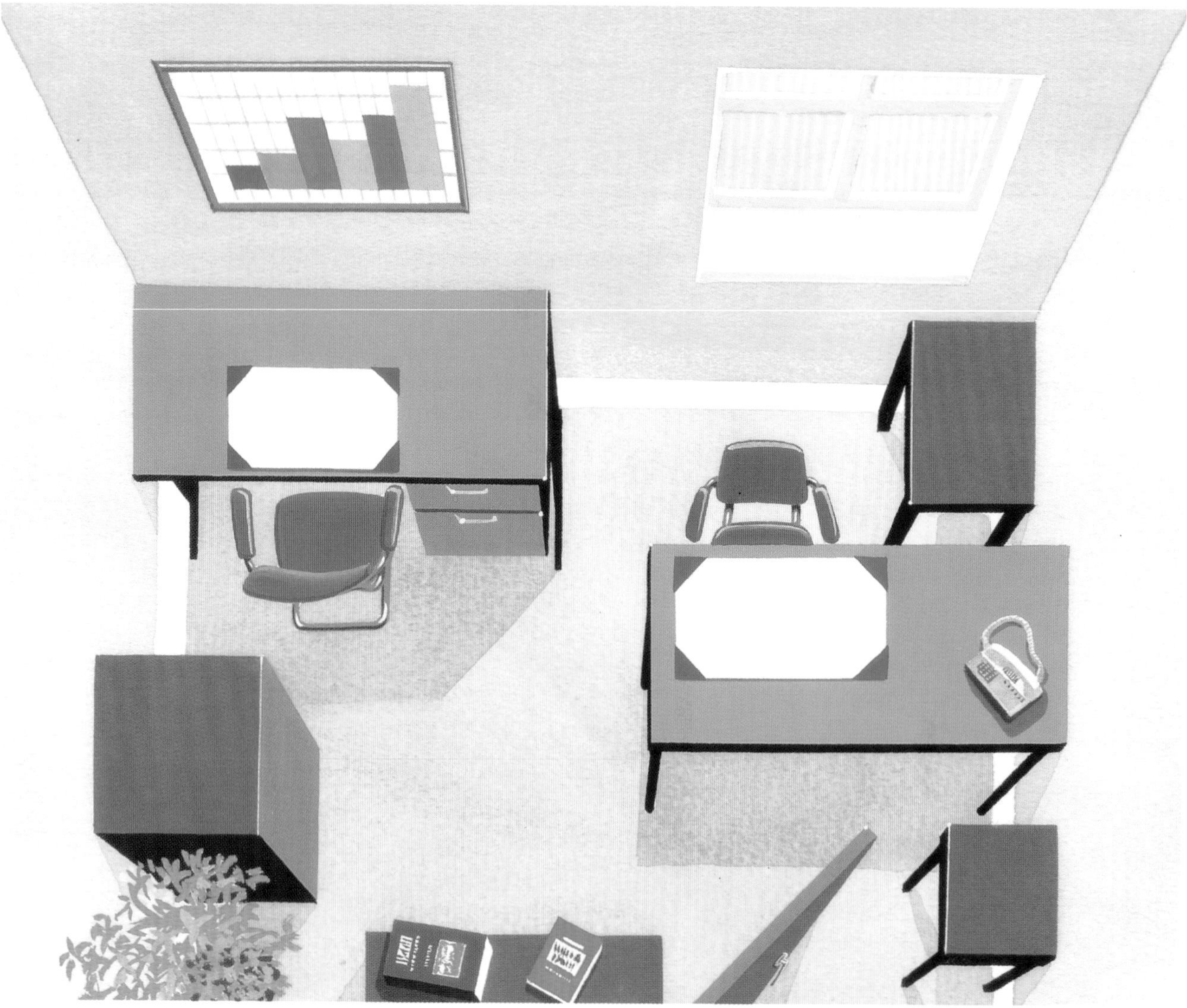

SPEAKING 4
Expressing opinions

1 Look at these phrases from the listening text used to give opinions and agree/disagree. Decide which of the phrases in group 2 would be an appropriate response to each phrase in group 1, and which wouldn't, and why.

1 Ways of giving an opinion:

I think we should…
I don't think we should…
In my opinion we should…
Wouldn't it be a good idea to …?
If you ask me…

2 Ways of agreeing and disagreeing:

That's right.
So do I.
Nor do I.
Absolutely.
I think so too.
That's a good idea.
You've got a point there.
No, I'm sorry. I can't agree with you there.
I'm afraid I don't agree.

2 With your partner use the expressions above to give your opinion about some of these topics. Find out whether your partner agrees or disagrees and why.

- fast food
- keeping pets in a flat
- ballet dancing
- Picasso
- nuclear power
- computer games
- working in an office
- mass tourism
- Heavy Metal

GRAMMAR 3
So/Nor

1 Look at these pairs of phrases:

I don't know how much they cost. – Nor do I.

I think I should try one. – So do I.

I can't read this fax. – Nor can I.

I'd like a new computer. – So would I.

What are the rules for using *so* and *nor* when you want to agree with someone?

2 Agree with each of these statements using *so* or *nor*.

1 I think that car's very expensive.

2 I don't want to buy a new fax machine.

3 I'd like a larger desk.

4 I don't think it's going to rain today.

5 I can't read Kate's handwriting.

6 I'll have a cup of coffee, please.

7 I'm feeling rather tired.

8 I'd rather work outside.

9 I shouldn't eat so much chocolate.

10 I've had a very interesting morning.

11 I'm going to see a film this evening.

12 I've never been to the USA.

3 Look at this pair of phrases:

I can't read this fax.
Can't you? It looks clear enough to me.

Match each of theses non-agreement responses **a–l** to the statements **1–12** in exercise 2 above.

a Don't you? I think it is, actually.
b Can't you? It's not as bad as yours!
c Are you really? We've got a long way to go yet.
d Will you? I think I'll wait till later, actually.
e Really? I don't think you eat that much, do you?
f Are you? I didn't think there was anything good on.
g Really? I thought you'd been a number of times.
h Do you? I think it's quite good value, actually.
i Don't you? I think it's a really good idea.
j Would you? It seems big enough to me.
k Would you? I'm quite happy here really.
l Really? Mine's just been so boring.

4 Practise reading the statements 1–12 with your partner and agree or disagree with each other.

HELP WITH WORD FORMATION 2

1 There are many ways of making nouns from verbs. Here are some examples:

verb	noun	
a express	expression	(verb + sion)
b equip	equipment	(verb + ment)
c predict	prediction	(verb + tion)
d discover	discovery	(verb + y)

Sometimes one or two letters from the verb are changed or lost in the change.

Example:
include   inclusion

2 Look at the verbs below and decide if they are the same as type **a**, **b**, **c** or **d** above.
Two of the verbs are of a different type. Which type is it?

observe	explore	improve
organise	complete	assemble
connect	design	explain
solve	inform	deliver
programme	invent	distribute
encourage	develop	describe
employ	produce	calculate
replace	decide	create
destroy	discuss	

Example:

verb	type	noun
observe	c	observation

3 Look at the words in the box and underline the part which is a suffix.

Is the first part of the word:

a a noun?
b a verb?
c an adjective?

drinkable	swimming	
sweeten	tasteless	friendship
handful	upward	modernise
manager	hopeful	

4 Complete this table using the suffixes you underlined. Add another word as an example.

meaning	suffix	another example
a state	*ship*	*membership*
to change	*ise*	*computerise*
1 a person who does something		
2 without		
3 you can do/be it		
4 an activity		
5 a direction		
6 a quantity		
7 how you feel		
8 to make more		

5 Complete the gaps by adding a suffix to the word in capitals to make a new word.

Example:
Although it doesn't rain much, the local tap water is quite ___*drinkable*___ . **DRINK**

1 The road is being _____ to cope with increased traffic.　**WIDE**

2 The _____ of the office will make our work easier.　**COMPUTER**

3 _____ of the club is open to all who live in the village.　**MEMBER**

4 The factory has four _____ lines working at any one time.　**PRODUCT**

5 He's tired because his new job is so _____ .　**STRESS**

6 The bad weather will move _____ during the day.　**EAST**

7 Add a _____ of sugar to the recipe if you have a sweet tooth.　**SPOON**

8 He gave up work at 55 and led an active _____ .　**RETIRE**

9 I came to this restaurant on the _____ of a friend.　**RECOMMEND**

10 One team member dropped out and we had to find a _____ .　**REPLACE**

■6 Read the text below. Use the word given in capitals at the end of each line to form a word that fits in the space in the same line. There is an example at the beginning (0).

Coca-Cola

John Pemberton, a chemist from Georgia, was responsible for the (**0**) _invention_ of Coca-Cola in 1886. He decided	**INVENT**
to make a syrup that was both (**1**)_____ and thirst-quenching.	**ORIGIN**
In his drugstore, he produced a (**2**)_____ of cola-nut extract,	**MIX**
sugar and caffeine. The exact (**3**)_____ is still a secret. A few	**COMPOSE**
months later, one of Pemberton's (**4**)_____ mistakenly	**ASSIST**
served Coca-Cola with (**5**)_____ soda water, which turned out to	**ADD**
be very (**6**)_____ . To market his new drink Pemberton decided	**SUCCESS**
to form a (**7**)_____ with Frank Robertson whose elegant	**PARTNER**
(**8**)_____ was used for the Coca-Cola trademark.	**HAND**
In 1985, the (**9**)_____ of an improved recipe called New Coke	**INTRODUCE**
did not meet with the (**10**)_____ of Coke drinkers and the old recipe was revived.	**APPROVE**

🔊 LISTENING 4
Multiple choice

■1 Talk to your partner.
Have you ever used an electronic organiser?
Which of the following might one be useful for?

as an address book	as a diary
translating words	telling the time/date
as a dictionary	checking spelling
listing telephone numbers	making calculations

■2 You will hear an interview about electronic organisers. For questions **1–7**, decide which of the choices **A**, **B**, or **C** correctly answers each question.

1 How is an electronic organiser like a computer?
A The size of the chip.
B The way it works.
C The quality of the screen.

2 Why are Cherry electronic organisers used in some shops?
A They are simple to operate.
B They are easy to carry.
C They are linked to a large system.

3 Why does the Cherry not make a very good address book?
A Typing skills are necessary.
B The screen is too small.
C The memory is limited.

4 The Blunt organiser is
A the same size as a diary.
B the same shape as a wallet.
C the same price as a calculator.

5 The Blunt organiser is very useful if you
A forget someone's name.
B get lost in a city.
C are late for an appointment.

6 What is Eric Newman's advice about electronic organisers?
A Give them to friends as a gift.
B Compare all the models available.
C Don't buy one at the moment.

7 How does the interviewer feel about electronic organisers?
A Doubtful.
B Keen.
C Confused.

PRONUNCIATION

/h/

1 Listen and decide which word, A or B, is being said.

	A	B
1	arm	harm
2	ill	hill
3	add	had
4	old	hold
5	air	hair
6	eat	heat
7	eye	high
8	eight	hate
9	is	his
10	am	ham

2 Practise reading the pairs of words with your partner.

3 Listen and repeat these sentences.

I haven't heard from Harry for ages.
I hate eating in the heat.
I hear that Mrs Hill is ill.
Is this his hat, or isn't it?
You can hold my arm if you don't hurt it.
Had he hurt his eye?
Yes, he'd hit it with a hairbrush.

4 Practise reading the sentences with your partner.

READING 3

Reading for main points

1 Discuss with your partner what you know about global warming and the greenhouse effect.

2 Read the article quickly to find the answers to these questions:

1 What do these pairs of numbers refer to?
80/½
2090/30
1988/24
150/24

2 What have been the main causes of global warming?

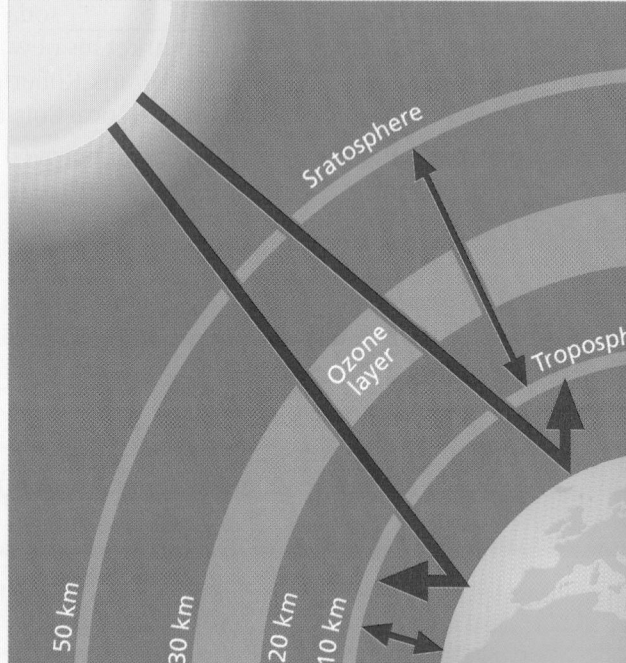

HOW THE GREENHOUSE EFFECT WORKS

1 The sun's shortwave radiation can penetrate even large amounts of CO_2 and CFC in the troposphere – the part of the atmosphere nearest the earth. These rays are reflected from the earth as longwave 'heat' radiation,
5 much of which is trapped by the carbon dioxide and CFCs. So the climate gets warmer.

CLIMATE OF CHANGE

Of all these issues, many experts agree that the most pressing problem facing all of us, not just in Britain, is that of the gradual warming of the earth's atmosphere caused
10 mainly by the build up of carbon dioxide and CFCs producing what has become known as the greenhouse effect. Informed opinion is that the atmosphere is getting warmer. In the past 80 years the average temperature has increased by half of one degree Celsius.

15 Hardly the making of a heatwave, but the consequences are likely to be significant. Weather experts maintain that

the rate of increase in the warming process is <u>accelerating</u>.
Some predict that by 2090, the temperature in southern
Britain on a typical summer's day could be 26–30°C. (In
20 1988 the highest temperature recorded was 24°C.) Good
news, you may think, but there'd be a price to pay.

MELTING ICE CAPS

Even a small rise in temperature could, scientists say, have
a <u>dramatic</u> effect on ice in the polar regions. Pieces would
break off, float away and melt. Sea levels would rise and
25 Britain's low-lying coastal regions would be <u>flooded</u> unless
sea defences were built. But the effect of higher temperatures on other countries could be even more severe.

Hot countries which are already suffering from <u>droughts</u>
could get even hotter and drier, and more arid.

CREATING A GLOBAL GREENHOUSE

30 What Man has done to produce this warmer climate is to
burn fossil fuels (coal, gas and oil), cut down trees faster
than they are replaced, use aerosol sprays and buy food
packaged in rigid-foam containers.

He's also used refrigerators and freezers with CFC
35 coolants. Burning fossil fuels uses oxygen and produces
carbon dioxide. Trees that are growing use carbon
dioxide and produce oxygen. So there could be a healthy
balance.

But since the industrial revolution – about 150 years
40 ago – that balance has been <u>upset</u> as more fossil fuels
have been burned and forests cut down and burned at an
<u>unprecedented</u> rate. Both processes produce carbon
dioxide (CO_2). The result is that carbon dioxide in the
atmosphere has increased by 24% over the past 150 years.
45 Some CO_2 is essential to life – to help plants grow and to
retain some heat. But the very large amounts now present
are, in part, responsible for trapping even more heat in the
earth's atmosphere – the so-called 'greenhouse effect'
(see illustration).

50 Other important 'greenhouse gases' are CFCs
(chlorofluorocarbons), especially the types which have been
used in aerosols, some food trays, domestic freezers and
refrigerators, supermarket refrigeration systems and most
air conditioning systems. Some CFCs are at least 10,000
55 times more powerful than carbon dioxide in trapping heat in
the earth's atmosphere.

3 Read more carefully and match the underlined words from the text on the left with the
meanings on the right.

Example:
heatwave   long period of hot weather

1	pressing	a	getting faster
2	build up	b	not really
3	hardly	c	covered with water
4	maintain	d	serious
5	accelerating	e	never seen before
6	dramatic	f	absence of water
7	flooded	g	disturbed
8	drought	h	strongly believe
9	upset	i	important
10	unprecedented	j	increase

4 Divide these into

a **causes** of global warming
b **results** of global warming
c **solutions** to the problem of global warming

1 cutting down fewer trees
2 melting ice caps
3 using aerosols
4 droughts in hot countries
5 eating frozen and chilled food
6 rising temperatures
7 building sea defences
8 planting more trees
9 using alternative sources of energy
10 flooding in Britain

5 Now complete the three paragraphs below in
your own words. Try to use the passive form
of verbs where it seems appropriate.

1 Global warming is caused by

_____

_____

_____

_____

2 This has resulted in

_____

_____

_____

_____

3 Some solutions would be

_____

_____

_____

_____

GRAMMAR 4
Conditionals 2

■ **1** Look at these pairs of sentences about global warming. For each pair say what the difference is in meaning and in form.

1 **a** If temperatures rise any more, the polar ice-caps will melt.
b If temperatures rose any more, the polar ice-caps would melt.

2 **a** If the ice caps melt, parts of Britain will be flooded.
b If the ice caps melted, parts of Britain would be flooded.

3 **a** If more trees are cut down, the level of carbon dioxide will rise.
b If more trees were cut down, the level of carbon dioxide would rise.

When do we use the first conditional and when do we use the second conditional?

■ **2** Often we decide to use the first or the second conditional depending on how we feel about the situation. In each of these situations decide which is better for you – first or second conditional – and complete the sentences.

1 If I win/won lots of money, I will/would…

2 If it snows/snowed this winter, I will/would…

3 If I don't/didn't do my homework, I…

4 If I don't/didn't have to come to school next week, I…

5 If I can/could be a famous person for a day, I…

6 If I have/had the chance to travel next year, I…

7 If I have/had to choose a new sport or pastime to learn, I…

8 If I pass/passed the exam, I…

■ **3** In one of the sentences only the second conditional is possible. Which sentence is it and why?

HELP WITH WRITING
Giving opinions

■ **1** Read this article on the subject of global warming, and then fill in the spaces in the plan.

Do you agree that global warming represents a serious problem for the future of the world?

1 Introduction

2 **a** Scientists do not agree
 b _____
 c _____

3 **a** _____
 b _____
 c _____

4 Conclusion

Limits of our knowledge

In recent years a lot of publicity has been given to the problem of global warming caused by the so-called greenhouse effect.

It is worth pointing out, however, that not all scientists agree about the causes of warming or, **indeed,** if it is happening at all. **Moreover, it is important to remember** that reliable records have only existed for 130 years, which is a very short period in climatic terms. **While** this has been a particularly warm decade, we know that there have been other warm, and cold, periods in history, **although** we have no precise records about them.

In other words, recent changes in the climate could be explained by natural variations. **Besides** the lack of convincing evidence, **there is a tendency for** this type of issue to get too much publicity and to become fashionable, which, **in my opinion,** does not help the scientists. Science is about making calculations and predictions and building up theories that must be tested, and often only time will tell us the real answer.

So, bearing this in mind, it is important to be aware of the possible consequences of problems like global warming, **but** it is also necessary to remain realistic about the nature of scientific research and the limits of our knowledge.

■ **2** Look carefully at the words in bold type. How are they important?

■**3** Choose one of these topics for an article for a class magazine:

1 'Most people will soon be working from home, using a computer terminal.' Do you think this is a realistic prediction?

2 Describe some of the effects of the growth of satellite TV. What are the prospects for the future?

3 Do you think it is a good idea to have a telephone in your car? Explain your reasons.

■**4** Find a partner who has chosen the same question as you. Find out if you agree or not.

Make a plan for your article in the grid below.

1	Introduction
2	a _____
	_____
	b _____
	_____
	c _____
	_____
3	a _____
	_____
	b _____
	_____
	c _____
	_____
4	Conclusion

■**5** Before you write your article, look again at the words underlined in the text and other similar expressions on pages 13, 14, 68 and 69. Try to use them in your article.

▭ LISTENING 5
Short extracts

You will hear people talking in five different situations. For questions **1–5**, decide which of the choices **A**, **B** or **C** is correct.

1 You will hear part of an interview with a woman who has carried out a travel survey. What kind of travel is she talking about?

  A coach travel
  B air travel
  C train travel

2 You will hear Mary, a secretary, complaining about a new computer system she is using. Who is Mary talking to?

  A a computer engineer
  B another secretary
  C her boss

3 You will hear an advertisement for a place tourists might like to visit. What type of place is it?

  A a shopping centre
  B a restaurant
  C a museum

4 You will hear a woman talking about her dishwasher. How does she feel about the dishwasher?

  A She regrets buying it.
  B She wishes she'd bought it sooner.
  C It took time to get used to it.

5 You will hear someone talking to a group of students about an exhibition centre. What's special about the exhibition?

  A It's all about music and sound.
  B You can touch the exhibits.
  C People explain science to you.

SPEAKING 5
Expressing and justifying opinions

Talk to your partner. Discuss the following comments made by British students and say whether you agree or disagree with the comments they make. Look again at the phrases on page 121.

● People who like science should specialise in science subjects.

● Everyone should study all subjects until the age of 18.

● More time should be devoted to teaching technology in schools.

● Students need more help in choosing the right subjects to specialise in.

● It's useless to study foreign languages unless you are good at your own language.

● Students should study things which will prepare them for the world of work.

● All students should do their homework on a word processor.

READING 4
Multiple matching

Here are some comments made by science and technology students from different countries who are studying in Britain. For questions **1–15**, write the name of the student who expresses this view. When two students express the same view, there are two spaces. There is an example at the beginning (**0**).

The city has links with my home town. (0) _Nelson_

I was attracted by the length of the course. (1) _____ (2) _____

I received financial help. (3) _____

The course was recommended to me. (4) _____

The university is known to be good. (5) _____ (6) _____

I prefer the British system. (7) _____ (8) _____

It is better to live inside the college. (9) _____

I live a long way from the college. (10) _____

The classes are not too big. (11) _____

The facilities in my accommodation are good. (12) _____ (13) _____

There is a good range of things to eat. (14) _____ (15) _____

What is it really like to live and study in the UK? We asked some international students to give us their views.

Name: Nina
Home country: Poland

My father decided to send me to Cambridge College on the advice of a friend whose daughter had studied here and got very good results. I am studying accountancy and computer studies.

I did really badly in the courses I took in my own country, but the system of study here is much better. The workload is not too heavy and we are assessed each week by the teachers to make sure we really understand what we've been taught. There are only eight students in the class, which means there are fewer distractions and the teacher has more time to spend with each individual. I find the teachers very helpful.

Name: Marcel
Home country: Brazil

I wanted to come to Edinburgh both because the town is attractive and because the university has a good reputation, especially for medicine, which is my main subject.

I live in a student house which is self-catering and not too expensive. The only drawback is the distance it is from the faculty – it takes me about 35 minutes to walk between the two. I could complain about the weather, but I knew when I came here that Scotland had a colder climate than Brazil, so it wouldn't be fair.

Name: Juan
Home country: Spain

This is my fourth year studying in Britain. I have already got a National Diploma and I am now studying for a Higher National Diploma in sound and video technology. I would never have been able to do a course like this in Spain. I was a really bad student at home – there was less choice of subjects and I was not interested in what I was doing. The British system is much more flexible, which suits someone like me. Here I will be able to create a career for myself.

I am currently living in a rented house found for me by the college. I share it with two Greek students. The accommodation is cheap, but it is important to look around. I pay £30 a week for this house, but I have paid a lot more.

Name: Sabrina
Home country: Italy

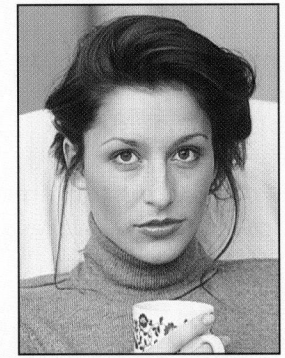

Being an English teacher as well as a maths teacher I was keen to experience UK education and culture first hand. I wanted to go to a university of repute and was selected for a scholarship.

Everything is very well organised here – from the library to travel facilities, which are excellent. Clothes and food for all tastes are available, so being a vegetarian is not difficult. Even the cold is not a problem because there is central heating everywhere.

Name: Nelson
Home country: Argentina

Although I am an Argentinian, my great grandparents were Scottish, so when I had the opportunity to go on my home town university's exchange programme with Edinburgh, I jumped at the chance. As well as seeing what life is like in the UK, I particularly wanted to study the Scottish scientific heritage.

I live in a student flat – it is one of the new ones, which means it has a shower, which is less usual in the UK than in South America. It is self-catering and very reasonably priced, so I am really happy with it. I've learnt to cook a bit, but there's also a good range of takeaway places just across the road.

Name: Eleni
Home country: Greece

It is quite prestigious to study overseas, and the range of facilities at UK universities is good. I wanted to come to Buckingham because degrees are two years instead of three or four.

I live in a hall of residence, which is very convenient and well equipped. Ideally I would prefer to live out with a group of friends, but it's too much hassle to move. My friends come from a wide variety of cultures, mainly European, Asian and African. It is very easy to make friends in a small university. I met most of my friends during a pre-sessional course, although I am also very involved in the Greek Society.

Name: Haider
Home country: Pakistan

Because Pakistan is a Commonwealth country, our education system is quite similar to the English one. I chose to study at Milton because for my subject it has the second largest faculty in the country after Cambridge, and you can complete your degree in only two years.

I live in halls of residence. In my opinion, it is better to live on campus than off it. Students here are very friendly – about half of us are from overseas, so you make friends from all over the world in this, sort of, international community. I think people who live away from the college, in the town, can feel lonely or isolated – I wouldn't like that.

■**1**   Choose one of the following subjects for a magazine article. Write your
article in 120–180 words in an appropriate style.

1   'Computerisation is changing the world for the worse not for the better.'
What is your opinion?

2   'Television is producing a generation which does not read, write or talk
enough.' Do you agree?

3   Why have most important inventions and discoveries been made by men?
Do you think this will continue in the future?

■**2**   Read the text below and decide which word **A**, **B**, **C** or **D** best fits each
space. There is an example at the beginning (**0**).

Are you using the best tool for the job?

Derek Puplett (**0**) _____ *C* _____ why he still sees a long and busy life
(**1**) _____ for the office typewriter, (**2**) _____ the introduction of
the PC.

No one can (**3**) _____ the benefits that a PC (**4**) _____ to an office
when there are large, multi-page word processing projects to be completed.
But there is increasing (**5**) _____ that managers and secretaries are
beginning to (**6**) _____ that they threw out all their typewriters in favour
of PCs and printers.

The PC, it seems, is not as good a (**7**) _____ as many companies had believed. For there are some jobs that an electronic typewriter can do faster and
more efficiently (**8**) _____ a PC.

Indeed, managers are at (**9**) _____ accepting what their secretaries and
typists have been (**10**) _____ them all along. That, in (**11**) _____ ,
using a PC to produce one-off letters and short memos is like using a sledge-
hammer to crack a nut; that it often takes longer to (**12**) _____ the word
processor software than it does to type the words; that a PC and printer are not
the right tools for (**13**) _____ in forms where accuracy of position is very
important; and that most printers are not good at (**14**) _____ envelopes.

As a (**15**) _____ , an increasing number of UK businesses are planning
to include a typewriter as an essential tool for typists and secretaries. Not as a
replacement, but in addition to a PC.

0	**A** expects	**B** tells	**C** explains	**D** talks
1	**A** ahead	**B** advance	**C** forwards	**D** along
2	**A** despite	**B** although	**C** however	**D** whereas
3	**A** refuse	**B** deceive	**C** revenge	**D** deny
4	**A** leads	**B** brings	**C** carries	**D** fetches
5	**A** evidence	**B** appearance	**C** notice	**D** demonstration
6	**A** disappoint	**B** forgive	**C** regret	**D** doubt
7	**A** explanation	**B** solution	**C** treatment	**D** reaction
8	**A** of	**B** than	**C** that	**D** as
9	**A** last	**B** end	**C** final	**D** late
10	**A** mentioning	**B** speaking	**C** telling	**D** saying
11	**A** exercise	**B** practice	**C** habit	**D** custom
12	**A** put	**B** load	**C** charge	**D** place
13	**A** completing	**B** answering	**C** writing	**D** filling
14	**A** touching	**B** handling	**C** pulling	**D** drawing
15	**A** result	**B** final	**C** product	**D** decision

3 Read the text below and look carefully at each line. Some of the lines are correct, and some have a word which should not be there. If a line is correct put a tick (✓). If a line has a word which should not be there, write the word in the space on the right. There are two examples at the beginning (**0**) and (**00**).

Global Warming

Dear Ms Salt

I was very interested to read the your recent	**0**	*the*
article about global warming in the local newspaper.	**00**	✓
I'm afraid I am don't agree at all about a number	**1**	
of points you mention in your letter. Firstly, you say that	**2**	
some leading scientists they do not believe in this	**3**	
theory. But who are just these scientists? I	**4**	
have never heard of any of them. Secondly, it is	**5**	
not true that global warming have receives too	**6**	
much publicity. On the contrary, we really do need to	**7**	
make the public more aware of such as dangers.	**8**	
We must all put to pressure on the authorities	**9**	
if we want something to will be done about the world's	**10**	
problems. Lastly, you seem to suggest not doing	**11**	
nothing in case the scientists are wrong. Well, have you	**12**	
thought that if they are in right, it will be too late	**13**	
by the time we find ourselves out! We must act now	**14**	
if we are to have any chance of avoiding disaster.	**15**	

Yours sincerely

Dr Pepper

4 Read the text below. Use the word given in capitals at the end of each line to form a word that fits in the space in the same line. There is an example at the beginning (**0**).

Telephone Calls

Today an enormous amount of (**0**) _personal_ and	**PERSON**
business (**1**) _____ takes place by telephone and fax machine.	**COMMUNICATE**
It's usually quite easy to make a call to (**2**) _____ right on the	**ONE**
other side of the world because these days most long- (**3**) _____	**DISTANT**
calls travel via satellite. Fifty years ago, however, an (**4**) _____	**NATION**
call was far more difficult. It could sometimes take the (**5**) _____	**OPERATE**
a very long time to make a (**6**) _____ , and even then the	**CONNECT**
(**7**) _____ was often rather poor. Telephones at that time	**RECEIVE**
could only work between places connected by (**8**) _____	**CONTINUE**
wires which had to cross the oceans. The world's (**9**) _____	**LONG**
cable still stretches (**10**) _____ for fifteen thousand kilometres	**WATER**
beneath the Pacific Ocean.	

Working out

SPEAKING 1

Talking about photographs

Work in pairs. Decide who is Student A and who is Student B.

1 **Student A:** Look at photographs 1 and 2. Compare and contrast the two photographs and tell your partner if you think these are good ways of exercising.

2 **Student B:** Look at photographs 3 and 4. Compare and contrast the two photographs and tell your partner if you think these are good ways of exercising.

Listen to your partner and say if you agree.

HELP WITH SPEAKING

■1 In Part 3 of the Speaking test you have to discuss something with your partner. Remember:

1 Talk to your partner (not to the examiners).

2 Speak clearly so that the examiners can hear you.

3 Listen to what your partner says and answer appropriately.

4 Give your partner a chance to speak (especially if he/she is rather shy).

5 Help your partner if you can – it is not a competition!

6 You can agree and disagree but at the end try to reach a compromise so that your discussion has a conclusion.

7 Don't agree on a conclusion immediately – remember you have to talk together for three minutes! Discuss all the possibilities before coming to a conclusion.

Useful words and phrases:

> Where shall we begin?
> Let's start with X, shall we?
> What do you think about X?
> What about X?
> I think X is best, don't you?
> I agree with you.
> I'm sorry, I don't agree with you.
> Well, we'd better come to a decision.
> So, I think we agree, don't we?

■2 A local school has been given some money to equip a new health and fitness centre. You can buy any three of the things listed below. Talk to your partner and decide which three things would represent the best use of the money. You have three minutes to reach your decision.

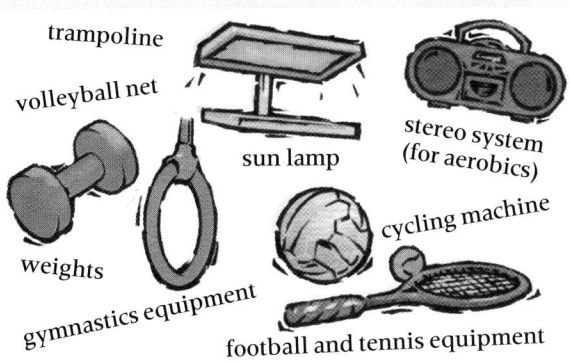

trampoline

volleyball net

sun lamp

stereo system (for aerobics)

weights

cycling machine

gymnastics equipment

football and tennis equipment

■3 Discuss with a partner how effective each of these activities is as a way of keeping fit and healthy:

very quite not very
effective effective effective

jogging

cycling

walking to work/school

eating less

a high-fibre diet

playing a sport regularly

sleeping late

not smoking and drinking

living in the country

Which would be more suitable for

- children?
- teenagers?
- parents?
- grandparents?

Gapped text

1 Discuss these questions with your partner:

1   What is a marathon?

2   Why is it called a marathon?

3   How long is a marathon?

4   Why has marathon running become such a popular sport in the last few years?

5   Have you ever run a long distance? How does it feel during the run and afterwards? What training is necessary?

2 You are going to read an article about the marathon. Seven sentences have been removed from the article. Choose from the sentences **A–H** the one which fits each gap **1–6**. There is one extra sentence which you do not need to use. There is an example at the beginning (**0**).

The Marathon Man

The marathon is a phenomenon of our time which has motivated thousands of men and women to copy the epic run of a Greek soldier named Pheidippides who, in 490BC, ran non-stop from the plains of Marathon to Athens, a distance of approximately 39 kilometres (24 miles).

THESE DAYS WHY, you may ask, do thousands of people punish their aching limbs over a distance of exactly 26 miles and 385 yards? **0** **H** When the event was introduced at the revival of the Olympic Games in Greece, in 1896, it covered the historic route from the plains of Marathon to Athens. Its introduction caught the imagination of runners throughout the world and races were later run in many countries. **1**

In 1908, the modern Olympics came to London and the marathon was set to be run over a 26-mile course between Windsor Castle and London. On the day of the event, Queen Alexandra decided that she would not be able to see the race clearly from her seat and asked for the starting line to be moved back so that she could get a better view. The organisers readily agreed to her request and the starting line was moved back a distance of 385 yards. **2**

What of the man Pheidippides however? Was he really the epic figure described by legend? Pheidippides, a champion runner, was employed as a messenger. **3**

He was serving with the Greek army which had scored a notable victory over their old enemy the Persians at the Battle of Marathon, in spite of being heavily outnumbered. Pheidippides was given the task of taking the joyous news back to Athens. **4**

A Unbelievably, the distance the runners covered that day has been officially recognised as the marathon distance ever since.

B After many hours running, he fell dead on the outskirts of the city, gasping 'Rejoice, we conquered!'.

C Such speculation is pointless, however, for whatever his fate, thousands of people follow his example each year, most of them not knowing of his existence.

D The distances covered varied depending on the route and the ideas of the organisers, but were usually between 20 and 25 miles.

E His task was to run between armies and the cities to deliver urgent messages.

F In addition, his journey would have been over rough rocky tracks, not smooth roads, with few spectators to encourage him on his way.

G Marathon racing is far more tiring than track or cross-country running, because it is all on hard roads.

H The explanation is even more incredible than the popularity that this event has achieved in recent times.

Unlike his modern counterparts, poor Pheidippides would not have attended a pasta party on the evening before the run to build up his strength, or benefited from the vast range of specialist clothing and equipment that is now available. 5☐
Even so, if it had not been for Pheidippides' sad end after proclaiming the good news to the citizens of Athens, it seems likely that this episode in history would have been forgotten long ago.

6☐ The statistics of modern marathon running show, however, that deaths have been rare – in spite of the fact that thousands of people of all ages have taken part in the event, a great many of them inadequately prepared.

3 Find words that mean

1 not exactly

2 arms and legs

3 bringing back to life

4 very important

5 very happy

6 people doing a similar thing

7 very large

8 a number of things to choose from

9 not very common

10 not very well

4 Mark the stressed syllable in these words from the text and practise saying them with your partner.

marathon	imagination	equipment
motivated	throughout	available
approximately	organisers	inadequately
revival	messenger	unbelievably
introduction	specialist	explanation

⏸ LISTENING 1
Short extracts

You will hear people talking in six different situations. For questions **1 – 6** choose the best answer **A**, **B** or **C**.

1 You will hear part of a radio programme about fitness.
What type of programme is it?

  A The introduction to a report.
  B Part of an advertisement.
  C A sports commentary.

2 You will hear a man talking about a trip he made.
How was he travelling?

  A By balloon.
  B By boat.
  C By bicycle.

3 Listen to this telephone message from a businesswoman to a client.
Why has she phoned?

  A To suggest new ideas.
  B To turn down an invitation.
  C To propose a change of plan.

4 You will hear a woman talking about her job.
What is her job?

  A A doctor.
  B A nurse.
  C A dentist.

5 You will hear an advertisement on the radio.
What is being advertised?

  A A restaurant.
  B A shop.
  C A pub.

6 You will hear two people, Rob and Jane, discussing a course they have seen advertised.
How does Rob feel about the course?

  A He refuses to go.
  B Jane convinces him to go.
  C He is not keen to go.

READING 2
Reading for specific information

█ 1 Discuss with your partner:

Have you ever been sunburnt?
How does it feel?
How can it be prevented?

█ 2 Read the article and decide if the sentences which follow are true or false.

Play it SAFE

This Morning's Liz Earle on protecting your child in the sun

It is estimated that about half our total lifetime's sun exposure happens during childhood. Long summer holidays and lots of outdoor activities mean that children are at far greater risk of over-exposure than adults. Children's skin is very sensitive to sunburn. Not only is this painful and damaging to the skin, but just one case of severe sunburn during childhood is thought to double the risk of developing skin cancer in later life.

Follow this safe tan code:
● Don't let children play outside in the midday sun without some form of protection. It may be easier to slip on a lightweight shirt and hat than to apply sunscreen.
● Look for sunscreens that have the highest SPF numbers. Don't use less than SPF 15 on young vulnerable skins.
● Sunscreens for toddlers should say on the label

that they have been especially formulated for children. These products contain fewer chemical ingredients and so are less likely to irritate children's delicate skin.
● The sun's rays pass through water, so always use the waterproof sunscreens while swimming and make sure children re-apply them frequently.
● Babies under six months should never be exposed to strong sunshine. This is because their skin hasn't fully formed the melanin-producing cells that protect the skin. Protect older babies with sun hats and pram parasols.

1 Children spend more time in the sun than adults.

2 Children are more likely to get skin cancer than adults.

3 Light clothes do not provide protection from strong sun.

4 Sunscreens with SPF 15 or less are best for young children.

5 You can buy special sunscreens for very young children.

6 Sunscreens contain chemicals that may irritate the skin.

7 Children should put on more sunscreen after swimming.

8 Babies get sunburned more easily than older children.

GRAMMAR 1

Present perfect continuous

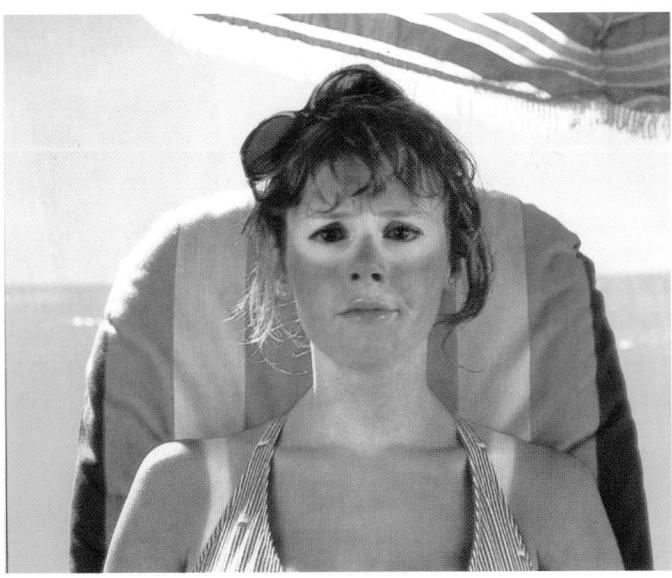

■ 1 Look at the woman in the photo.

Where do you think she comes from?
Where is she now?
What mistakes has she made?
How does she feel?
Is she going to enjoy the rest of her holiday?

■ 2 What has she been doing this morning? Make sentences like the example.

Example:
She/sit/in the sun
She's been sitting in the sun.

1 She/swim/a number of times.

2 She/wear/a bikini.

3 She/read/a book.

4 She/listen/music/Walkman.

5 She/drink/Coke.

6 She/not sit/under an umbrella.

7 She/not use/sunscreen lotion.

8 She/sleep/in the sun.

■ 3 Present perfect or present perfect continuous?

1 Why are the sentences in the above exercise in the continuous form?

2 Why are the following sentences not continuous?

  a She has just woken up.
  b She has lost her sunglasses.
  c She has finished her Coke.
  d She's already finished one book.
  e She's written four postcards.
  f She hasn't posted them yet.

■ 4 In the following sentences decide which is best – the present perfect continuous or the present perfect simple, or if it makes no difference.

1 I (write) five letters this morning.

2 I (write) letters all morning.

3 I (lose) my pen somewhere in this room.

4 I (use) this sunscreen for years. It's the best.

5 Janice (work) in another office this week.

6 Janice (work) in five different offices since joining the company.

7 I (learn) English for two years.

8 Louise (phone) me twice this morning.

5 Make a note of:

1 Some things you have been doing this morning/afternoon/evening – this week or recently.

2 Some things you've done in the same period.

Now tell your partner.
Do you agree with your partner's use of the simple or continuous form?

6 Look at the postcard below from Jenny to Sue. Change each of the verbs in brackets into the best tense: present simple, present continuous, present perfect simple, present perfect continuous or past simple.

Word formation

Complete each space with one word from the box combined with the word *sun* to form a new word.

rise	screen	roof
shine	bathing	glasses
set	tan	flower

Example:
He liked to get up very early and walk along the beach at *sunrise*.

1 In the evening the clouds disappeared and there was a beautiful _____ over the sea.

2 You could tell he'd been on holiday from his deep golden _____ .

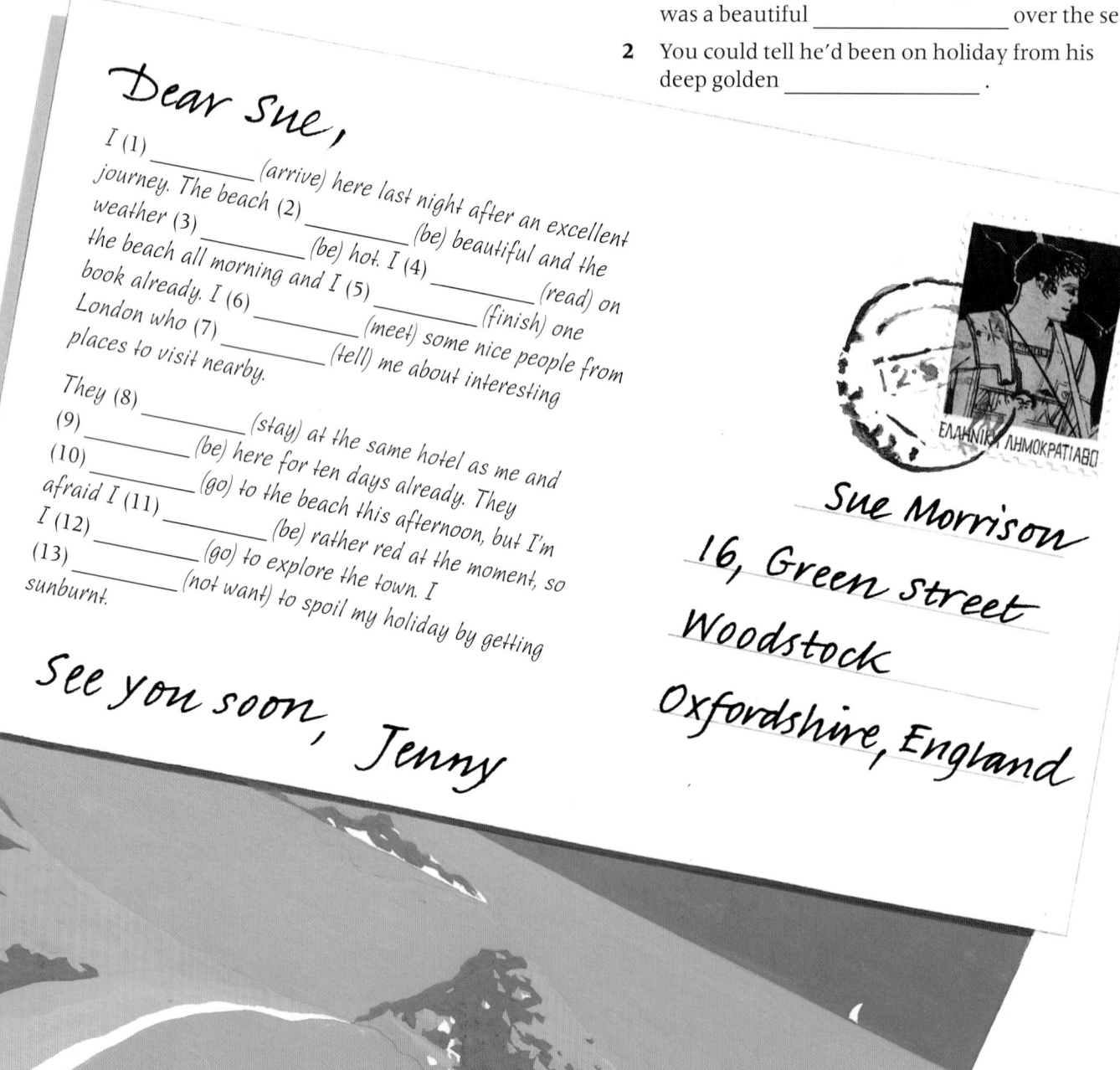

Dear Sue,

I (1) _____ (arrive) here last night after an excellent journey. The beach (2) _____ (be) beautiful and the weather (3) _____ (be) hot. I (4) _____ (read) on the beach all morning and I (5) _____ (finish) one book already. I (6) _____ (meet) some nice people from London who (7) _____ (tell) me about interesting places to visit nearby.

They (8) _____ (stay) at the same hotel as me and (9) _____ (be) here for ten days already. They (10) _____ (go) to the beach this afternoon, but I'm afraid I (11) _____ (be) rather red at the moment, so I (12) _____ (go) to explore the town. I (13) _____ (not want) to spoil my holiday by getting sunburnt.

See you soon, Jenny

Sue Morrison
16, Green street
Woodstock
Oxfordshire, England

ΕΛΛΗΝΙΚΗ ΔΗΜΟΚΡΑΤΙΑ 80

3 It's difficult to read on the beach without
_____ .

4 It was such a nice morning he decided to
have breakfast outside in the warm
_____ .

5 To get more air in the car she opened the
_____ .

6 The roof of the hotel was an excellent place to
go _____ .

7 The seed of the _____ is used to
make cooking oil.

8 _____ is a lotion that protects your
skin from burning.

LISTENING 2

Selecting an answer

Listen to the conversation and decide whether
these statements are true or false.

1 Jenny is sorry that Sue didn't go with her.

2 Jenny bought some sunscreen before she left.

3 Jenny forgot to buy sunscreen when she arrived.

4 Jenny stayed on the beach for longer than she
had intended.

5 Jenny was unable to go back to the beach but
found lots of other things to do.

6 Jenny read books all day in the hotel.

7 Jenny doesn't even have a suntan.

GRAMMAR 2

Regrets

1 Look at these phrases from the listening text.

I wish you had come with me
I wish I'd taken a few books with me
I wish I'd stayed at home
If only I hadn't been so stupid

1 Which tense is used after *I wish* or *If only*?
2 What time is referred to?
3 What feelings are expressed?

2 Complete the second sentence so that it has a
similar meaning to the first sentence. Use the
word given and other words to complete each
sentence. You must use between two and five
words. Do not change the word given.

1 I regret going to bed so late last night.
wish
I _____ to bed
so late last night.

2 If only I had taken that job in the bank.
regret
I _____ in the bank.

3 Jenny regrets not buying some sunscreen before
her holiday.
wishes
Jenny _____ some
sunscreen before her holiday.

4 He regrets not telling people it was his birthday.
wishes
He _____ people
it was his birthday.

5 I regret not booking the seats in advance.
only
If _____ the seats in advance.

6 I wish I'd gone on holiday with my friends.
regret
I _____ on
holiday with my friends.

7 They regret ever getting married.
never
They wish _____ married.

8 If only I had been more careful.
regret
I _____ more careful.

9 I wish I hadn't gone to that party.
only
If _____ to that party.

10 Larry regrets not telling his girlfriend where he
was going.
had
Larry _____ his
girlfriend where he was going.

3 When is it better to use *I wish* or *If only* and
when is it better to use *I regret*?

4 Do you have any regrets in your life? Make a
list of some of the things you regret – you can
invent them if you like!

Now tell your partner.

LISTENING 3

Note-taking

1 What has happened to the pensioner?

2 What has happened to his money?

3 Why do you think this has happened?

Listen to this radio programme where the story is discussed, and fill in the information in the numbered spaces below.

Pensioner Leaves Secret Fortune to Aromatherapist

MR EDWARD GREY, (87), of Newton Street, who died last month, has left a fortune of £1,008,279 to his local aromatherapist. Members of his family were shocked at the size of the fortune and enraged not to receive any of it.

Name	Relationship to Mr Gray	Amount left in will	Purpose	Reason
Rosemary Lacey	Aromatherapist	£1,008,279	1	he got relief from aromatherapy
2	nephew	£50	3	4 ....
5	6	£100	to spend on second-hand furniture	7 ....
Cecilia Grey	daughter	8	for her old age	9 ....

GRAMMAR 3

Conditionals 3

1 Look at these sentences from the listening text and answer the questions.

1 *If he'd paid back the £50, he would have inherited a much larger sum.*
   a Did he inherit a larger sum?
   b Why was this?
   c Can he change the situation?

2 *If she'd been more patient, she'd have got the furniture.*
   a Did she get the furniture?
   b Why was this?
   c Can she change the situation?

3 *If she'd agreed to look after him, she'd have inherited the house.*
   a Did she inherit the house?
   b Why was this?
   c Can she change the situation?

4 Which tenses are used in third conditional sentences? What time do they refer to?

2 Read this article.

Why did June Booker have to go to hospital twice in one day?

WHAT A BARGAIN

When June Booker bought a new frying pan at 30% off in the sales, she thought she had got a real bargain. But as it turned out that was only the beginning of a very expensive day. First, she dropped the pan on her foot on the way home and was taken to hospital. 'I had lots of shopping because I hadn't planned to buy a frying pan, and the pan was very heavy, I just couldn't carry it all,' said June. At the hospital her foot was bandaged and she was sent home in a taxi.

Then, when she eventually got home, she decided to use the new pan to cook dinner. 'I'd just put some oil in it and started to heat it up when the phone rang. I only left the kitchen for a couple of minutes but when I came back there were flames coming out of it' said June. So she picked up a bowl of water and threw it onto the pan. 'I know it was a stupid thing to do, but I panicked,' said June, 'and the flames got bigger.'

Fortunately, her neighbours saw smoke and called the fire brigade, who arrived and dealt with the fire in minutes. Although she will need a new kitchen, the rest of June Booker's flat was only slightly damaged by smoke. A shocked but unhurt Mrs Booker was taken to hospital for routine tests. 'They were rather surprised to see me back again so soon,' she said.

3 Complete each of the phrases from **A** with one of the phrases from **B** to make a third conditional sentence about the story.

A

1 If Mrs Booker hadn't bought a frying pan in the sale, ☐ e
2 If the frying pan hadn't been in the sale, ☐
3 If she hadn't dropped the pan on her foot, ☐
4 If the pan hadn't been heavy, ☐
5 If she had had less shopping, ☐
6 If the phone hadn't rung, ☐
7 If she hadn't panicked, ☐
8 If she hadn't thrown water onto the pan, ☐
9 If her neighbours hadn't seen smoke, ☐
10 If the fire brigade hadn't come so quickly, ☐
11 If she had turned off the cooker, ☐

B

a they wouldn't have called the fire brigade.
b she wouldn't have dropped the pan.
c she wouldn't have left the kitchen.
d it wouldn't have hurt her foot.
e she wouldn't have gone to hospital twice in one day.
f the rest of the flat could have been seriously damaged.
g the oil wouldn't have caught fire.
h she wouldn't have been taken to hospital.
i Mrs Booker wouldn't have bought it.
j she wouldn't have thrown water into the pan.
k the flames wouldn't have spread.

4 Complete the second sentence so that it has a similar meaning to the first sentence. Use the word given and other words to complete each sentence. You must use between two and five words. Do not change the word given.

1 The picnic was cancelled because it rained.
   have
   If it hadn't rained, the picnic
   _____ cancelled.

2 Without his father's help, he wouldn't have got that job.
   him
   If his father _____ ,
   he wouldn't have got that job.

3 The car crashed because it was travelling too fast.
   been
   If the car _____
   so fast, it wouldn't have crashed.

4 I couldn't phone you because I'd lost your number.
   have
   If I hadn't lost your number, I
   _____ you.

5 John caught a cold because he didn't wear a coat.
   had
   If _____ , he
   wouldn't have caught a cold.

6 He found the treasure as he was digging in his garden.
have
If he hadn't been digging in his garden,
_____ the treasure.

7 I only knew about her wedding because I met her mother in the street.
not
If I hadn't met her mother in the street,
_____ about her wedding.

8 I lost my key so I had to wait outside in the snow.
have
If I hadn't lost my key, I _____
to wait outside in the snow.

9 I couldn't give him a lift because I didn't have my car.
had
If _____ my car, I could
have given him a lift.

10 Ray didn't pass the exam, because he didn't work hard enough.
harder
If Ray _____ , he would
have passed the exam.

SPEAKING 2
Expressing opinions

1 Label each of these things in the pictures below.
PLUG   SOCKET   FLEX   ADAPTOR   SWITCH   HEATER

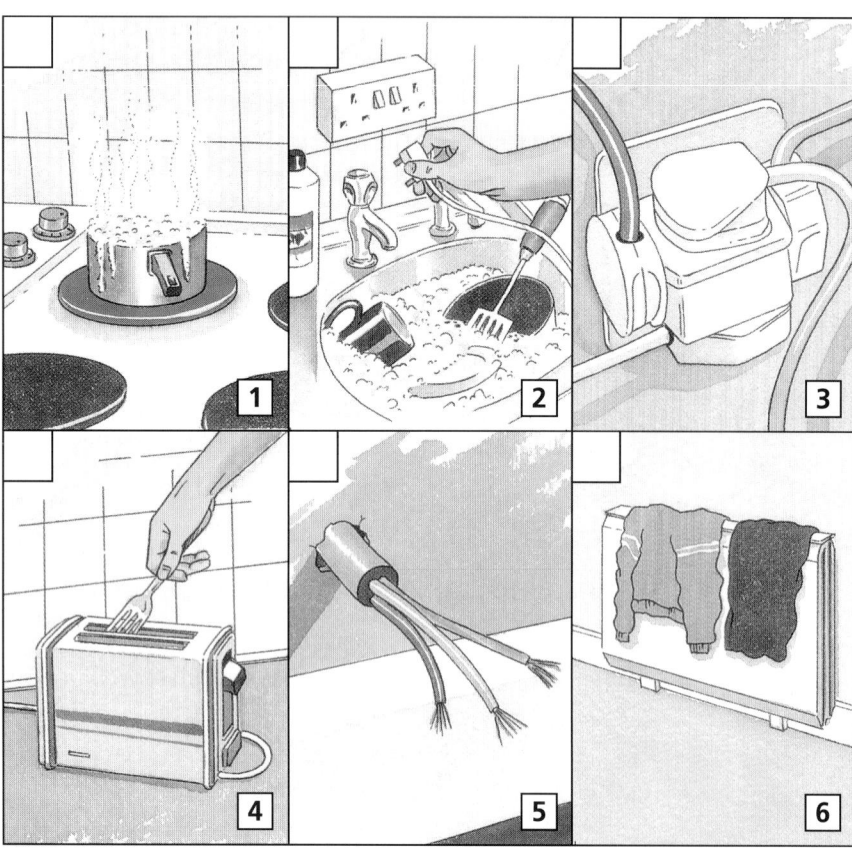

2 Talk to your partner. Which of these situations do you think is the most dangerous? Why?

3 In what other ways can electricity be dangerous in the home?

4 What other things can be dangerous in the home?
Think about:

- old people
- children
- babies
- gas
- fire
- water

LISTENING 4
Matching information

1 Listen to the telephone conversation and tick (✓) the pictures mentioned below.

2 Listen again and answer these questions.

1 Mrs Platt is Mrs Grey's
  A neighbour.
  B social worker.
  C relative.

2 Mr Fields is Mrs Grey's
  A friend.
  B son.
  C nephew.

3 What is wrong with the sockets in Mrs Grey's house?
  A They are not safe.
  B There are too few of them.
  C They do not work properly.

4 What is Mr Fields going to do?
  A Take Mrs Platt's advice.
  B Ask for his aunt's opinion.
  C Have some work done.

5 How does Mr Fields feel about the phone call?
  A Offended.
  B Embarrassed.
  C Bored.

SPEAKING 3
Expressing opinions and giving advice

1 Stomachache is sometimes a symptom of food-poisoning. What other parts of the body can ache?

2 Look at these symptoms. Can you diagnose this illness? Use a dictionary to help you.

sore throat   sneezing   runny nose
aching limbs   coughing   shivering

1 What is the cure for this illness?

2 What can you do to relieve the symptoms?

3 What can you do to prevent yourself getting this type of illness?

4 Are these good ideas for getting rid of this type of illness?

- take a warm shower and a cold shower at regular intervals
- hold your face over a bowl of steam
- take very large doses of vitamin C
- eat lots of garlic
- eat nothing for 48 hours

READING 3
Reading for main points and specific information

1 Read the article below quickly to find out:

1 Which of the ideas in the list above is described.

2 What these numbers from the text refer to.

50   26–40   18–24   12–18   35   46   23   100

Build Up with a Cold Spray

1 **Cold showers are not everybody's favourite way to start the day, but even a half-hearted attempt, using a cold spray on your arms and legs, will help stave off a cold.**

5 Researchers at Munich university medical school took 50 men and women aged between 20 and 50, divided them into two similar groups, and taught one group a simple hydrotherapy method to use at home five times per week. This was their schedule:

10 **Week 1:** Arms and legs only, five-minute warm shower (26–40°C) followed by a 30-second cold shower (18–24°C). Repeated twice.

Week 2: Five-minute whole body warm shower followed by 30-second cold shower (same
15 temperatures as above).

Week 3 – Week 26: Five-minute whole body warm shower followed by 30-second cold shower (12–18°C), with the cold shower being gradually lengthened to two minutes over the following two to
20 three weeks.

The second group was given no instructions and were only monitored as to their incidence of colds. The results were exciting.

It was expected that, on average, everybody would
25 have two colds during the six months of the study (50 colds in each group of 25 people). What actually happened was that the hydrotherapy group had only 35 colds, while the non-hydrotherapy group had 46. And when the six-month time scale was divided into two, an
30 even more significant discovery emerged.

During the first three months the hydrotherapy group had 25 colds, compared with 23 in the other group. But during the second three months the hydrotherapists had only ten, while there were 23 colds in the untreated
35 group. This clearly shows that there is a "hardening" effect from this method which builds up slowly and is really evident after three months of regular use.

Severity of the colds was also reduced among those having regular hot and cold showers, with the average
40 length of their colds being just under six days, compared to seven-and-a-half days, with the colds becoming shorter as the treatment programme progressed.

Prof Ernst Edzard, the chief researcher, believes that,
45 *"An efficient, practical and inexpensive prophylaxis against one of the most frequent and expensive diseases in man has been identified at last."* (Physiotherapy, April 1990).

The fact that this same method has been advocated by naturopaths for 100 years should not be forgotten in
50 the euphoria of this medical "discovery". But now we have objective proof that we can increase our hardiness and reduce our susceptibility. You can help even more by regular vigorous "skin-brushing" using a damp towel, a light brush or a loofah. This will stimulate the
55 skin and its amazing eliminative function, as well as help to improve overall circulatory efficiency.

2 Read more carefully and decide if these statements are true or false.

1 The two groups were of equal size.

2 The length of the warm shower was gradually reduced.

3 The second group took only warm showers.

4 Over six months the hydrotherapy group had fewer colds.

5 Over the first three months the two groups had about the same number of colds.

6 The non-hydrotherapy group had more severe and longer colds.

7 The Munich research took place over 100 years ago.

8 Damp towels are a common cause of colds.

3 Find words in the text which mean

1 not very enthusiastic (paragraph 1)

2 protect yourself from (1)

3 timetable (2)

4 made longer (5)

5 checked (6)

6 how many times it happens (6)

7 important (7)

8 making harder (8)

4 Complete this table with the correct word.

Adjective	Noun	Verb
long	length	
	hardness	
wide		to widen
	depth	to deepen
fresh		
large		to enlarge
		to strengthen
weak		
		to soften
	darkness	
bright		

Multiple matching

1 What is an allergy? What types of things can people be allergic to? What particular allergies affect people in your country? Are they worse at certain times of year? What solutions are there to these problems?

2 Read this magazine article about hay fever (an allergic reaction to pollen). Choose the most suitable heading from the list **A–I** for each part **1–7** of the article. There is one extra heading which you do not need to use. There is an example at the beginning (**0**).

When your body goes haywire

ONE IN FOUR of us will be sniffing, sneezing and crying our way through what should be the most enjoyable time of the year. Must summer always mean hay fever? Julie-Anne Ryan reports.

0	A

The weather's warmer, the grass needs cutting and students are doing their exams. Oh, and the pollen count is being given out on the radio and in the newspapers. Yes, it's hay fever time again.

1

In fact, it's such an awful disruption to normal life for so many people that it's high time we understood it better. Doctors and researchers refer to hay fever as SAR, which stands for Seasonal Allergic Rhinitis. At certain times of the year an allergic response causes rhinitis – inflammation of the lining of the nose.

2

Different people are allergic to different things, and the time of your worst symptoms will help pinpoint what causes your allergy.

"Brighter flowers are less likely to cause a problem because they are pollinated by bees, which are attracted to them by their colour, and so don't need to produce so much pollen," explains Dr Jean Emberlin of the Pollen Research Unit. "Wind-pollinated plants – trees, grasses and some wild plants – cause a greater problem because they have to produce a lot more pollen."

3

The chances are that if one member of your family gets hay fever, then so will others – it's a hereditary condition which affects at least 10% of the population at some time in their lives around the world. The group worst affected is the 15 – 44 age group, although people younger and older do suffer, too. As you grow older symptoms tend to

A   Summer means hay fever

B   How to avoid hay fever

C   What to do if you have hay fever

D   A strange fact

E   Who suffers from hay fever?

F   Why more people are being affected

G   Why hay fever makes you cry

H   The various sources of pollen

I   What is hay fever?

---

decrease because we 'de-sensitise'. This means that through repeated exposure the body adapts to the pollen and stops the over-reaction.

4

Hay fever has increased greatly over the years. One hundred years ago it was only those in the country during harvest time who suffered. Research started in the early 1960s reports a doubling in the number of people who go to their doctor about hay fever each decade.

Experts differ in their opinions about the cause. Southampton University's Dr Peter Howarth, an expert in breathing allergies, says, "There are more people consulting doctors about hay fever, and it may well be that in a polluted area symptoms may be worse. Also, over the years we have changed from being a largely agricultural population to one which lives indoors, so we don't have the de-sensitisation that exposure to pollen over a long period used to bring us."

5

But Dr Tom Smith, author of the article *Trends in Hay Fever*, believes pollution is the problem. He emphasises the irony that "over the past three decades, when the amount of grassland has fallen and pollen counts have gradually dropped, the number of people with hay fever has risen steeply. Not only that, but the rise has been in the cities and not the country."

6

To help keep air pollen-free, keep windows at home, in the office and in the car closed. Air vents in the car draw in the air from outside and so can concentrate the pollen in your car by up to 50%. A seaside environment helps – there are fewer pollen-producing plants growing on sand and the breeze helps clear the air.

7

If you are badly affected, consider buying an air filter. Used correctly they can significantly reduce the pollen in the air in your living room. You can buy smaller ones for your car. In recent years there have been major drug advances, so consider taking advice on what is available.

Reports

1 Look back at the article and write a word or short phrase in each space 1–10 to complete the notes about hay fever.

Symptoms of hay fever:

1 _____

2 _____

3 _____

4 _____

Causes of hay fever:

5 _____

6 _____

7 _____

Remedies for hay fever:

8 _____

9 _____

10 _____

2 Compare your notes with your partner's.

3 Without looking back at the article, use your notes to write a short report about hay fever for your school magazine. Write about 125 words.

Use this plan:

1 Introduction –   what is hay fever?

2 Causes of hay fever –   who gets it and why?

3 Remedies for hay fever – what you can do if you suffer from hay fever

4 Conclusion

Expressing feelings

Talk to your partner:

1 In which of these situations would you feel most nervous?

- on the day of an important exam or test
- waiting for a race, competition or sports match to begin
- meeting new people at a party
- speaking in front of a large group of people
- travelling alone
- at an interview for a job
- speaking in a foreign language
- before a long journey
- being at home alone at night
- acting or playing a musical instrument in public

2 How do you feel when you're nervous? Have you ever experienced these things?

- butterflies in your stomach
- a frog in your throat
- knees knocking together
- a fit of the giggles
- being tongue-tied

Tell your partner about a time when you felt especially nervous. Try to explain how you felt.

3 Read the text below and think of the word which best fits each space. Use only one word in each space. There is an example at the begining (**0**).

On Wednesday, the actor John Smithson, (**0**) ___who___ is starring (**1**) _____ a play in London's West End, suddenly froze on stage and stood still (**2**) _____ several minutes before apologising (**3**) _____ the audience for experiencing stage fright. (**4**) _____ a few minutes in his dressing room, he pulled himself together and continued (**5**) _____ the play.

Actors are (**6**) _____ the only ones to suffer (**7**) _____ nerves. Last year a performance of a Mozart opera at the Royal Opera House in London was interrupted (**8**) _____ one of the cast, a large bird of prey called Jesse, who (**9**) _____ so nervous during a long aria (**10**) _____ she fell (**11**) _____ her perch.

All that the audience (**12**) _____ see was one leg tied (**13**) _____ a branch and a cloud of feathers falling to the ground.

A spokesman for the Royal Opera House said that the bird had stage fright in much the same (**14**) _____ that singers sometimes get frogs in (**15**) _____ throats, but when birds of prey become very nervous they play dead and fall off their perches.

LISTENING 5
Multiple matching

You will hear five different people talking about stage fright. For questions **1–5**, choose which of **A–F** each speaker is doing when they speak. There is one extra letter you do not need to use.

A describing a successful cure	Speaker 1
B remembering a colleague who suffered	Speaker 2
C describing the feelings	Speaker 3
D explaining the causes	Speaker 4
E suggesting types of treatments	Speaker 5
F warning against temptation	

READING 5
Multiple choice

1 Read this newspaper article about the experience of a visitor to Africa. The article tells a story in which each of the following things happened. As you read, underline the parts where each of the things happened for the first time.

a meeting	a surprise
an apology	a rescue
an attack	an accident
a defence	a warning

African Adventure

• • • • • • • • • • • • • • • • • • • •

1   The village of Nagaro, on the River Dunga, forms the southern boundary of one of Kenya's great national parks. At its small airfield I
5   was met by Alison Smith. Dr Smith is a biologist working on the Kenya White Rhino Project. She and her husband have built a small house on the banks of the river and the
10   household includes a large dog (a second dog has been eaten by a crocodile), two cats and a mongoose, which had enjoyed the run of the camp before taking up the habit of
15   attacking people.
    Since Dr Smith had mentioned its bad character, I was unpleasantly surprised to see this animal appear underneath the wooden wall of the
20   outdoor shower where I had limped

2 Look at the article again and find:

   A the names of animals
   B the names of parts of the body
   C some verbs describing different ways of moving
   D some verbs describing different ways of biting

3 Now read the article more carefully. Here are some unfinished statements each with four possible ways of finishing. Choose the one which fits best **A**, **B**, **C** or **D**.

1 The mongoose which attacked the writer was

   A a family pet which had started biting people.
   B a wild animal which had entered the house.
   C an animal which had never been violent before.
   D always attacking people in the shower.

2 The writer felt at a disadvantage because

   A he was in a strange country.
   B he didn't know how to handle the animal.
   C he had already injured his foot.
   D he didn't know the animal was unfriendly.

3 Dr Smith didn't come immediately because

   A she was with her baby.
   B she didn't hear the writer calling.
   C she didn't know where the animal was.
   D she was taking her pet for a walk.

4 When Dr Smith came

   A she wasn't able to catch the mongoose.
   B the mongoose bit her too.
   C she slipped and fell over.
   D she was too embarrassed to enter the shower.

5 Dr Smith and the writer

   A were very embarrassed about the situation.
   B were angry with each other.
   C found the situation very funny.
   D both needed medical treatment.

just before dusk. There was no doubt about its intention, which was to bite me as quickly as possible, and sure enough it ran into the
25 shower and nipped my heel.
   A mongoose is much too quick even for a cobra, let alone an injured man in a small shower slippery with soap. With a twisted
30 and swollen ankle I was already at an enormous disadvantage.
   I called out to Dr Smith that she could find her mongoose near the shower. She replied that she had
35 meant to take 'Goose' for a walk and started to call it. The mongoose completely ignored her, darting in and out of sight under the shower door. I flicked hot water at it and
40 made threatening noises, but it disappeared for a moment and then rushed in from another angle and sank its teeth into my toe. 'Is Goose biting you?' called Dr Smith,
45 'I'm so sorry!' She said she was feeding her baby, but would come and fetch the mongoose in a minute.

   I picked up a steel bucket and banged it down in front of the
50 animal. This drove him back a little, but did not deter him. My toe was bleeding and my ankle hurt. Although I did not want to kill the

pet by bashing its brains out with
55 a bucket, I was considering this when it ran out of sight for a moment and shot in again from another angle, fixing itself on my left foot with a terrific bite. There it
60 stayed until I kicked it away, crying out in pain.
   Perhaps worried about her pet, Dr Smith appeared almost at once and joined me in the shower. On
65 the soapy floor she slipped over and crashed into the wooden wall. Looking up, now soaked in water, she saw her guest trying to cover himself with the bucket. 'Sorry,' she
70 said, starting to laugh, and I laughed too. 'I have no secrets,' I said, reaching for a towel. 'Just remove that mongoose'. I pointed at my bloody foot and with suspicious
75 speed – I suspected that an emergency mongoose-bite first-aid kit was always ready – Dr Smith was back at the shower door with bandages and disinfectant.

WRITING 3
Reports

■1 You have been asked to prepare a report for your class on one of the topics **1–3**. Talk to a partner who has chosen the same title and make a list of points to include.

1 Young people should not be allowed to watch films which contain scenes of violence. Do you agree?

2 Bicycles may be a dangerous form of transport. Do you agree?

3 What are some of the best ways in which people can keep fit and healthy in modern society?

■2 Which points will you include in each paragraph of your report?

■3 Write between 120 and 180 words in 45 minutes. Use some of the words/expressions from the box.

although	however
despite	moreover
whereas	besides
whilst	in my opinion
therefore	on the other hand

PRONUNCIATION
th sounds

The spelling *th* is used to represent two different sounds in English.

1 Listen to the difference:

A / θ/ /θ/ is a sound made only with the tongue and the teeth.

B / ð/ /ð/ is a sound made in the same way, but using the voice.

2 /θ/ is used in many ordinal numbers, like **fourth**. Practise reading the words in the box with your partner.

fourth	fifth	length	seventh
eighth	warmth	teeth	bath
thick	through	three	mouth
faith	twelfth	cloth	

3 /ð/ is used at the beginning of many grammatical words, like **that**. Practise reading the words in the box with your partner.

the	this	that	there
then	though	these	those
they	rather	mother	further
them	clothes	weather	

4 If /θ/ and /ð/ do not exist in your language, you may be making the wrong sound. Practise saying these pairs of words and listen to your partner.

three	tree
mouse	mouth
thick	sick
path	pass
there	dare
they	day
first	thirst
free	three
tin	thin
Marta	Martha

5 Read these phrases to your partner.

- 30,000 theatre tickets.
- Thursday 30th at 3.30 pm.
- My mother would rather have wet weather.
- Those clothes give winter warmth.
- Thirty-three thirsty fathers.

EXAM PRACTICE 9

1 Read the text below and think of the word which best fits each
space. Use only one word in each space. There is an example at the
beginning (**0**) .

Staying Fit

At 34 years of (**0**) __*age*__ , Graham Simpson, the Foxton United captain,
(**1**) _____ just led his team to the Second Division championship. Now,
one year away (**2**) _____ retirement, he is a model (**3**) _____
fitness. He explains his enduring success (**4**) _____ pointing to a
healthy lifestyle. He is still exactly the (**5**) _____ weight as he was ten
years (**6**) _____ and still as fast.

(**7**) _____ many highly trained athletes, Graham likes to get
(**8**) _____ least nine hours sleep a night, plus a regular couple of hours
in the afternoon.

Graham is also careful (**9**) _____ his diet. He likes to eat food that gives
a (**10**) _____ of energy but which is low (**11**) _____ fat. He
(**12**) _____ eats a lot of bananas and tuna fish and has (**13**) _____
up fish and chips.

Graham is to retire from playing football (**14**) _____ year, but he is
(**15**) _____ likely to be collecting his old age pension just yet!

2 Read the text below and look carefully at each line. Some of the lines are
correct, and some have a word which should not be there. If a line is
correct, put a tick (✓). If a line has a word which should not be there,
write the word in the space on the right. There are two examples at
the beginning (**0**) and (**00**).

Dear Kathy

I'm sorry I couldn't come to your birthday party last week.	**0**	✓
I haven't been to very well for the last fortnight and I	**00**	*to*
just couldn't face it going out on Friday night. I think	**1**	
I've got some 'flu, but I went to the doctor and she said	**2**	
it's just a bad cold and there isn't much I can do except	**3**	
stay in bed and take down some aspirins and lots of hot	**4**	
drinks. It is all started with a really bad headache about	**5**	
two weeks ago, and then I started up getting aches	**6**	
and pains in my arms and legs and a really sore throat.	**7**	
I went to the work for the first few days but then I	**8**	
started looking so bad that my boss he told me to go	**9**	
to home and stay there until I felt completely better!	**10**	
The doctor said that there are lots of people going	**11**	
down with this sort of a summer cold and the only thing	**12**	
she could give me was some of medicine for the sore	**13**	
throat – it was really very painful and I lost my voice	**14**	
completely for both two days. (Too much talking, my	**15**	
mum said!)		

Hope to see you soon.

Erica

3 Read the text below and decide which word **A**, **B**, **C** or **D** best fits each space. There is an example at the beginning (**0**).

Couch-potatoes are getting fatter

An important (**0**) _C_ has recently confirmed a (**1**) _____ national stereotype – people in the USA are fat. The researchers (**2**) _____ out that a third of people in the USA are more than 20% above their (**3**) _____ weight. Twenty years ago the (**4**) _____ of over-weight adults was about one in four. Among young people the figures are even more (**5**) _____ .

The research is a poor advertisement for the slimming industry in the United States which (**6**) _____ $40 billion on marketing diet products every year. This (**7**) _____ in the country's waistline is the (**8**) _____ of an increasingly inactive lifestyle and the fact that food is (**9**) _____ available all day. The US food industry produces 3,700 calories per day for every US citizen, but a woman's energy (**10**) _____ is half of that, and a man can easily live (**11**) _____ 2,500 calories.

The experts say that television, use of cars and the (**12**) _____ of compulsory physical education in schools have all (**13**) _____ down the activity (**14**) _____ of people in the USA, and this situation is (**15**) _____ even worse by people's habit of eating more while they are watching television.

0	**A** composition	**B**	research	**C**	study	**D**	inspection
1	**A** normal	**B**	common	**C**	ordinary	**D**	average
2	**A** brought	**B**	gave	**C**	turned	**D**	found
3	**A** ideal	**B**	happy	**C**	top	**D**	real
4	**A** measure	**B**	proportion	**C**	part	**D**	size
5	**A** worrying	**B**	anxious	**C**	annoying	**D**	concerned
6	**A** empties	**B**	costs	**C**	spends	**D**	passes
7	**A** growing	**B**	building	**C**	add	**D**	increase
8	**A** result	**B**	answer	**C**	end	**D**	reason
9	**A** gradually	**B**	partly	**C**	easily	**D**	surely
10	**A** want	**B**	request	**C**	need	**D**	wish
11	**A** on	**B**	by	**C**	through	**D**	above
12	**A** end	**B**	finish	**C**	last	**D**	close
13	**A** come	**B**	got	**C**	cut	**D**	let
14	**A** amount	**B**	level	**C**	degree	**D**	height
15	**A** brought	**B**	done	**C**	held	**D**	made

It's a bargain

SPEAKING 1

Talking about photographs

1 Talk to your partner. Look at these pictures and compare two of them. These questions will help you.

1 What type of shop is this?

2 What are the people doing?

3 What things can you buy in this type of shop?

4 How is it organised?

5 What would you expect to find in different parts of the shop?

LISTENING 1

Short extracts

You will hear three people talking about shops. Decide which situation each of the people is talking about, **A**, **B**, **C** or **D**.

1 _____

2 _____

3 _____

Expressing and justifying opinions

Talk to your partner. You plan to visit Selfridges, a shop like the one in picture D. Here is your shopping list. All of the items can be found in six departments. Divide the items into six groups of five according to which department they can be found in. Give each department a name. The first one has been done for you.

Shopping List

ink	saucepan	rubber	plug	jam
kettle	shampoo	bracelet	light bulb	peanuts
brooch	necklace	smoked salmon	ruler	bath foam
teaspoons	shaving foam	garlic	corkscrew	watch
headphones	adaptor	earrings	pepper mill	envelopes
toothpaste	batteries	pencil sharpener	sponge	mushrooms

FOOD HALL

Note-taking

You will hear a series of announcements made to customers in a department store. As you listen, complete the information in the grid below.

Department	Product	Offer	Floor
Food Hall	bread	Reduced	1 _____
2 _____	soft furnishings	20% off	3 _____
4 _____	Brighthouse Cleaning Products	5 _____	basement
Restaurant	6 _____ £3.20	set meal	7 _____
8 _____	*The Miltons* by J. Bakerson	signed copy	9 _____
10 _____	suits	11 _____	12 _____

READING 1
Multiple choice

Talk to your partner.

1 How many pairs of shoes do you buy each year? Do some people need more pairs of shoes than others?

2 Make a list of the different types of shoes you can buy.

Read the article quickly to find out:

a How many different types of shoes or footwear are mentioned.
b How many pairs of shoes Gloria has.
c Why she has so many.
d Which are her favourite type.

HIGH-HEEL FREAK
The owner of 150 pairs of shoes, Gloria Hunniford is a high-heel freak!

"My mother always said that in life you should buy good shoes and a good bed – because if you weren't in one you'd be in the other," laughs Gloria Hunniford.

Wise words – and they could explain Gloria's passion for shoes as well as her fondness for the exclusive Pinet shoe shop in London's Bond Street.

With its marble steps and antique furniture the shop oozes with luxury and glamour. "I love the atmosphere, the service and knowing that whatever I buy there will be the best. I'll look good and feel good – and that's coming from someone who's a high-heel freak."

At her home in the countryside cupboards have been fitted with row upon row of shoe racks to house the 150 pairs that Gloria has collected.

When her daughter ("now she's a real shopaholic") moved out recently to get married, Gloria took over her bedroom, turning it into a room "for the overspill. I simply can't throw them away. I've got every colour and type imaginable, although most are high heels. I sometimes look at some of the outrageously high ones and wonder how on earth I ever managed to walk on them."

For some time after Gloria moved to London from Northern Ireland she'd return to shop in Belfast. "London was still a maze, and it took me a while to find my way around."

Since discovering Pinet, she heads for the shop whenever she needs shoes to match an outfit. "I'll take in a piece of fabric and Trevor Goodlad, the deputy manager, who has been helping me choose shoes for years, sees it as a great challenge to match it up."

Avoiding the satin rhinestone numbers at £79, the gold hand-painted pumps or even the handmade silk evening shoes selling between £200 and £300 – "I'd never spend that much money. My average is just over £100, and around £40 for sale shoes" – she usually heads for the Weitzmann collection.

"They're very stylish and flattering, especially to someone like me who has absolutely horrible feet," she says, shaking off her shoes to reveal neat pointed toes.

3 Now read the article more carefully and for questions **1–5** choose the answer which you think best fits according to the passage.

1 What type of shoes did Gloria's mother recommend?

A High-quality shoes.
B Shoes which look expensive.
C Shoes from a particular shop.
D Shoes which made her look good.

2 What does Gloria keep in her daughter's bedroom?

A Her daughter's shoes.
B Only high-heeled shoes.
C The shoes she has no space for.
D Shoes which are worn out.

3 Why did Gloria go back to Belfast to shop?

A She thought the shops were better.
B She needed to match shoes to fabrics.
C She could get higher heels in Belfast.
D She found London large and confusing.

4 How does Trevor Goodlad help Gloria?

A By finding shoes with pointed toes and high heels.
B By making shoes especially to match her clothes.
C By finding shoes in the colour and style she wants.
D By advising her on clothes to match her shoes.

5 Why does Gloria like Weitzmann shoes?

A They are very comfortable.
B They make her feet look nice.
C She can buy them in a sale.
D They are made by hand.

4 Find words or phrases in the passage that mean:

1 a type of stone (paragraph 3)
2 is full of (3)
3 more than will fit (5)
4 extremely (5)
5 labyrinth (6)
6 goes directly to (7)
7 a set of clothes (7)
8 makes you look good (9)
9 well designed and fashionable (9)
10 to show (9)

GRAMMAR 1
Obligations

1

trolley	checkout	cashier
till	carrier bag	aisle

1 Name as many things in the photograph as you can. Begin with the words in the box.

2 What are the advantages and disadvantages of shopping in this type of place?

3 Think of some things you have to do/need to do in this type of shop compared to other types.

4 Think of some things you needn't do/don't have to do.

2 Read the leaflet on page 155 from Tesco, a large supermarket.

For each phrase **1–10**, decide whether this is something you have to do or don't have to do according to the leaflet, if you want to take advantage of Multisaver.

1 keep the discounted items separate
2 buy exactly the number printed on the sign
3 buy at least the number printed on the sign
4 tell the cashier you have discounted items in your shopping
5 take your receipt to a special desk
6 buy all the items on the same visit to the shop
7 show this leaflet to the cashier
8 go to a special Multisaver cashier
9 buy items that have a Multisaver sign on them
10 buy a particular product or range of products

WHAT IS MULTISAVER?

MULTI SAVER

Multisaver is the convenient way to make savings on your everyday shopping.

Throughout this store you'll see Multisaver signs on dozens of essential items and some of your favourite luxury goods as well. Offers will apply to single items or groups of products.

Simply buy the number of items shown on the Multisaver sign and you will automatically receive the discount indicated.

Discounts are automatically deducted from your bill by our scanning system – even if the Multisaver items are spread throughout your shopping, provided they are purchased at the same time.

The savings you make will be shown both on the till screen and your receipt, indicated by the word "Multisaver" and a negative value.

THE MULTISAVER SIGN

BUITONI ITALIAN TAGLIATELLE **79p** 500 gram each	**MULTI SAVER** 2 for **£1.28** 12.8p per 100 gram	BUY 2 SAVE **30p**
The name of the product or range of products which qualify for the Multisaver offer	The number you need to buy	The discount you will receive

QUESTIONS AND ANSWERS

Q Do I need to purchase all of the items on the same trip?

A Yes. All items must be purchased in a single transaction.

Q Do I need to put the items together at the checkout?

A No. The discount will be deducted from your bill even if the Multisaver items are spread throughout your shopping. If the offer is "BUY 3 SAVE 10p". the discount will be shown after the 3rd item on your receipt.

Q If the offer is "BUY 3 SAVE 10p" and I buy 6, what will happen?

A You will qualify for the discount twice ie. 20p will be deducted. Any exception to this will be described on the Multisaver sign.

Q How will I know that I have received the discount?

A The savings you make wiil be shown both on the the till screen and on your receipt.

---

3 Find words from the leaflet that mean

1 easy and comfortable
2 in all parts
3 necessary
4 also
5 individual
6 shown
7 taken away
8 distributed
9 as long as
10 bought

4 Match each of the expressions on the left with a phrase on the right which means the same thing.

1 You need to go
2 You have to go
3 You must go
4 You can go
5 You should go

It is necessary for you to go
It is possible for you to go if you like
It would be better if you went
You have no choice but to go

Which two phrases on the left have the same meaning?

5 Match each of the expressions on the left with a phrase on the right which means the same thing.

1 You don't have to go
2 You needn't go
3 You don't need to go
4 You can't go
5 You shouldn't go
6 You mustn't go

It isn't necessary for you to go
It isn't possible for you to go
It would be better not to go
It is forbidden!

Which three phrases on the left all mean the same thing?

6 Complete these sentences about supermarkets with one of the words or phrases from the box.

have to	don't have to	need to	can
should	can't	mustn't	must
needn't	shouldn't	don't need to	

1 You _____ push your own trolley.

2 You _____ change the price labels on the goods.

3 You _____ use a basket or trolley.

4 You _____ choose your own vegetables.

5 You _____ put things straight into your shopping bag.

6 You _____ push in front of people in the queue.

7 You _____ sit down while the assistant finds things for you.

8 You _____ bring boxes and bags to take your goods home.

9 You _____ compare prices with other supermarkets.

10 You _____ queue up at busy periods.

11 You _____ buy large quantities, and if you do you _____ go shopping so often.

12 You _____ allow children to eat the food before you reach the checkout.

🔊 LISTENING 3
Selecting an answer

Listen to the conversation and decide whether these statements are true or false.

1 Anne thinks Liz's top was expensive.

2 You are not allowed to try clothes on in the shop.

3 If you bring them back you can exchange them for other goods.

4 To get a refund you have to prove the clothes do not fit.

5 The shop only accepts payment in cash.

6 Ferguson clothes are only sold in Ferguson's.

7 Liz persuades Anne to go to the shop.

8 Anyone can have a Ferguson's card.

Make, let, allow

1 Look at these phrases from the listening text.

they make you pay in cash
they don't let you try things on
you're allowed to pay it off
you're not allowed to try things on

When do we use *make, let* and *allow*?

2 Put the correct form of *make, let* or *allow* in the spaces in these sentences.

1 Oh, I hate piano recitals. Please don't _____ me go.

2 You're not _____ to eat or drink in the computer room.

3 When I was young, I was _____ to wear horrible long woollen socks.

4 Her father is strict, he won't _____ her wear make-up.

5 He is not _____ to go out after nine o'clock in the evening.

6 They _____ that dog climb all over people who visit them.

7 At that school they don't _____ the students wear high-heeled shoes.

8 I wasn't _____ to go to a pop concert until I was sixteen.

3 Discuss these questions with your partner:

1 Should people be allowed to choose their own birthday presents?

2 Should parents let their teenage children smoke at home?

3 Should all teenagers be made to have a bank account?

4 Should children be made to help with the house-work?

5 Should parents let children buy whatever clothes they want?

VOCABULARY 1
Vocabulary in context

1 Read this story and choose a word from the box to fit into each of the numbered blanks.

instalments	bill	sale	discount
deposit	currency	cost	afford
buy	cash	exchange	bargain
price	debt	worth	spending
pay	wallet	bank	~~receipt~~

Bruce walked out of the travel agency and looked at the (1) *receipt* he had been given. It had been so easy to book the holiday in the Caribbean. The assistant had been very helpful and persuasive. He had been attracted by the 25% (2) _____ offered on the (3) _____ in the brochure if you booked before the end of the month. He had only had to pay a (4) _____ of £100 to be followed by four monthly (5) _____ of £75, surely he could (6) _____ that?

He realised, however, that he had forgotten to ask about the (7) _____ of living on the island or about the (8) _____ rate of the local (9) _____ . These were important because he had only booked bed and breakfast and so would have to (10) _____ other meals out of his (11) _____ money.

He took his (12) _____ from his pocket and remembered that he had to go to the (13) _____ because he had run out of (14) _____ . Oh dear, and there inside was the electricity (15) _____ that he had forgotten to (16) _____ .

He stopped and looked up. He was outside a very smart clothes shop. In the window there was a big sign with (17) '_____' written on it and there next to it was a lovely lightweight jacket. It would be just the thing for the Caribbean, and at only £55 it was a real (18) _____ . Even if it meant going into (19) _____ , he couldn't resist such a good chance to save money. He walked into the shop. 'This holiday had better be (20) _____ it,' he said to himself.

HELP WITH WRITING
A transactional letter

In FCE Paper 2 you must answer Question 1. This consists of some instructions and notes. You have to write a letter using some of the information given. The letter might be semi-formal – to a company or to someone you have never met, or it might be informal – to a friend. You will always be asked to write the letter for a specific reason which is given in the instructions.

1 Look at this advertisement for a coach trip to a shopping centre. Discuss with your partner what things might go wrong on a trip like this.

Special Day Trip

Happy Coaches Ltd

HAPPY COACHES

Enjoy an exciting day out at Britain's newest covered shopping complex.

Newton Stilton has 133 different retail outlets including all your favourite high street stores and many speciality shops.

The coach leaves Milton Bus Station at 08.30 and travels through the beautiful Cole Valley. Return 17.30.

Price: £9.50.
19th December

■**2**   Read this letter written by somebody who went
on the coach trip advertised above.

Dear Sir or Madam

I am writing to complain about a Happy Coaches day trip which I went on to the Newton Stilton
shopping complex on December 19th.

According to your leaflet, the coach was supposed to leave at 8.30 in the morning. I arrived at 8.20 to
find no coach waiting, and it did not arrive until after 9.00. **To make matters worse**, when eventually
we left, the coach went at such speed along the country lanes that I felt nervous and uncomfortable
(although the journey still took nearly three hours). Is there not a more direct route?

As if this were not enough, when we finally arrived at Newton Stilton I found that half the new
shopping complex was still closed. Many of the best shops will not be opening until the spring. I am
afraid that your leaflet is rather misleading in this respect.

On top of everything, the coach broke down on the return journey and we had to wait for an hour before another coach was sent.

You can imagine how disappointed I am to have wasted a day in this way, and I feel that your company
is directly to blame. I am, therefore, writing to request an immediate refund of the £9.50 I spent on the
ticket.

I look forward to receiving your prompt reply.

Yours faithfully

D Stanton

D. Stanton

Why has it been written?
Give each paragraph in the letter a title.

1   Introduction
2   _____
3   _____
4   _____
5   _____

■**3**   Look at the phrases which are in **bold** type.
How are they important to the letter?

■**4**   Look at these informal expressions. For each
one find the formal equivalent in the letter.

1   your leaflet says
2   it doesn't tell the truth about this
3   I'm really fed up about it
4   it's your fault
5   so I want my money back
6   write back soon

■5 You recently ordered something from a mail-order clothing company. You receive a package and this note:

Tulip Casual Clothes Co.

Delivery note

Goods:	Type:	Colour:	Size:

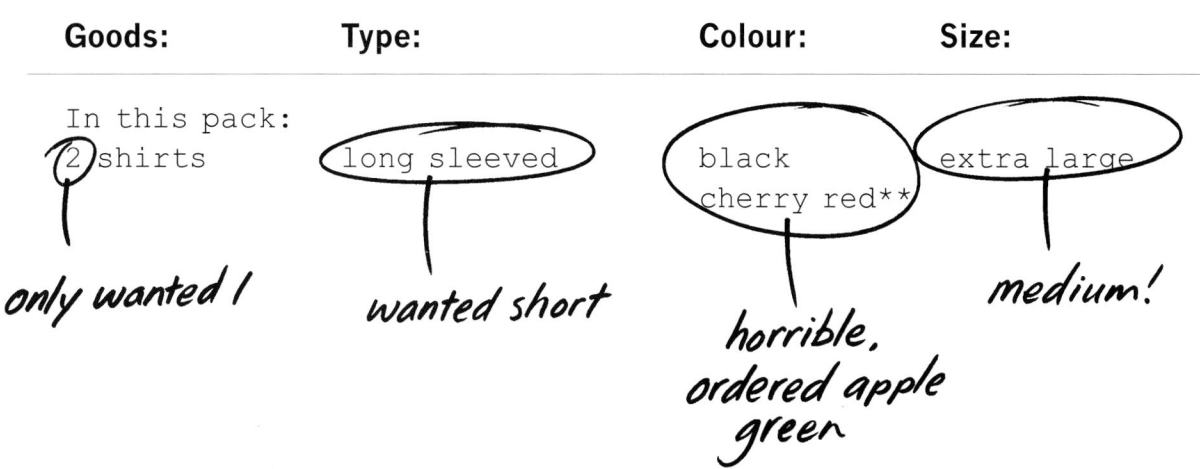

In this pack:
(2) shirts   (long sleeved)   black / cherry red**   extra large

only wanted 1   *wanted short*   *horrible, ordered apple green*   *medium!*

** Sorry! Your first choice of colour was not available.

Catalogue says they deliver in 4 days - I've waited 3 weeks. Don't like these colours - ask for something else.

■6 Read the note which came with the goods carefully and the notes which you made for yourself. Then write to the company explaining the problem and covering the points in your notes.

Write a letter of between 120 and 180 words in an appropriate style. Do not write any addresses.

SPEAKING 3
Expressing opinions

1 Talk to your partner.

1 Have you ever complained in a shop? Why did you complain and what was the result?

2 Look at this list of complaints that people make in shops. Say which of these complaints you would expect to hear most often in your country – tell your partner your opinions and experiences of these things.

- unhelpful or rude shop assistants
- shop assistants standing around chatting to each other
- not enough shop assistants
- pushy shop assistants who don't give you time to look
- shop assistants who know nothing about the goods they sell
- long queues to pay
- poor choice of goods
- poor quality goods, high prices or poor value for money
- limited range of sizes, colours or styles
- goods out of stock

2 What are the advantages and disadvantages of using credit cards? Do you know anyone who has had a bad experience with a credit card?

READING 2
Gapped text

1 You are going to read a newspaper article about one man's experience of shopping with a credit card. Choose from the sentences **A–I** the one which fits each gap **1–7**. There is one extra sentence which you do not need to use. There is an example at the beginning (**0**).

A The radio is playing 'Love is all around' by Wet Wet Wet. Toby begins to sing quietly along.

B He smiles with the enthusiasm of a man who is being paid on commission.

C I do actually know this, but I get out my wallet, open it and look inside.

D Moments later, I come back from the changing room and present myself, wallet at the ready.

E His name is Toby, according to the friendly badge so firmly attached to his chest.

F Now it just declines your credit card, ruining your whole day in the process.

G Every single person in the shop turns to look at me now.

H It is extraordinarily difficult to describe the pure sarcasm with which Toby manages to say the word 'sir'.

I The last one I bought I held on to for many years.

PROBLEMS WITH PLASTIC

The other afternoon I went into town and thought I'd buy myself a new suit. This is not something I do very often [0][I]

Anyway, there I am in the changing room, trying on jacket and trousers, going out to the mirror and then back behind the curtain and stripping off again. I am enjoying myself a lot, but the assistant is not much help. [1][ ]

Despite this he has an air of seeming to regard dealing with the public as some sort of deeply unpleasant necessity. The fact is that every time I ask for another suit, he sighs deeply and looks at his finger nails before going to get it. Toby is silently thinking, "Ten thousand suits in the shop and this chap is going to try on every one."

In the end I choose a tasteful suit in a striking dark red colour. Toby immediately cheers up. [2][ ] He congratulates me warmly on the excellence of my choice. The trousers will need to be let out just a bit he says, but that's OK.

3 ☐ I hand over my credit card and Toby puts it through a machine beside the cash register which bleeps every few seconds. A little time passes. We stare at each other. I notice that his eyes are just a little too close together.

He drums his fingers on the top of the cash register. **4** ☐ The credit card machine interrupts him. It begins to bleep wildly as it bursts into life and gives out a slip of paper. Toby takes the paper and looks at it. His eyes widen. He stares at me accusingly.
"Your credit card has been declined," he says.
"What?" I say.
"YOUR CREDIT CARD HAS BEEN DECLINED," Toby repeats, slowly, loudly emphasising every syllable. **5** ☐

"DECLINED," Toby says again, pushing the piece of paper into my hand.
"YES ... LOOK. DECLINED!"
I stand by the counter, head hung low in shame. Then I look up pitifully. I am nervous.
"I don't know how this could have happened," I stammer.
"Huh," he says.
He looks up at the ceiling, then folds his arms

and closes his eyes. "I don't suppose you have another credit card?" he sighs.
I don't have another credit card.

6 ☐ All I can find is a five pound note, a photograph of the dog and some peppermint chewing gum. I tell him I've forgotten all my other credit cards. He makes an unkind noise. I offer to go and get cash from my bank. Toby's eyebrows go up practically to meet his hair line. "Cash? I can't take cash now. I've put it through as a credit card sale."

"Well," I say, "I'll come back tomorrow then. Thanks."
"Yes, sir," he says. "Why don't you do that, sir. Thank you very much, sir."
7 ☐ It was a terrible moment. It was just as though a large hand had come bursting through the ceiling with its long finger pointing accusingly at me. I leave the shop feeling like a major criminal.

■ **2**   Complete this summary of the article. Use the word given in capitals at the end of each line to form a word that fits in the space in the same line. There is an example at the beginning (**0**).

When he was out shopping, Joe (**0**) _*decided*_ to buy a new	**DECIDE**
suit. He went into the (**1**) _____ room in the shop to	**CHANGE**
try on some suits. Although the shop (**2**) _____ was	**ASSIST**
rather (**3**) _____ , Joe had soon made	**HELP**
his (**4**) _____ of suit, and took it over to	**CHOOSE**
the counter, offering his credit card as (**5**) _____ .	**PAY**
(**6**) _____ , the credit card machine did	**FORTUNE**
not accept his card. So, feeling very (**7**) _____ ,	**EMBARRASS**
Joe pretended that he had (**8**) _____ all his	**FORGOT**
other credit cards and he left the shop without (**9**) _____	**BUY**
the suit. He felt like some kind of (**10**) _____ .	**CRIME**

⊟ LISTENING 4

Note-taking

▣1 Listen to a man making a complaint in a shop and make notes under the following headings.

1 What did he buy?

2 What is his complaint?

3 What happened as a result?

4 Why did it happen
   - according to the assistant?
   - according to the customer?

5 What exactly does the customer want?

6 Why is this not possible?

7 What does he decide to do?

8 What else will he complain about?

▣2 Listen again and then plan the paragraphs of the letter the customer will write to the manager.

▣3 Now write the letter.

⊟ PRONUNCIATION

Word linking

When we speak quickly in English, some sounds at the beginnings and ends of words join on to each other or are lost.

▣1 Listen to these examples. (The parts that change are underlined.)

   It's next week
   I went last night
   I prefer baked potatoes
   It's stopped raining
   She's finished, has she?
   Who asked the question?
   I'll leave it for you
   Don't talk about it

▣2 Listen and repeat the phrases and then practise saying them with your partner. You have to speak fast.

⊟3

Listen to these phrases and mark the letters that have joined together or been lost.

1 You can't do that

2 He didn't throw it

3 I'm going next year

4 Do you want a small glass or a big glass?

5 I'll look for him outside

6 The problem with this exercise is …

7 He asked the teacher a question

8 She looked through the window

9 I like boiled potatoes

10 He isn't taking the exam

▣4 Compare with your partner. Listen to check and then practise saying the phrases with your partner.

⊟ LISTENING 5

Note-taking

▣1 Listen to the phone-in programme and make notes under these headings.

	Name	Wish	Reason
1st caller			
2nd caller			
3rd caller			
4th caller			

▣2 Compare your notes with your partner, then listen again to check.

GRAMMAR 3

Wishes

▣1 Look at these sentences from the listening text and answer the questions.

1 *I wish I could ski.*
   Can she ski?
   How does she feel about it?

2 *I wish I was rich.*
   Is she rich?
   How does she feel about it?

▣2 Listen again and make a note of four other sentences using *I wish*.

   How many different types of sentence are there?
   How are they different?
   Ask yourself questions as in the example.

3 Match eight of the sentences **1–10** with one of the phrases **a–h** to show the meaning. Note that there are two sentences which cannot be matched.

1	I wish I could ski.	**a**	But I'm not.
2	I wish you luck.	**b**	But I don't.
3	I wish I knew what to buy.	**c**	But I didn't.
4	I wish I had blonde hair.	**d**	But I can't.
5	I wish I was rich.	**e**	But I haven't.
6	I wish they'd be quiet.	**f**	But they won't.
7	I wish you a happy birthday.	**g**	But he does.
8	I wish you could come with me.	**h**	But you can't.
9	I wish he didn't always sing in the bath.		
10	I wish I had asked more questions.		

4 Which two sentences from **1–10** cannot be matched? Why? What other things can you wish people in this way?

Which of the sentences **1–10** expresses past regrets (see page 139)?

5 Is there anything about yourself or other people you would like to change?

6 Finish the sentences below with your wishes.

1 I wish I was _____

2 I wish I could _____

3 I wish I had _____

4 I wish _____ would

_____

5 I wish _____ could

_____

7 Now tell your wishes to as many people in the room as possible.

Can you find someone with the same wish as you?

8 Complete the second sentence so that it has a similar meaning to the first sentence. Use the word given and other words to complete each sentence. You must use between two and five words. Do not change the word given.

1 I'm sorry that you can't come to the party.
wish
I _____ to the party.

2 He keeps interrupting me, which is very annoying.
wish
I _____
interrupting me, it's very annoying.

3 Ingrid would like to be able to swim, but she can't.
wishes
Ingrid _____
swim.

4 I hope that you are successful in your exams.
luck
I wish _____
in your exams.

5 My hair's short and dark, but I'd prefer long blonde hair.
wish
I _____
long blonde hair.

6 Eric doesn't see his grandchildren very often, which makes him sad.
wishes
Eric _____
more often.

7 I'm sorry that he won't accept the job he's been offered.
wish
I _____
the job he's been offered.

8 I have very little patience, which is a shame!
were
I _____
patient.

9 This continual rain is making me feel depressed.
stop
I _____
raining – it makes me feel depressed.

10 The print in this book is so small that I'm afraid I can't read it.
was
I wish the print in this book _____
_____ , then I could read it.

🔊 LISTENING 6

Multiple matching

1 Talk to your partner.

What is a vending machine?
What types of vending machines can you find in your town or village?
What is the strangest vending machine you've ever seen?
What are the advantages and disadvantages of vending machines?

2 You will hear five different people talking about vending machines. For questions **1–5**, choose from the list the comment **A–F** which best summarises the point each speaker is making. There is one extra letter which you do not need to use.

A Vending machines can be useful in an emergency

B An example of an unsuccessful vending machine

C There's nothing new about vending machines

D The range of goods available from vending machines

E Why vending machines are becoming more common

F What to do if there is a problem with a vending machine

Speaker 1 ☐
Speaker 2 ☐
Speaker 3 ☐
Speaker 4 ☐
Speaker 5 ☐

READING 4

Multiple matching

You are going to read some information about places to buy Christmas presents. For questions **1–14**, choose from the extracts **A–J**. Some of the places may be chosen more than once. There is an example (0) at the beginning.

In which of the places can you:

get a special Christmas service?	**0** B		
buy jewellery?	**1** ☐	**2** ☐	**3** ☐
get something made specially for you?	**4** ☐	**5** ☐	**6** ☐
receive an after-sales service?	**7** ☐		
have the products delivered to your home?	**8** ☐		
buy things from other cultures?	**9** ☐	**10** ☐	**11** ☐
get old-fashioned things?	**12** ☐		
buy the work of local people?	**13** ☐	**14** ☐	**15** ☐

Christmas Presents

■ **A** Bicycle Doctor

1 *(68 Dickenson Road, Manchester)*
Is your nearest and dearest fed up with the traffic congestion? Buy them a bike. This shop has bicycles
5 for all, with prices going from £70 for a modest machine, up to the thousands for the full mountain bike. The best point about this bike shop is that it offers free of charge
10 repairs for a year after purchase. So next time they wrap themselves round that lamp-post, Bicycle Doctor will medicate the machine.

■ **B** British Airways Santa Flights

If you want this one you've got to
15 book now, it gets full in a minute. It's a 45 minute flight, 10,000 metres up on a Boeing 737 (with red nose and antlers), aims to track down Santa as he goes about his
20 work, and then 'beams' him aboard. A pre-flight magic show and gifts for kids of all ages, including a little food and drink too, will cost you £50, and babies under two years old get
25 to go free. Goody!

■ **C** The Garden of Life

(258 Upper Chorlton Road, Manchester)
African art has always been big business, but now in these two
30 shops you can get the art with the history and meaning behind beautifully carved structures, instruments, and glorious clothes. From baskets, to books, to utensils,
35 to pictures and in a price range which allows everyone purchasing power.

D The Dazzle Contemporary Exhibition

in Manchester's Royal Exchange, is exactly what it says. A yearly event, where over 2000 pieces of work
40 from top designers from this region and from across the UK, are displayed before you – and you think you can leave empty handed? I really don't think so! There are
45 some brilliant bits of silver and some innovative uses of other precious metals and stones which are great for gifts or personal treats to wear yourself. Go there, you
50 should see something you like.

E The Design Centre,
Royal Exchange

The fashion design centre in the Exchange is worth a look too. At upmarket *Afflek's*, the clothes are
55 slightly more expensive, but worth it for the quality and innovative designs. There are a lot of designers from our city here who would welcome the support and deserve
60 it too. There's a Design Centre up-stairs and one downstairs. Both have clothes outlets such as *Arc* and *Wear It Out*, where there are some really reasonably priced funky
65 designs. Well worth a look round.

F Design Goes Pop

is situated under Cafe Pop *(34 Oldham Street, Manchester)*. If you're into retro, this is the place to go. Virtually all the items in use or on
70 display are original classic designs from the '40s to the '70s. And the shop downstairs sells more wild and wacky goods, everything from every era. Prices go from £1 to
75 £600, so there is something for every pocket. Be individual and give unique presents from the past.

G Manchester Craft Centre

(Oak Street, Manchester) is full of interesting and original presents
80 which make a change from bath salts and socks. The artists are all local, and their inspirations range from Marco Polo to Pythagoras. Brooches, necklaces, earrings,
85 sculpture, oil lamps and hand-painted silk waistcoats are just some of the things available, and there is something in every price range. And if you want something
90 unique, the designers can be commissioned. There will be extended opening hours throughout December.

H Ochio-Rios

(44 Belthorne Avenue, Manchester)
95 This has got to be a treat amongst treats. Check the scenario: three or four guys come into your house, take over your kitchen, prepare a meal of your choice for as many or
100 as few of you as you desire, but they bring the music, the cutlery, the plates, the ambience, and all the feel-good factor you could imagine! Everything is pre-arranged; the
105 food can be anything from Italian, to African, to English, to Japanese, and the menu and price is tailored to suit you and yours. I've had it done and believe me – the feel-fine factor
110 lasted for days. Give them a call.

I Shared Earth

(51 Piccadilly, Manchester)
Situated in the heart of the city centre, this shop shares the crafts, music and literature from many
115 parts of the world – for a price, of course, although it's not overly expensive. There are bright and colourful clothes, cards and books, candles, bracelets and rings, sweet-
120 smelling incense, and equally varied music from Fela Kuti to Billy Bragg, to Latin American to Ambient Dub.

J Worldwide Songwriters

(71 Longford Road, Manchester)
Here's a novel gift for your loved
125 one; how about a personalised song? Fourteen musicians, vocalists and songwriters, directed by Clive van Cooten, will write and record a song especially tailored to your
130 needs. Fill out the form: Where'd you meet? S/he got broad shoulders and green eyes? What sort of personality have they got? Etc. CD or cassette, it will cost you around
135 £250, but you got it to give 'cos you love 'em, right?

1 Read the text below and decide which word **A**, **B**, **C** or **D** best fits each space. There is an example at the beginning (**0**).

Teenage Tycoon

With his mobile phone, (**0**) ____*B*____ cards and smart leather briefcase, Peter Elliot looks just (**1**) _____ a successful company executive. (**2**) _____ , the fast-growing advertising business which he started a year ago, when he was just 15, is (**3**) _____ from his school classroom during the breaks between lessons.

After walking through the town centre himself with a sandwich board for a local dry cleaner's (**4**) _____ his neck, Peter decided to (**5**) _____ up his own sandwich board (**6**) _____ . But a massive increase in (**7**) _____ meant he recently had to (**8**) _____ on twelve of his school friends as (**9**) _____ went up by more than 40% each month.

His clients, mostly local shops, are (**10**) _____ by Peter's brochure, produced on his Dad's home computer. Peter's clients (**11**) _____ a standard fee for each hour that their board is displayed and a small (**12**) _____ charge for handing out leaflets to passers by.

'It's a cheap and effective way for local shops and cafes to advertise because we go up to people when they are (**13**) _____ out shopping. They see the sandwich board and go (**14**) _____ into the shops,' said Peter, who got (**15**) _____ an exam in Business Studies last summer. 'It may be old-fashioned, but it really works.'

0	**A** industry	**B** business	**C** invitation	**D** firm
1	**A** as	**B** so	**C** like	**D** than
2	**A** Despite	**B** However	**C** Although	**D** Otherwise
3	**A** run	**B** done	**C** followed	**D** made
4	**A** across	**B** around	**C** between	**D** above
5	**A** fixed	**B** set	**C** grew	**D** put
6	**A** shop	**B** industry	**C** house	**D** firm
7	**A** need	**B** request	**C** claim	**D** demand
8	**A** take	**B** bring	**C** carry	**D** let
9	**A** incomes	**B** benefits	**C** increases	**D** profits
10	**A** appealed	**B** attracted	**C** invited	**D** included
11	**A** pay	**B** hand	**C** deposit	**D** hire
12	**A** super	**B** attached	**C** additional	**D** extension
13	**A** before	**B** previously	**C** earlier	**D** already
14	**A** straight	**B** direct	**C** immediate	**D** instant
15	**A** through	**B** passed	**C** over	**D** by

2 Read the text below and look carefully at each line. Some of the lines are correct, and some have a word which should not be there. If a line is correct, put a tick (✓). If a line has a word which should not be there, write the word in the space on the right. There are two examples at the beginning (**0**) and (**00**).

Shopping in Cambridge

You asked for a few suggestions about where to go	**0**	✓
shopping when you will come to Cambridge next month.	**00**	*will*
Well, this is really quite a small town but there are two	**1**	_____
main areas with a good range of the shops. First, there	**2**	_____
are lots of shops in the city centre by itself. This is	**3**	_____
where you can find it branches of all the main stores as	**4**	_____
well as quite a lot of specialist shops – a big lot of them	**5**	_____
stock up clothes and gifts which visitors like to take away	**6**	_____
as these souvenirs. There are some big department	**7**	_____
stores and a really great open-air market which is good	**8**	_____
at for fruit and vegetables but sells a whole range of	**9**	_____
things from hats to a second-hand books at good prices.	**10**	_____
The other area is a modern shopping complex about	**11**	_____
15 minutes' walk far from the centre – it's especially	**12**	_____
popular if the weather is bad as the whole place	**13**	_____
is too indoors. There's a food area and a multi-screen	**14**	_____
cinema for when do you get fed up with shopping! Or	**15**	_____
for a change of scene you can always go to London – it's		
only an hour away on the train.		

3 Read the text below. Use the word given in capitals at the end of each line to form a word that fits in the space in the same line. There is an example at the beginning (**0**).

Money

Before the (**0**) *invention* of money, people used to get **INVENT**
the goods and services they wanted by (**1**) _____ things **SWAP**
with others. This system was entirely (**2**) _____ on an **DEPEND**
(**3**) _____ between both people, who each needed to **AGREE**
have what the other wanted.

The system of (**4**) _____ started to work much more **CHANGE**
smoothly with the (**5**) _____ of money. By using precious **INTRODUCE**
metals, which had been (**6**) _____ weighed and made **OFFICIAL**
into coins, it (**7**) _____ possible to sell what you produced **COME**
in return for coins, then use the coins to buy (**8**) _____ **ANY**
you wanted from a third party.

Some societies have developed (**9**) _____ substitutes **ACCEPT**
for coins by using things which, in (**10**) _____ , have a **REAL**
fixed value such as salt or cigarettes.

SPEAKING 1
Talking about photographs

Talk to your partner. Look at this photograph and discuss the following points. Give reasons for your opinions.

1 The picture in general:

Where was the picture taken?
What time of year or day is it?
How are the people dressed?
How do they feel?
How do they feel about each other?

2 Looking beyond the picture:

What has just happened?
What have the people been doing?
What is going to happen?
What are the people going to do?

3 Extending the theme:

What is the main character doing?
Is it a good idea? Why?
How would you feel in this situation?
Could this happen in your town?

LISTENING 1
Short extracts

You will hear the woman in the photograph talking about her experience of wearing a smog mask.

How does she feel about the mask?

A keen on it
B unsure of it
C negative about it

SPEAKING 2
Expressing and justifying opinions

Discuss with your partner the advantages and disadvantages of each of the following solutions to the problem of air pollution. Think about a big city in your country, or a city like London or Los Angeles.

1 Increase tax on petrol.
2 Limit each family to one car.
3 Close the city centre to traffic.
4 Improve the bus services.
5 Create special roads for bicycles.
6 Build underground railways.
7 Build bigger car parks.
8 Use electric cars.

READING 1
Multiple choice

1 Read the article and underline the parts where these questions are answered:

1 What do the masks do?
2 Who is already using them?
3 Who should be wearing them?
4 What does the BLF predict?
5 Who is thinking about using masks?
6 Who doesn't the mask work for?
7 Who thinks the mask is not the solution?
8 What other solution is proposed?

2 Find words which mean:

1 poisonous (line 1)
2 frightening (7)
3 a mixture (15)
4 part of the body (organ) (19)
5 likely to suffer from (30)
6 most important thing (33)
7 where nothing can pass (40)
8 reduced (53)

3 For each of the following questions choose the best answer, **A**, **B**, **C** or **D**.

1 What does Dr Malcolm Green think?

   A London has as much air pollution as Athens.
   B Smog masks solve the problem of air pollution.
   C People working outside should wear a mask in London.
   D A mask is necessary after twenty minutes in London.

2 Why does Liz Marriot have doubts about the masks?

   A They do not work so well for cyclists.
   B The number of cars is always rising.
   C The masks do not fit everyone perfectly.
   D The masks do not work over a long time.

3 What do Friends of the Earth think?

   A People cannot be forced to wear masks.
   B World Health Organisation levels are too low.
   C A new generation of cleaner vehicles is needed.
   D People must use their cars less.

---

1 **SMOG** masks which filter toxic gases out of the air we breathe could soon be a common sight on city streets, air pollution experts say.

5 Space-age masks are already a frequent accessory for cyclists. But, with toxic ozone levels now rising at an alarming rate, experts say pedestrians should be wearing them too.

10 The Clean Air Act of 1956 that followed the deaths of 4,000 people due to a London pea-soup smog has almost wiped out emissions of deadly sulphur dioxide.

But concern is mounting over invisible 15 "ozone smog", a poisonous cocktail created when car fumes such as nitrogen dioxide and carbon monoxide are heated by sunlight.

Last week the British Lung Foundation 20 (BLF) predicted that London could become as polluted as Los Angeles and Athens within 15 years.

Dr Malcolm Green, BLF chairman, said if the current pollution levels continued, 25 all city dwellers, who were outside for 20 minutes or more, would have to wear masks. Traffic wardens, cyclists, messengers and transport police should be wearing them already, he warns, particularly 30 those prone to chest infections, asthma or bronchitis.

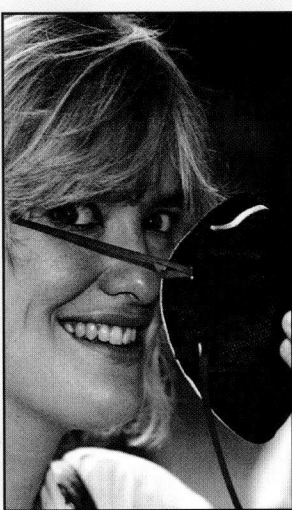

Are you safe to go out without a smog mask?
by Cathy Scott-Clark

Pollution at danger levels, say experts

"The reduction of air pollution must be our first priority, but this takes time. Masks are a sensible way of protecting the lungs."

35 A Metropolitan Police spokeswoman confirmed that smog masks for officers and traffic wardens in London are now being considered.

But Liz Marriot of the London Cycles Campaign says their use is limited.

40 "Unless a mask makes a perfect seal on your face, it doesn't work.

Where does that leave men with beards, people who wear glasses or someone with a big nose?"

Curbed

45 Friends of the Earth air pollution experts say wearing of masks is not a long-term solution.

"Nobody wants a world in which people have to wear masks in the street," says campaigner Fiona Weir.

50 "This is a new generation of pollution. Numbers of vehicles are constantly rising and ozone pollution is rising very, very rapidly – car usage has to be curbed."

Government success at ending the Fifties 55 pea-soupers has led to complacency at the growing danger of toxic vehicle fumes which make up ozone, she claims.

FoE is concerned that toxic ozone levels in Britain now regularly exceed World Health 60 Organisation safety guidelines.

VOCABULARY 1
Prepositions

Put a preposition in each of the numbered spaces.

Recently, the authorities (**1**) _____ Athens were forced (**2**) _____ ban all cars (**3**) _____ the city centre (**4**) _____ one day because (**5**) _____ the levels of air pollution.

Meanwhile, (**6**) _____ California, a law has been passed saying that no car manufacturer will be allowed (**7**) _____ sell cars (**8**) _____ the state after 1998, unless (**9**) _____ least two percent (**10**) _____ its sales are in Zero Emission Vehicles (ZEVs). This percentage will rise (**11**) _____ ten percent (**12**) _____ subsequent years.

The only true ZEVs are electrically-powered cars that run (**13**) _____ batteries and most car manufacturers are now working (**14**) _____ electric models.

Other US states have followed California's example which suggests that the electric car may be the car (**15**) _____ the future.

WRITING 1
Discursive writing

■ **1** Choose one of these writing tasks.

1 What can be done to solve the problems of smog in large cities?

2 What are the advantages and disadvantages of wearing smog masks?

3 The only solution to the problem of urban smog is to limit the use of cars. Do you agree?

Find a partner who has chosen the same topic, and make a list of the main points you will want to mention.

■ **2** Compare your list with another pair in the class who have chosen the same title.

■ **3** You are now ready to write your composition (120–180 words).

GRAMMAR 1
Reported speech: Statements

■ **1** In the pictures below decide which person is using each of the tenses in this list. Some people use more than one tense. What happens to each of these tenses in reported speech?

present simple	past simple
present continuous	past continuous
present perfect	
present perfect continuous	
'going to' future	

■ **2** Rewrite each of the sentences below, using reported speech, to show what each of the people in the pictures said.

ALICE: I support Friends of the Earth and other environmental movements.

_____

_____

_____

ANDREW: I have been living in Athens for ten years and I've noticed the pollution getting worse.

_____

_____

_____

NORMAN: I was living in London during the famous smogs of the nineteen fifties.

_____

_____

_____

JANE: I was visiting Los Angeles last year and was very surprised by levels of atmospheric pollution there.

_____

_____

_____

ALAN: I'm going to buy a car that uses unleaded petrol next time.

_____
_____
_____
_____
_____

LIZ: I'm organising a campaign in favour of banning cars from our city centre.

_____
_____
_____
_____
_____

SALLY: I have always supported the idea of using public transport instead of private cars.

_____
_____
_____
_____
_____
_____

3 Look at these reported statements about other things that each of the people in the pictures said. Try to decide what their actual words were.

Example:
Alice said that she had raised a lot of money for environmental charities since 1990.

Alice said: 'I've raised a lot of money for environmental charities since 1990.'

1 Andrew said that there were going to be further restrictions on traffic in Athens.
Andrew said: '_____

2 Norman said that London was much cleaner than it had been in 1960.
Norman said: '_____

3 Jane said that underground railways were being built in California.
Jane said: '_____

4 Alan said he had been trying to use his car less.
Alan said: '_____

5 Liz said that she had been using the bus every day for ten years.
Liz said: '_____

6 Sally said she never used her car unless it was really necessary.
Sally said: '_____

LISTENING 2

Note-taking

1 Listen to Part One and decide which of the speakers uses each of these modal verbs.

	Lidia	Les
1 can		
2 may		
3 must		
4 will		

1 What happens to these verbs in reported speech?

2 Listen again and make a note of the main point each speaker makes.
Lidia: _____
Les: _____

3 Now write a sentence that summarises that main point in reported speech (use the modal verbs above).
Lidia said _____
Les said _____

2 Listen to Part Two and compare your sentences with the interviewer's.

3 Now listen to Part Three and decide which speaker uses each of these modal verbs.

	Gordon	Mary
1 should		
2 would		
3 could		
4 might		
5 ought to		

1 What happens to these verbs in reported speech?

2 Listen again and make a note of the main point each speaker makes.

Gordon: _____

_____

Mary: _____

_____

3 Now write a sentence in reported speech summarising each main point using the verbs above.

Gordon: _____

_____

Mary: _____

_____

4 Compare your sentences with your partner's.

GRAMMAR 2
Reported speech: Time changes

1 What other words change in reported speech?

Example:
'I had a lovely surprise yesterday' said Karen.

Karen said she had had a lovely surprise | the previous day.
| the day before.

2 Match the direct speech word or phrase on the left with its reported speech equivalent on the right.

1	yesterday	**a**	then
2	tomorrow night	**b**	three years previously
3	tonight	**c**	the previous day
4	here	**d**	that
5	now	**e**	the following week
6	this	**f**	the night before
7	next week	**g**	that night
8	these	**h**	there
9	last night	**i**	those
10	three years ago	**j**	the following night

LISTENING 3
Selecting an answer

Talk to your partner.

1 What does recycling mean?
What materials are recycled?
What other things could be recycled?
What are the advantages and disadvantages of recycling?

2 Label the car on the next page using the words in the box.

bonnet   boot
bumper   aerial
windscreen   dashboard
sunroof   headlights
number plate
rear-view mirror
windscreen wiper

3 Listen and decide whether these statements are true or false.

1 The metal part of a car is already recyclable.

2 25% of a car is not made of metal.

3 Some new cars are made entirely of plastic.

4 Car bumpers usually get replaced after an accident.

5 The local garage makes new bumpers from the damaged plastic.

6 New plastic is put onto the old bumpers.

7 Most of the plastic from damaged bumpers is not used for new bumpers.

8 Drivers whose bumpers are recycled get new bumpers free.

9 Some recyclable car parts are very valuable.

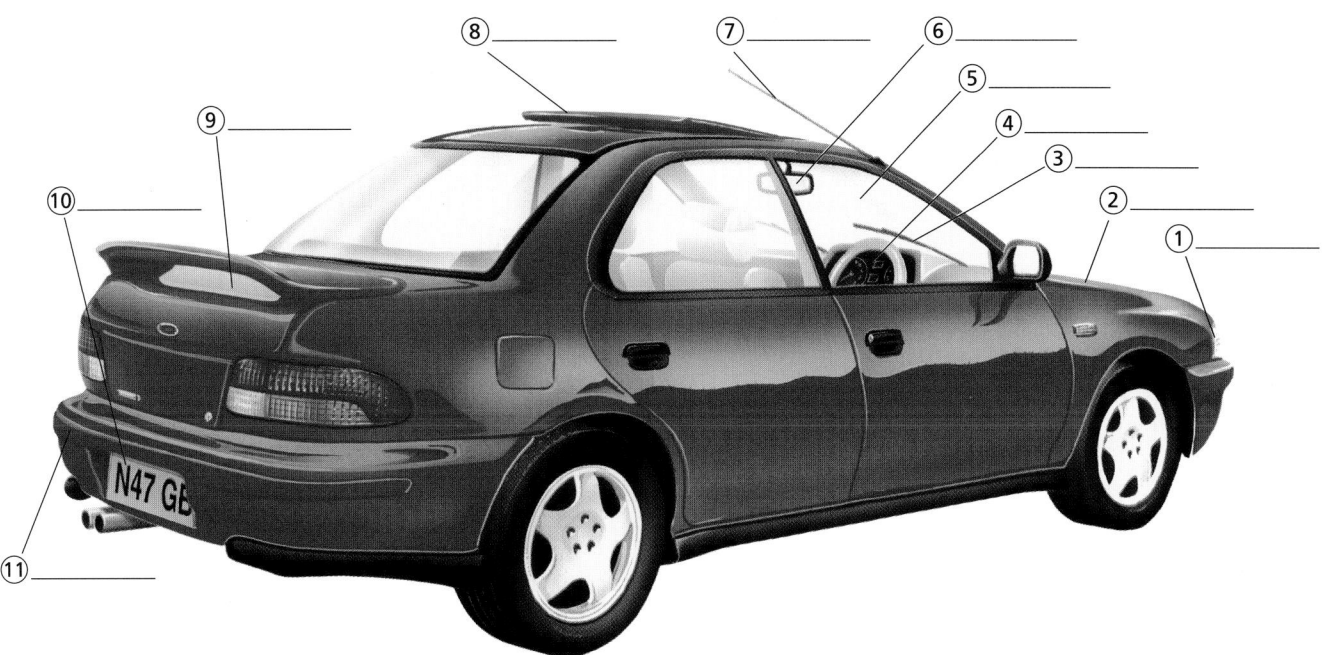

GRAMMAR 3
Reported questions

1 What questions does Nick ask Jenny? Listen again and make a note of his questions.

2 How do we put questions into reported speech? Write in reported speech the five questions Nick asked Jenny.

Which one is different? Why is it different?

3 Complete the second sentence so that it has a similar meaning to the first sentence. Use the word given and other words to complete each sentence. You must use between two and five words. Do not change the word given.

1 'What time is it, Frances?' said Tim.
asked
Tim _____ it was.

2 'Are you coming to the party tonight, Joanna?' said Adam.
if
Adam asked Joanna _____ to the party that night.

3 'Can I borrow your pen please, Sam?' said Jill.
if
Jill asked Sam _____ pen.

4 'Do you know what's on at the cinema, James?' said Pam.
knew
Pam asked James if _____ on at the cinema.

5 'Have you finished your homework yet Robin?' said Sandra.
whether
Sandra asked Robin _____ homework yet.

6 Julia asked Phil if he would feed her cat while she was on holiday.
you
Julia said: _____ while I'm on holiday?'

7 Sara asked me to get her some stamps from the post office.
me
Sara said: _____ some stamps from the post office, please?'

8 Karl asked me what time the meeting would end.
will
Karl said: _____ end?'

9 Elena asked the waitress for another knife.
could
Elena said: _____ , please?'

10 Luke asked Valerie if she had got a car.
you
Luke said: _____ a car, Valerie?'

4 In reported questions when can we use

1 *if / whether?*

2 an infinitive (eg *to go*)?

3 a question word (eg *when*)?

Look again at **1–5** in exercise 3. Can they be rewritten using alternative forms?

READING 2

Grammar in context

Talk to your partner.

1 What is happening to the tropical rainforests? Why is this a problem? What can be done?

2 Match the words on the left with the definitions on the right. Use your dictionary if necessary.

1	timber	**a**	plants grown for food
2	species	**b**	wood used for making things
3	crops	**c**	something you buy
4	decade	**d**	a family of plants or animals
5	currently	**e**	a period of ten years
6	a purchase	**f**	at the moment

3 Read the article and circle:

a 3 words connected with water.

b 2 types of shop.

c 3 illnesses.

d 3 things made from wood.

e 3 industries.

f 3 ways in which people have been killed.

Why we must fight the destruction

When rainforests are cleared and burned millions of tonnes of carbon dioxide are released into the atmosphere affecting climatic conditions and threatening us all with severe flooding, drought and crop failure.

The rainforests contain at least half of the Earth's species. At the current rate of devastation an estimated 50 species worldwide become extinct every day.

One in four purchases from your chemist is derived from the rainforests. Scientists are currently caught in a race against time to find rainforest treatments for cancer, AIDS and heart disease — before they are lost forever.

Tribal people in the rainforests have been shot, poisoned and infected with disease to which they have no resistance — to make room for logging, mining and dams.

If this destruction continues only nine of the 33 countries currently exporting rainforest timber will have any left by the end of the decade.

Almost everyone will have part of the rainforests in their home, as DIY stores still supply and the construction industry still uses tropical hardwoods for doors, window frames and even toilet seats.

What Friends of the Earth has done

Friends of the Earth's Tropical Rainforest Campaign has been fighting to save the rainforests for ten years. In that time, we've achieved a great deal.

◆ We've forced the British Government – and even timber trade organisations themselves – to acknowledge just how short-sighted the devastation is.

◆ We have persuaded major international companies to stop industrial activities that harm the rainforests.

◆ And by mobilising consumer pressure, we have helped reduce imports of tropical timber into the UK by nearly a third.

Please help us save the tropical rainforests now, before it's too late. There's still a lot more to do. With your help, we can build on our success.

4 Read again and underline the verbs which are in the passive.

Why has the passive been used in each case?

5 Using the passive, write three sentences describing things that Friends of the Earth has achieved.

_____

_____

_____

_____

Expressing and justifying opinions

Talk to your partner.

1 You have decided to enter this competition which you have seen in a magazine.

Which of these photographs would make a good poster for Friends of the Earth to use in your country?

Win Fantastic Prizes in our Great Competition!

All you have to do is select a picture which you think can be used to encourage people to give money and help save the rainforests in all countries where they are threatened with destruction.

It's easy, first choose which you think is the best picture, then write and tell us why you made your choice.
Write 120 – 180 words.

2 With your partner decide the good points and bad points of each picture as a way of encouraging people to give money to help the rainforests.

3 Make notes about the good and bad points of each picture.

WRITING 1
Reports

Use your notes to write your report (approximately 120–180 words). Start the paragraphs of your report in this way:

I would choose picture number _____ because

_____

_____

_____

_____

My second choice would be

_____

_____

_____

_____

I certainly would not choose

_____

_____

_____

_____

GRAMMAR 4
Impersonal passive

1 Look at these sentences. In what situation would the second sentence be more appropriate?

1 *Friends of the Earth say that fifty species become extinct every day.*

2 *It is said that fifty species become extinct every day.*

2 Look at the sentences in the box.

> His wife is believed to be from the USA.
> She is understood to be very lonely.
> He is reported to be living in Florida.
> It is said that he cooks very well.
> It is thought that a cure for cancer may be found.

1 How certain are we about the information?

2 What is the source of the information?

3 What are the advantages of using this type of phrase?

3 Complete the second sentence so that it has a similar meaning to the first sentence. Use the word given and other words to complete each sentence. You must use between two and five words. Do not change the word given.

1 People say that Lorna has many friends in London.
is
Lorna _____
many friends in London.

2 People think that he is living abroad.
be
He _____
living abroad.

3 Graham is said to be very generous.
that
Everyone _____
very generous.

4 The world is believed to be getting warmer.
that
People _____
getting warmer.

5 Britt is understood to be a supporter of Friends of the Earth.
understand
I _____
a supporter of Friends of the Earth.

LISTENING 4
Multiple choice

1 Talk to your partner.

Why are so many animal species in danger of extinction? What can be done to help them?

When did dinosaurs live?
Why did they become extinct?

2 You will hear part of a radio programme about the extinction of the dinosaurs. For each of the questions 1–4 choose the best answer **A**, **B** or **C**.

1 The extinction of the dinosaurs

    A was caused by disease.
    B happened very quickly.   ☐ 1
    C followed a volcanic eruption.

2 Where has iridium been found?

    A In areas near to volcanos.
    B In rocks about 65 million years old.   ☐ 2
    C In rocks formed under water.

3 Why did the animals die?

    A They were covered in dust.
    B There was nothing to eat.   ☐ 3
    C They could not see the sun.

4 Why is the crater difficult to find?

    A There may be more than one.
    B It has been destroyed by the sea.   ☐ 4
    C It is buried under more recent rock.

3 Read the text below and think of the word which best fits each space. Use only one word in each space. There is an example at the beginning (**0**).

The End of the Dinosaurs

About 66 million years (**0**) ___*ago*___ , seventy percent of all living creatures including the dinosaurs are (**1**) _____ to have disappeared (**2**) _____ the surface of the Earth.

Scientists believe that this may (**3**) _____ been caused by a natural disaster on a very large scale. One possible explanation is (**4**) _____ the earth was (**5**) _____ by an enormous asteroid about six miles in diameter as it travelled through space.

Side effects of this disaster could have been the destruction of (**6**) _____ ozone layer, acid rain, global warming and the pollution of the atmosphere (**7**) _____ dust which blocked out the sun.

Either one or a combination of these effects could have (**8**) _____ to the disappearance of the various species.

Scientists are (**9**) _____ searching for the site of the crater (**10**) _____ the asteroid must have (**11**) _____ . This may be buried (**12**) _____ more recent rocks, or be lost somewhere on the seabed. Wherever (**13**) _____ is, it seems probable that the dinosaurs died out (**14**) _____ a result of an environmental disaster lasting only a (**15**) _____ years.

Gapped text

1 Talk to your partner. Look at the list of natural disasters in the box and discuss the causes and results of each of them. What can we do to protect ourselves from events like this?

volcanic eruptions	drought	famine
earthquakes	floods	hurricanes

2 You are going to read a newspaper article about a natural disaster. Choose from the sentences **A–I** the one which fits each gap **1–7**. There is one extra sentence which you do not need to use. There is an example at the beginning (**0**).

A This in turn led to an explosion of violence which reduced the food supplies still further.

B This gave them the false confidence that they could survive the much longer one which destroyed them.

C But the colonists refused to change their social system.

D History is not man-made, it is the planet itself which shapes our destiny.

E But none of this would have produced a revolution if the country had not been faced with famine.

F Instead of improving their agriculture, their rulers fought endless wars to win more land.

G This led to a massive lowering of temperature for several years.

H An intelligent civilisation will be safe from any but the most severe climatic change.

I This in turn, produced two decades of war and, indirectly, two centuries of conflict in Europe.

3 Find words or phrases which mean:

someone who studies volcanoes (line 3)
for a short time (11)
financially ruined (13)
for the reason that (22)
made angry (28)
very heavy rain (33)
lived through a difficult period (54)

Revolution that erupted from two volcanoes

1 CAN A VOLCANIC eruption on the other side of the world affect politics? According to two French vulcanologists the answer is yes. Despite a distance of thousands of kilometres and a gap of six
5 years, they say that in 1783 eruptions of a volcano in central Japan and another in southern Iceland, helped set off the French Revolution. **0 I**

Like the eruption of Mount Pinatubo in the Philippines in 1991, these eruptions blew large
10 amounts of sulphurous ash into the atmosphere, partly blocking the sun's rays and temporarily cooling the climate.

France in 1789 was already bankrupt because of a long war in America. The government was threatened
15 by a plot to organise riots financed by an ambitious aristocrat who wanted to become king. **1** The result of the eruptions was several years of cold, wet weather in Europe. Two violent storms in 1788 and 1789 destroyed the harvest in many parts of the
20 country, and the resulting shortage of corn was made worse by the Finance Minister's refusal to import corn from abroad on the grounds that the state could not afford it.

2 When the people of France saw wagons full of
25 corn go through their village streets they said, 'There is plenty of corn, but not for us: it's for the king, the aristocrats, the rich who have plenty to eat while we

4 Mark the stressed syllable on these words from the text.

eruption	threatened	civilisation
opposite	revolution	organise
Scandinavian	intended	atmosphere
ambitious	aristocratic	collapsed
government	Indonesia	Eskimo
exceptionally		

go hungry.' And then the maddened people would throw the sacks of corn into the nearest river.

30 Another volcanic eruption – in Indonesia in April 1815 – may have helped cause Napoleon's defeat at the battle of Waterloo. **3**☐ 1816 was called the 'year without a summer'. Torrential rains marked the beginning of the Waterloo campaign, creating
35 deep mud which for many hours prevented Napoleon from moving his big guns.

The French revolution is one of many examples where a change of climate was the final blow to an already threatened society.
40 The Little Ice Age, which started about AD 1400, threatened the Scandinavian colony in Greenland. **4**☐

They might have survived if, instead of sticking to their aristocratic society, they had moved from
45 farming to hunting, like the Eskimos who replaced them.
At about the same period the great civilisation of the Mayas in Yucatan faced ever worsening droughts. **5**☐ This had the opposite effect to that intended,
50 since forcing people into the army meant they had to leave their land.

The Bronze Age empire of Mesopotamia also collapsed from drought about 3000 years ago. People successfully survived two fairly short periods
55 of drought. **6**☐

What lessons can be drawn for the future? **7**☐ The exceptionally violent eruption of Krakatoa in 1883, for example, caused no social disasters. Only societies which behave stupidly will fail when nature
60 turns bad.

🔊 LISTENING 5

Short extracts

1 You will hear eight short dialogues. For questions 1–8, decide which of the choices, **A**, **B** or **C** best summarises what is said.

1 **A** He warned me not to go near the dog.
   B He advised me not to go near the dog.
   C He persuaded me that I shouldn't go near the dog.

2 **A** He recommended the restaurant to me.
   B He persuaded me to go to the restaurant.
   C He invited me to go to the restaurant.

3 **A** He encouraged me to go in for the competition.
   B He reminded me to go in for the competition.
   C He told me to go in for the competition.

4 **A** He persuaded me to work harder.
   B He told me to work harder.
   C He advised me to work harder.

5 **A** He warned us to take our passports.
   B He reminded us to take our passports.
   C He advised us to take our passports.

6 **A** He offered her a cup of coffee.
   B She persuaded me to have a cup of coffee.
   C She reminded me to have a cup of coffee.

7 **A** He admitted stealing the money.
   B He denied stealing the money.
   C He apologised for stealing the money.

8 **A** He promised to buy her a present.
   B He offered to buy her a present.
   C He refused to buy her a present.

2 What is the difference in meaning between these verbs?

   A persuade/encourage
   B advise/warn

3 Look again at the verbs used above in questions 1–8 and decide if they are type **A**, **B** or **C**, or a different type.

type A	verb + person + infinitive with 'to'
example:	He asked me to go to the cinema.
type B	verb + infinitive with 'to'
example:	She agreed to type the report.
type C	verb + '-ing'
example:	He regretted dropping the vase.

READING 4
Multiple choice

1 Talk to your partner.

What environmental problems can be caused by fast-food restaurants?

What solutions would you suggest to these problems? Think about:

- position of litter bins
- making new laws
- redesigning the restaurants
- changing the packaging
- educating the public
- training the staff

2 Read the article quickly and underline these things:

1 four ways of serving chips
2 where the new packaging is made
3 what it is made from
4 where it has been tried in the UK
5 what needs to be changed for the British market

3 Now read more carefully and answer these questions.

1 Why do fish and chips cause environmental pollution?

   A People buy more than they can eat.
   B People prefer to use plastic plates.
   C People are careless with the wrapping.
   D The plates and wrapping are not used again.

2 How will the new product solve the problem?

   A It can be used again.
   B It is a different shape.
   C People can eat it.
   D It lasts longer than paper.

3 What is the new product made of?

   A Paper that tastes of salt.
   B Things usually eaten with chips.
   C Mostly natural ingredients.
   D It is a secret.

4 Chips served in the new product

   A will be larger than those served abroad.
   B will taste better than those served in plastic.
   C will cost more than those served in paper.
   D will be easier to eat than other chips.

The chips are down for fast-food wrappers

1 That international symbol of British cuisine – fish and chips wrapped in paper – may never be the same again. The industry associated with the national delicacy is facing increasing pressure to reduce the environmental pollution
5 caused by its discarded packaging.

An estimated 3.6 billion containers for take-away British chips and their continental cousins, French fries and pomfrites, are thrown away each year. Apart from conventional paper wrapping, it is estimated that almost
10 one billion plastic and cardboard plates are dumped each year in Britain alone after fish and chip lovers have had their fill.

Later this month, a new product will be launched which, its manufacturers claim, will help reduce the 22,000 tons of
15 European paper waste associated with the food. The new product, an edible chip cone, is biodegradable and, say its makers, even tastes like a chip. Fast food shops will now be able to serve portions in the new cone, which can be eaten itself after its contents have been consumed, therefore
20 leaving no litter.

The Dutch manufacturers , Viko, point out that if people prefer not to eat the product they can throw it in a litter bin where it will decompose naturally within a few days.

The new cone — at approximately 10 inches high, the
25 right size for a medium portion of chips — is made from powdered potato, wheat flour, vegetable oil and salt. A

secret coating on the inside makes it impervious to vinegar and sauces.

Bruce Kirk of Belfast was the first-known British trade user
30 of the cone and claims that the product "will catch on". But, he points out, the packaging is more expensive than the conventional wrapping and the consumer may have to foot the bill for the extra cost.

The cones, already launched successfully in Holland and
35 Germany, are now being stock-piled in their millions for their British launch.

Many local authorities on the Continent already make the use of biodegradable take-away food packaging a prerequisite for granting food and drink licences to outside
40 events such as exhibitions and pop concerts.

Elaine Gilligan of Friends of the Earth welcomed the product in principle, but pointed out that even "environmentally friendly products cause pollution when they are made".
45 At Birmingham's Jolly Fryer customers gave the cone a mixed reception. Some claimed it tasted like "salted paper", while others said that they "wouldn't eat it" but their "dog might". Some said the product was "a good idea" and that they "would certainly eat it to save the environment".
50 The makers are already planning to re-examine the size of the cone for the British market, where the custom is for larger portions than those demanded by continental chip lovers.

Once they've been adapted to the larger British appetite, the future of the humble, edible chip looks promising –
55 especially after expected changes in the law make fast food traders responsible for litter caused by the products they sell.

■4 Find words in the article that mean:

1 food speciality (line 1)

2 thrown away (line 5)

3 traditional (line 9)

4 thrown away (line 10)

5 introduced (line 13)

6 which you can eat (line 16)

7 it decomposes naturally (line 16)

8 quantity of food (line 18)

9 eaten (line 19)

10 waste paper (line 20)

11 liquids cannot pass through it (line 27)

12 a condition (line 39)

13 look again (line 50)

14 changed (line 53)

■5 Mark the stressed syllable on these words from the passage and practise saying them with your partner.

international	estimated	successfully
associated	containers	exhibitions
environmental	conventional	reception
pollution	manufacturers	appetite
packaging	approximately	expected

▭ LISTENING 6 ▬▬▬▬▬▬▬▬▬▬▬▬

Selecting an answer

You will hear a member of a college ecology society talking at a student meeting.

1 Listen and tick (✓) to show which of the things on the list she proposes.

- Stop using photocopied handouts
- Recycling waste paper
- Using plastic cups and plates
- Better facilities for cyclists
- Using paper bags instead of plastic
- Not using products tested on animals
- Changing cleaning materials
- Recycling used batteries
- Changing the central heating system
- Providing more vegetarian menus

2 Here is a report of the meeting which appeared in the college magazine. Unfortunately, it is not very accurate because the reporter was late for the meeting and missed the talk. He got the story from a friend who was there.

> At last week's meeting, Tanya Butler from the college ecology society made some dramatic proposals about how we should make the college more environmentally-friendly.
>
> Ms Butler said that most of the handouts prepared by the teachers and photo-copied for students were rubbish. She reported that most of them got thrown away and should be used to make recycled paper.
>
> Ms Butler also claimed that a lot of paper was being wasted in the college office because the secretaries did not type on both sides of the paper. She suggested that they type on the back of old student work-sheets instead!
>
> Ms Butler went on to propose that the college cafeteria should serve only vegetarian meals and that students should wash up the plastic plates and cups instead of throwing them away!
>
> These are just some of Ms Butler's crazy ideas. While we all agree that the environment is an important issue, shouldn't the ecology society be putting forward more practical ideas than this?

Listen to the talk again, and underline any incorrect information in the article.

WRITING 2 ▬▬▬▬▬▬▬▬▬▬▬▬▬

Letters

You decide to write to the magazine to complain about the article, to correct the information and to ask for an apology.

■1 Look at the incorrect information in the article and decide what Tanya really said. You may need to listen to the talk again to do this.

■2 What type of language do you need to use in the letter?

1 Write a plan of the letter.

2 Compare plans with your partner.

3 Write the letter from the plan. Remember to use reported speech when necessary.

GRAMMAR 5

It's time

1 Look at these sentences from the listening text:

It's high time a range of vegetarian dishes was on offer.
It's time we had a balance of meat and vegetarian dishes.

1 What time is referred to?
2 Which grammatical form is used?

2 Compare these two sentences. What is the difference in meaning?

It's (high) time we went.
It's time to go.

3 Complete the second sentence so that it has a similar meaning to the first sentence. Use the word given and other words to complete each sentence. You must use between two and five words. Do not change the word given.

1 This room hasn't been cleaned for ages.
time
It's _____
cleaned.

2 The college has not been redecorated for years. It really needs doing.
time
It's _____
redecorated.

3 I haven't had anything to eat all day. I'm very hungry.
had
It's time _____
to eat.

4 It's late, I should have left for home an hour ago.
high
It's _____
for home.

5 My car's filthy, I really should have it cleaned.
time
It's _____
my car cleaned.

6 It's months since James had his hair cut.
time
It's _____
cut.

7 Rosemary hasn't been on holiday for years.
high
It's _____
on holiday.

READING 5

Reading for main points and specific information

1 Talk to your partner.

Do people in your country wear animal furs?
What are the arguments for and against wearing fur?
What are the alternatives?
Which animals are fur coats made from? Use a dictionary to find their names in English.

2 Look at the article quickly and find the answers to these questions:

1 What is Lynx?

2 Who are these people:
- Carol McKenna
- Yasmin Le Bon
- Mike Allen
- Rifat Ozbek

3 What do these numbers refer to?
5000   2   6   millions

Anti fur group to bury 5000 coats

1 **Campaigners are to bury thousands of fur coats in a ceremony to mark the end of the fur trade in Britain.**

2 Anti-fur group Lynx declared an "amnesty" two years ago, encouraging women to hand over their coats.

3 The campaigners have now collected 5000 – made from the fur of mink, leopard, squirrel and wolf, Carol McKenna, Lynx campaign director, said they will all be buried at an animal sanctuary next month.

4 "Every year millions of the world's most beautiful wild animals are electrocuted, gassed, strangled and trapped just for fur," she said.

5 "Thousands of people have taken advantage of Lynx's fur amnesty. In shock and horror they gave their coats to Lynx asking for them to be destroyed." The campaign against fur for fashion has grown in the last few years with many celebrities giving their support.

6 Models like Yasmin Le Bon and Paula Hamilton, fashion designers like Katherine Hamnett and Rifat Ozbek and actors including Sir John Gielgud have all refused to wear or use furs.

7 Lynx claims its campaign has led to the closure of six out of ten of fur retail outlets in Britain. Harrods closed its fur department some time ago, saying it was no longer profitable.

8 Mike Allen of the Fur Education Council representing fur traders, also blamed a series of warm winters for a drop-off in demand.

9 "When we have cold weather we sell more fur coats. There is still a good market in North America, Germany, Italy and Spain. Unfortunately, Lynx has intimidated British women into being self-conscious about wearing fur coats."

3 Now read more carefully and find words that mean:

1 represent (paragraph 1)
2 to give (2)
3 a safe place (3)
4 famous people (5)
5 shops (7)
6 economically healthy (7)
7 reduction (8)
8 feeling uncomfortable (9)

4 What has caused fur coats to become less popular:

1 according to Lynx?

_____

2 according to Mike Allen?

_____

3 What has been the result?

_____

SPEAKING 4

Expressing opinions

1 Choose three of the ideas below to discuss with your partner:

1 Animal rights campaigners are crazy extremists.

2 It's time factory farming was banned.

3 We should close zoos and return the animals to their natural environment.

4 The world would be a better place if everyone was a vegetarian.

5 It's time to give up the stresses of modern life and go back to growing our own food.

6 If we don't do more to protect the environment, many species will soon be as dead as the dinosaurs.

2 Think for a few minutes and note down a few ideas on the topics.

3 Discuss each one for three minutes without stopping or changing the subject.

LISTENING 7

Multiple matching

You will hear five different people talking about a proposed funfair development on the beach in the seaside town of Blackstone. For questions **1–5**, choose from the list **A–F** the person who is expressing these views about the project. There is one extra letter which you do not need to use.

A council officer
B teacher
C conservationist
D shopkeeper
E senior citizen
F developer

Speaker 1	
Speaker 2	
Speaker 3	
Speaker 4	
Speaker 5	

PRONUNCIATION

Shifting stress

1 Listen to these phrases and mark the stressed syllable on each word in bold type.

John is unable to **control** that dog.

I can't **permit** you to enter.

It was a strange **object.**

The footballer got a free **transfer.**

Vegetable oil is one of our main **exports.**

I shall now **present** the winner with this silver cup.

2 Check with your partner. Is each of the words a noun or a verb?

3 Now listen to these phrases and mark the stressed syllable on each word in bold type.

I can't work the **controls** on this video.

I haven't got a **permit** to enter the building.

I **object** to the way he spoke to me.

I would like to **transfer** some money out of my bank account.

This country **exports** a lot of vegetable oil.

I got lots of **presents** for my birthday.

4 Check with your partner. Is each of these words a verb or a noun? Practise saying the words with the stress on a different syllable.

5 Mark the stress on the appropriate syllable of the words below in bold type.

It's a new world **record.**

I'd like to **record** that song.

I'd like to **contrast** the two photos.

There's quite a **contrast** between them.

I'd like to **protest** about this problem.

I'd like to make a formal **protest.**

There's been an **increase** in crime.

Crime has **increased** in recent years.

The police **suspect** him of burgling the house.

The police have arrested a **suspect.**

6 Check with your partner. Practise reading out the phrases.

1 Read the text below and decide which word **A**, **B**, **C** or **D** best fits each space. There is an example at the beginning (**0**).

The Car of the Future

A French company has recently published (**0**) _plans_ for a revolutionary car of the future which will (**1**) _____ the nature of inner-city transport. The car of the future will (**2**) _____ the good points of private and public transport, giving users the advantages of a private car, (**3**) _____ the cost of purchase or (**4**) _____ .

The car will be (**5**) _____ by users on a pay-as-you-go basis. Drivers will simply (**6**) _____ up the a car at a special station, (**7**) _____ to a taxi-rank, and leave it at another station, (**8**) _____ for their destination. Here it will be cleaned ready for the next user.

The electronically-powered car will be about half the length of (**9**) _____ mini cars and will improve traffic flow and (**10**) _____ pollution in crowded cities. At present, most cars in towns (**11**) _____ only one person who spends most of his or her time looking for a parking (**12**) _____ .

A 'magic key' personal remote control opens the car and contains the (**13**) _____ information to enable the car user's (**14**) _____ to be prepared. In the car the magic key also works to programme the mobile phone, radio and heating (**15**) _____ to the driver's preference.

0	**A** plans	**B** programmes	**C** projects	**D** plots
1	**A** turn	**B** change	**C** switch	**D** exchange
2	**A** conduct	**B** concern	**C** connect	**D** combine
3	**A** without	**B** lacking	**C** short	**D** subtracting
4	**A** maintenance	**B** conservation	**C** preservation	**D** protection
5	**A** paid	**B** let	**C** hired	**D** lent
6	**A** take	**B** pick	**C** lift	**D** put
7	**A** just	**B** like	**C** same	**D** similar
8	**A** convenient	**B** useful	**C** nearby	**D** close
9	**A** nowadays	**B** current	**C** already	**D** actual
10	**A** slice	**B** smash	**C** chop	**D** cut
11	**A** bring	**B** carry	**C** fetch	**D** drive
12	**A** stop	**B** place	**C** point	**D** site
13	**A** necessary	**B** needed	**C** needful	**D** necessity
14	**A** receipt	**B** bill	**C** charge	**D** cheque
15	**A** service	**B** system	**C** section	**D** structure

2 Complete the second sentence so that it has a similar meaning to the first sentence. Use the word given and other words to complete each sentence. You must use between two and five words. Do not change the word given.

1 The weather was so nice they decided to eat outdoors.
such
It was _____
that they decided to eat outdoors.

2 Although he had a bad cold he went to work
spite
He went to work _____
a bad cold.

3 What a pity you didn't come to my party.
wish
I _____ to my
party.

4 I wish I'd finished my homework at the week-end.
regret
I _____ my
homework at the weekend.

5 Simon ate too much lunch and felt sick.
have
If Simon hadn't eaten too much lunch,
_____ sick.

6 An electrical fault caused the train crash.
by
The train crash _____
an electrical fault.

7 'You should go to the dentist's for a check up, Lorna,' said Martin.
advised
Martin _____
the dentist's for a check up.

8 'Don't forget to take your packed lunches, children,' said the teacher.
reminded
The teacher _____
to take their packed lunches.

9 'Don't touch that dog, it's dangerous,' Uncle Tim said to me.
not
Uncle Tim _____
that dog because it was dangerous.

10 'I went to a disco last night,' Les said.
had
Les said _____
disco the previous night.

3 Read the text below. Use the word given in capitals at the end of each line to form a word that fits in the space in the same line. There is an example at the beginning (**0**).

Lucky Escape

Susan Hill was (**0**) ___unaware___ as she carried her handbag around **AWARE**
for more than two months that it contained a bomb (**1**) _____ **HIDE**
there before she bought the bag.
The bomb was (**2**) _____ planted by animal rights **PROBABLE**
(**3**) _____ in August when there were several minor **TERROR**
(**4**) _____ in local shops caused by fire bombs placed in **EXPLODE**
leather bags. Susan (**5**) _____ the bag in October and **BUY**
used it (**6**) _____ for two months. She only found the **REGULAR**
bomb when she was (**7**) _____ her bag after a Christmas **PACK**
shopping trip. She thought she had (**8**) _____ one of the **LOSE**
gifts she had bought and after (**9**) _____ the side pocket **ZIP**
for the first time, she (**10**) _____ the cassette-sized **COVER**
device inside. The police said that if it had gone off it could have
caused a lot of damage and Susan could have been seriously
injured.

Finishing touches

LISTENING 1

Note-taking

1 Listen to two people talking about themselves and complete the information in the grid.

	Paul	Catherine	You
Place of birth:			
Place of residence:			
Occupation:			
Hobby/Favourite subject:			
Ambition:			
Current project:			
Intention:			

2 Listen again and decide which of the tenses in the box Paul and Catherine use when talking about each piece of information.

past simple	present continuous
present perfect continuous	present perfect simple
verb + infinitive	past passive
present simple	

3 Fill in the column for yourself and then make a note of which tense you will use to give each piece of information.

SPEAKING 1

Giving personal information

1 Tell your partner your personal information. When you listen to your partner, check that the tenses are correct.

Ask your partner one or two questions to get some more detailed information.

2 Find a new partner and start again.

3 Write a paragraph about yourself including a few more facts. Check the tenses with your partner.

I was born in _____

_____

_____

_____

_____

_____

_____

Multiple matching

1 Talk to your partner.
- What is your star sign?
- Do you read your horoscope?
- What kind of information do horoscopes usually contain?
- Why are horoscopes so popular?

2 You are going to read some horoscopes. For questions 1–16, write the name of the correct star sign. Some of the star signs may be chosen more than once. There are two examples at the beginning (**0**) and (**00**).

Which star sign this month:

promises good luck with money (**0**) <u>Virgo</u> (**00**) <u>Aries</u>

advises people to spend time and money on themselves
(**1**) _____ (**2**) _____

promises people a meeting with someone who will change the way they think
(**3**) _____ (**4**) _____

advises people to delay making a decision
(**5**) _____

advises people to keep physically active
(**6**) _____

warns people that they will feel nervous at first
(**7**) _____

advises people to visit another country
(**8**) _____

advises people to change the way they look
(**9**) _____

warns people of difficulties with family or friends
(**10**) _____ (**11**) _____

warns people to be careful with money
(**12**) _____ (**13**) _____

advises people to accept more responsibility
(**14**) _____

encourages people to be strong with others
(**15**) _____

tells people to be honest with themselves
(**16**) _____

Horoscopes

Aries
(March 21 – April 19)

You must find some challenge or battle to engage your energies. You need a fight and if you haven't got many demands on your physical energy, you're likely to feel irritable and aggressive. Nevertheless, you're in a lucky streak financially, and this could bring you the means to satisfy a few personal needs as well as a chance to have a great time with your large circle of friends.

Taurus
(April 20 – May 20)

What a lovely month! Everything's looking bright and beautiful and full of opportunities. Search them out, take them no matter how unusual and weird they seem. It's time to break some of your personal rules and fight against that desire for security, and to trust fate to bring some really exciting possibilities within your reach. You're certainly going to have a great time as long as you don't overspend!

Gemini
(May 21 – June 21)

After a period of strange worries and unusual tension, where what might happen seems more threatening than what is happening, life should begin to settle down a bit and you'll feel your typical self confidence again. Decide nothing until after the end of the month. You'll then be clearer about your situation and more in tune with what you really want to do.

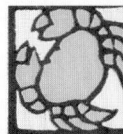

Cancer
(June 22 – July 22)

An active life and increased contact with friends makes this a wonderful sort of month. Do different things with different friends, get yourself out and about to widen your circle and meet new people. But keep a few pounds in reserve for the end of the month when even more exciting opportunities may present themselves.

Leo
(July 23 – August 22)

Unless you take care the next few weeks could be a bit trying and difficult. Those closest to you may seem hard to get along with, but this is probably your fault. Try and change your attitude a bit so that you don't get depressed. Opportunities to be responsible for others should not be avoided. Remember that you have definite creative gifts which could bring you status, recognition and popularity now.

Virgo
(August 23 – September 23)

Good fortune is starting to hammer on your door. Look at your life and see where the opportunities for change and growth are and then organise yourself to take full advantage of them. You can gain financially and personally, you can travel, learn and experience other ways of being and living. Don't let problems of study or work hold you back; plan a trip abroad to a place where you've never been before.

Libra
(September 24 – October 23)

There is a risk that problems could break out in some of your close relationships, as secrets come out and the past catches up with you, and even though you might fight hard to keep the peace, the unstoppable process of change brings some temporary chaos. You do stand to benefit through these changes, so the only person you hurt by pretending that everything is fine, if it obviously isn't, is yourself.

Scorpio
(October 24 – November 22)

Beware of tall dark strangers! This is a very passionate time, and you could find that you feel much more strongly towards all sorts of people, that you are emotionally demanding and very jealous. Don't shut off the possibility of new relationships; maybe only of a friendly rather than romantic nature, but no less important for that. New worlds can open out for you through who, rather than what, you know.

Sagittarius
(November 23 – December 21)

Try some of life's little luxuries that'll make you feel a bit spoilt and enable you to make more of your natural attractions. Don't be mean when it comes to anything that'll make you feel good, whether it's finding the time to go swimming or buying yourself some new clothes. Persuade your friends to get out into the fresh air, tune into the beauties of nature, work with them and you'll really have a great time and feel incredibly positive.

Capricorn
(December 22 – January 20)

Some specially exciting opportunity will land on your doorstep in the next fortnight. It's wacky, it's fun and it could change the way you do things, the way you feel about yourself and the way the world sees you too. This is a fortunate time for doing things like changing your hairstyle or anything involving your appearance. If you're normally a bit cautious about trying out new things this is the moment to take life's opportunities in both hands!

Aquarius
(January 21 – February 19)

Be firm and don't be afraid to seem unfair by laying down the law and saying 'No' occasionally. Also, use your powers of organisation to get things running smoothly: to arrange a party or to fix up home improvement schemes. It's as much up to you as anyone else to make your home as warm and hospitable as you can, so don't be hesitant about taking the law into your own hands.

Pisces
(February 20 – March 20)

Meetings with dark or scorpionic people could prove surprisingly pleasant, and make you feel quite differently about a situation or attitude that you've got used to. You have the power to make people like you, and to respond to your demands, so this might be an excellent time to work for charity or something else you believe in. The greater the enthusiasm you put in, the more you yourself will receive.

■ 3 These two tables contain words from the text. Complete the table by filling in the appropriate verb, noun or adjective in each case.

VERB	NOUN
warn	
advise	
encourage	
promise	
	enjoyment
	recognition
	attraction
persuade	
arrange	
	improvement
respond	
satisfy	

NOUN	ADJECTIVE
tension	
	threatening
confidence	
	exciting
popularity	
	romantic
	fortunate
	cautious
	hesitant
enthusiasm	
	irritable
	aggressive

LISTENING 2

Short extracts

You will hear people talking in four different situations. For questions 1–4 choose the best answer **A**, **B** or **C**.

1 You will hear someone talking to a group of people about taking a driving test.

What sort of people is he talking to?

A Teenagers
B Parents
C Driving instructors

2 You will hear the introduction to a radio programme.

What type of programme is it?

A A medical programme
B A scientific documentary
C A cookery feature

3 You will hear part of a report on a consumer programme.

What is the subject of the report?

A New fashions in food
B New hair care products
C New types of pets

4 You will hear a conversation between an employee and a customer.

Where does the conversation take place?

A At a hotel reception
B In a travel agency
C At an airport check-in

GRAMMAR 1

Question tags

1 Look at these sentences from the listening text.

You've booked a single, haven't you?
A deposit was paid by credit card, wasn't it?
I can pay the balance with my credit card, can't I?
It's included, isn't it?

2 These are statements with question tags. With your partner discuss the following:

1 What are the rules for forming question tags?

2 When are question tags used?

3

1 Add a question tag to each of these statements.

a You're Joe's sister, _____?
b It's a lovely day, _____?
c She's finished her course, _____?
d You went to that party, _____?
e He always drives to work, _____?
f You can give her a lift, _____?
g You won't forget to ring Lesley, _____?
h Let's play Scrabble, _____?
i You've met Mr Simpson, _____?
j You don't like tennis, _____?
k You haven't done your homework, _____?
l You'll have time for a cup of tea, _____?

2 Work in pairs reading the statements. Listen to check the question tag.

4 How well do you know your partner? Without asking any questions write down these things:

1 Five statements about your partner that you are sure are true.

Example: Your name's _____.

2 Five statements about your partner which you think might be true.

Example: You like _____ -ing.

3 Decide who is Student A and Student B.

Student A
Do not show your partner your list. Read the statements, adding a question tag to each one.

Student B
Respond to your partner's statements. If the information is wrong, correct it, using the language in the box to help you:

Yes, that's right.		
Well, actually no,	I'm not.	
	it isn't.	
	I don't.	(etc.)
(and give correct information)		

Find another partner and repeat the activity.

Expressing opinions

1 Talk to your partner. Do you have any pets?
What sort of animals make good pets for:

teenagers young families
old people people living alone
people living in cities

What sort of animals should people not be
allowed to keep as pets?

2 Read what 12-year-old David tells us about his pet water snake, Zoe,
and look carefully at each line. Some of the lines are correct, and some
have a word which should not be there. If a line is correct, put a tick(✓).
If a line has a word which should not be there, write the word in the space
on the right. There is an example at the beginning (**0**).

My pet snake

I got her from a reptile pet shop that when	0	*that*
she was a year and a half old. She is called Zoe.	00	✓
I was going for to call her something like Venom,	1	_____
but then I thought it puts people off if you would	2	_____
give a snake a bad name, so I changed it to Zoe.	3	_____
A month before I got her, I read in about nine	4	_____
thick books about snakes and when keeping them	5	_____
as pets. I am very careful with her as if you should be	6	_____
with any pet. Snakes are never stop being a bit shy.	7	_____
She is a very strong swimmer and, although	8	_____
she does not actually live in water, I put her	9	_____
in the bath and she goes swims very well.	10	_____
She normally lives in a heated tank with glass	11	_____
sliding doors. But snakes need any hiding	12	_____
places, or they tend to get very much nervous,	13	_____
so we found a teapot for her where to sleep in.	14	_____
She has not bitten anyone yet, she is a really nice friendly snake.	15	_____

READING 2
Multiple choice

1 Read this extract from a short story about pets and answer questions 1–3.

1 Who are these characters in the story?

Anna
Richard
Kate
Maria
Griselda
Melusina

2 What has happened ? How do each of these people feel about it?

Anna
Richard
Kate
Maria

3 What do you think is going to happen next?

The Cat Woman

Although no note awaited her on the doorstep, no letter came and there were no phone calls, Anna knew the cat woman would come back on the following evening. Richard had advised her to go to the police if any threats were made. There would
5 be no need to tell them she had been driving very fast. Anna thought the whole idea of going to the police bizarre. She rang up her friend Kate and told her all about it and Kate agreed that telling the police would be going too far.

The battered red car arrived at 7 pm. Maria Jakob was dressed as
10 she had been for her previous visit, but because it was rather cold, wore a jacket made of synthetic fur as well. From its harsh too-shiny texture there was no doubt it was synthetic but from a distance it looked like a black cat's pelt.

She had brought an album of photographs of her cats for Anna to
15 see. Anna looked through it — what else could she do? Some were recognisably of those she had seen through the windows. Those that were not, she supposed might be of animals now at rest under the wooden crosses in Maria Jakob's back garden. While she was looking at the pictures, Griselda, Anna's mother's cat, came in and jumped on
20 to the cat woman's lap. 'They're very nice, very interesting,' Anna said. 'I can see you're devoted to your cats.'

'They're my life.'

A little humouring might be in order. 'When is the funeral to be?'

'I thought on Friday. Two o'clock on Friday. My sister will be there
25 with her two. Cats don't usually take to car travel, that's why I don't often take any of mine with me, and shutting them up in cages goes against the grain, but my sister's two Burmese love the car, they'll go and sit in the car when it's parked. My friend from the Animal Rescue will come if she can get away and I've asked our vet but I don't hold
30 out much hope there. He has his goat clinic on Fridays. I hope you'll come along.'

'I'm afraid I'll be at work.'

'It's no flowers by request. Donations to the Cats' Protection League instead. Any sum, no matter how small, gratefully received. Which
35 brings me to money. You've got a cheque for me.'

'No I haven't, Mrs Yackle.'

'Miss. And it's Jakob. J, A, K, O, B. You've got a cheque for me for £799.'

'I am not giving you any money, Miss Jakob. I'm
40 very very sorry about your cat, about Melusina, I know how fond you were of her, but giving you compensation is out of the question. I'm sorry.'

The tears had come once more into Maria Jakob's eyes, had spilled over. Her face contorted
45 with misery. It was the mention of the wretched thing's name, Anna thought. That was the trigger that started the weeping. A tear splashed on to one of the coarse red hands. Griselda opened her eyes and licked up the tear.

50 Maria Jakob pushed her other hand across her eyes. She blinked.

'We'll have to think of something else then,' she said.

'I beg your pardon?' Anna wondered if she had
55 really heard right. Things couldn't be solved so simply.

'We shall have to think of something else. A way for you to make up to me for murder.'

'Look, I will give a donation to the Cats'
60 Protection League. I'm quite prepared to give them — say £20.' Richard would be furious but perhaps she would not tell Richard. 'I'll give it to you, shall I, and then you can pass it on to them?'

65 'I certainly hope you will. Especially if you can't come to the funeral.'

That was the end of it then. Anna felt a great sense of relief. It was only now that she realised quite how it had got to her. It had actually kept
70 her from sleeping properly. She phoned Kate and told her about the funeral and the goat clinic and Kate laughed and said, poor old thing. Anna slept so well that night that she did not notice the arrival of Griselda who, when she woke, was
75 asleep on the pillow next to her face, but out of touching distance.

■ **2** Read again more carefully. For questions **1–7**, choose the answer (**A**, **B**, **C** or **D**) which you think fits best according to the text.

1 Why had Anna not phoned the police?

  A Because she had been driving fast.
  B She wasn't sure if the woman would come back.
  C She hadn't been threatened in any way.
  D It seemed an unnecessary thing to do.

2 'synthetic' (lines 11 and 12) refers to which aspect of Maria's coat?

  A the material
  B the colour
  C the condition
  D the style

3 Why did Anna look through the photographs?

  A She recognised some of the cats.
  B She was very interested in them.
  C She didn't know how to behave.
  D Maria made her look at them.

4 What invitation did Anna refuse?

  A To attend a goat clinic.
  B To visit the Animal Rescue.
  C To go to a funeral.
  D To meet Maria's sister.

5 Why does Maria ask Anna for £799?

  A As a donation to the Cats' Protection League.
  B Because Anna can't attend the funeral.
  C Because Anna has killed one of Maria's cats.
  D Because Maria's car has been damaged.

6 What is Kate's reaction to the story?

  A She doesn't take it seriously.
  B She is relieved that it is over.
  C She feels sorry for Anna.
  D She finds it frightening.

7 What does 'it' (line 67) refer to?

  A Anna's guilt.
  B Richard's anger.
  C Maria's demands.
  D Melusina's revenge.

LISTENING 3
Note-taking

Listen to a quiz show on the radio where you will hear a person's life story, and complete the notes.

1 1756 _____ in Salzburg.

2 1762 First professional tour as a _____ .

3 1781 Moved to _____ .

4 1781–1787 Wrote two famous _____ .

5 1787 Became _____ .

6 1791 _____ .

GRAMMAR 2
Future in the past

1 Look at these sentences from the listening text.

He was going to become a brilliant musician.
He went on to become a prolific composer.
He was to write over six hundred musical compositions.

1 What time is referred to?
2 Which tenses are used?

These forms are used when we take a point in the past – the composer was 9 years old in the picture – and talk about what happened after that.

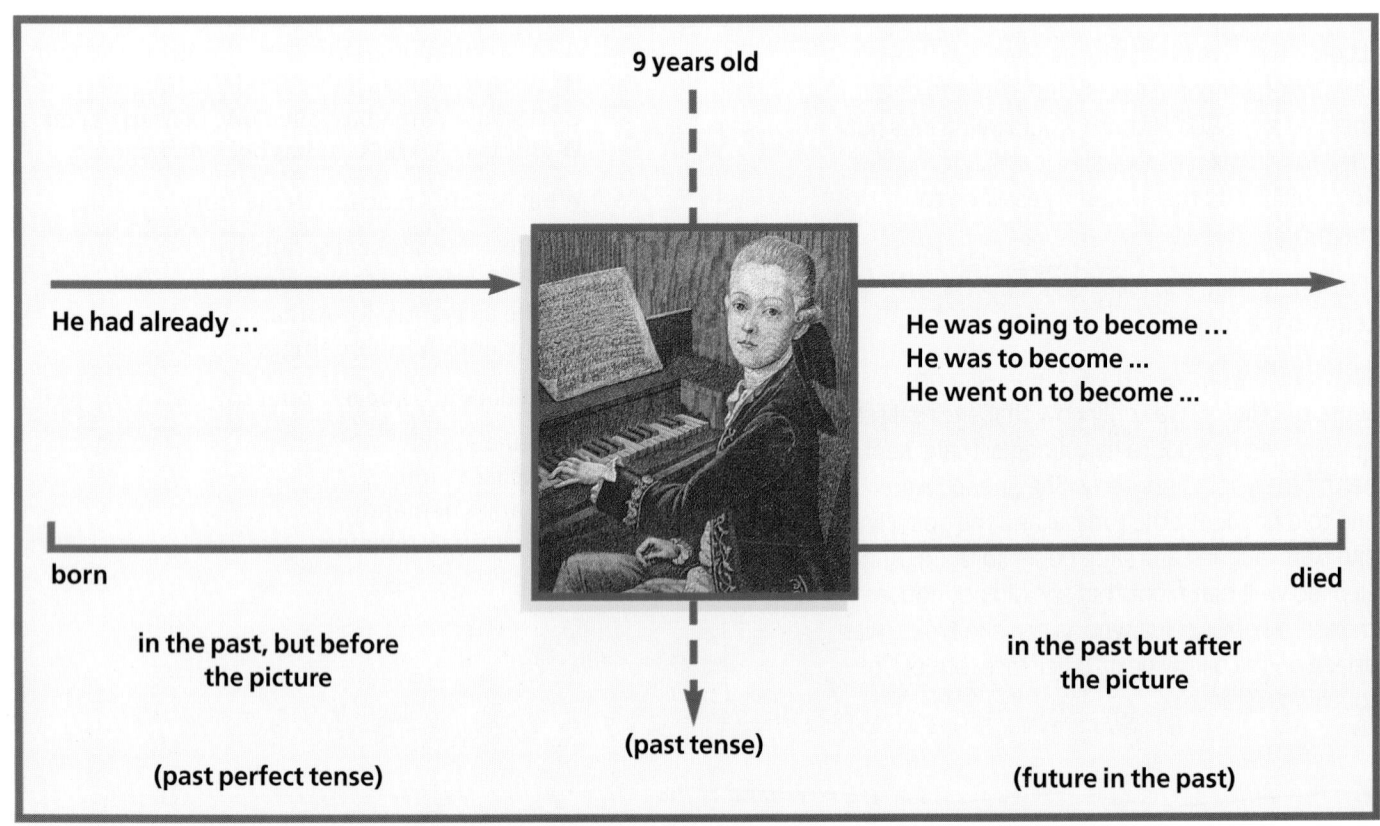

9 years old

He had already …

He was going to become …
He was to become …
He went on to become …

born   died

in the past, but before
the picture

in the past but after
the picture

(past tense)

(past perfect tense)

(future in the past)

■■2 Look at this information about the lives of two famous people. Choose one and write the script for the next part of the radio quiz using future in the past forms to talk about things which happened after the pictures were taken.

1

1911	Born at Tampico, Illinois Educated at Ureka College, Illinois
1937	Went to Hollywood Made his first film 'Love is in the Air'
1937 – 1962	Made over fifty films
1962	Joined the US Republican Party
1966	Became Governor of California
1980	Elected President of the USA
1981	Survived an assassination attempt
1984	Re-elected for a second term
1988	Retired as one of the most popular US Presidents ever

Reagan 1938

2

1879	Born at Ulm, Bavaria Studied at Munich and Zurich
1901	Took Swiss nationality
1902 – 1905	Worked for Swiss government
1905	Wrote his famous 'Special Theory of Relativity'
1909	Became a professor at Zurich Polytechnic
1914 – 1933	Director of Physics Institute, Berlin
1916	Published his 'Special Theory of Relativity'
1921	Awarded Nobel Prize for physics
1934	Left Europe to work in Princeton USA
1940	Became a US citizen and a professor at Princeton
1955	Died in USA

Einstein 1902

LISTENING 4

Talk to your partner. What do you know about Madame Tussaud's Waxworks in London?

Part 1   Blank filling

You will hear a historian talking about the life of Madame Marie Tussaud. For questions 1–10, complete the notes which summarise what the historian says by writing a word, number or short phrase.

Early Life:

Born in | *1761* | **0** | in France.

Her mother was | | **1** | to a doctor.

The doctor taught her how to | | **2** | .

She worked as | | **3** | to the King's sister.

French Revolution:

| | **4** | helped her to escape from the palace.

She made wax models of | | **5** | .

She wasn't | | **6** | of the revolution.

New Life:

Leaving her family, she | | **7** | .

She created a | | **8** | of waxworks.

In 1835 a | | **9** | was established in London.

Marie died in | | **10** | in London.

Part 2   Multiple matching

You will hear five people talking about Marie Tussaud and her work. For questions **1–5** choose from the list **A–F** what each speaker is talking about. Use the letters only once. There is one extra letter which you do not need to use.

A The making of wax models.
B Marie's sadness.
C Qualities of wax.
D Marie's attitude to wax modelling.
E Marie's character.
F Our reactions to wax models.

Speaker 1 | |
Speaker 2 | |
Speaker 3 | |
Speaker 4 | |
Speaker 5 | |

READING 3
Reading for specific information

1 Talk to your partner.

1 Choose one of these events and tell your partner about it:

- The day you first met someone important to you.
- The day on which a new chapter of your life started.
- The day you first tried a sport/pastime which became important to you.
- The day you visited somewhere special for the first time.
- An experience which changed the way you think or behave.

2 Was the event you talked about planned or did it happen by chance?

3 What changes would you like to make in your life at the moment?

2 You are going to read an article about parachuting. For questions **1–6**, on page 198, choose the answer (**A**, **B**, **C** or **D**) which you think fits best according to the text.

'Parachuting changed my life!'

1 When Su Woods stepped out on to the tarmac of Thruxton airfield one sunny afternoon to make her first
5 parachute jump, she was not only about to make her childhood dream come true, she was also leaving her old life for a new one. Achieving her ambition was
10 to transform her life. Eight years later, Su and her husband Dennis own the parachute club where Su made her first jump, and where they met.

15 'Parachuting has changed my life enormously,' Su says.' When I think back to the first day I came, watching all the experienced jumpers and free-fallers and
20 feeling so nervous, I have to keep telling myself that the club's all ours. I've made 100 jumps now – that's quite a lot. But there are plenty of members here who
25 are much more advanced than I am.

'It's so exhilarating you don't get frightened. Everything to do with parachuting in this country
30 is so highly regulated. You can't just go up in a plane and jump out of it. You must have proper training. Safety precautions are rigorously enforced. At first, you
35 have a static line attached to your parachute linking it to the aeroplane. As you fall free, the line pulls the parachute open. It's not until you've reached a certain
40 standard that you're allowed to open your own parachute, so there's not really any danger. A feeling of fear at the thought of jumping out of a plane at 762
45 metres is only natural sometimes!

'When you're first told you're ready to go up, you get really nervous. You step out on to the
50 platform, the instructor says "Go", and then you're in the air. It's so exhilarating, you can't imagine what you were afraid of. Even now, I get nervous when I
55 go up for a jump. But as soon as you're coming down, peace all around you, the earth below, it's wonderful.'

Juggling her career as editor of an
60 internal newspaper for a major British company with sorting out a new house, managing the parachute club and pursuing her favourite hobby, means that
65 things like housework and washing up can get badly neglected. 'But then,' Su says, 'it's a question of priorities. I'd rather parachute than spend
70 Saturdays cleaning the house.

'We try to travel the 40 miles from home to the club as often as we can and, of course, we're there all weekend. That's the
75 best time. It's a very sociable place – families come to watch and take part, and we have a lot of charity jumps, which is nice.'

1 What reasons did Su have for beginning parachuting?

   A It was something she had always wanted to do.
   B She had wanted to change her life completely.
   C She wanted to show her children what she could do.
   D She had married the owner of the club.

2 What happens when you start jumping?

   A You jump with the parachute already open.
   B You always jump with another person.
   C You are not allowed to open your own parachute.
   D You remain connected to the ground.

3 What does Su say about the emotions involved in parachuting?

   A You never get over the fear of falling.
   B You get very nervous before jumping out.
   C You are only nervous the first few times you jump.
   D You are more nervous with the instructor.

4 How has parachuting changed Su's life?

   A She has given up her job.
   B She now jumps for a living.
   C She now owns the parachute club.
   D She goes parachuting every day.

5 'juggling' (line 59) means

   A replacing.
   B resigning.
   C combining.
   D organising.

6 How does Su spend most of her weekend?

   A Looking after her family.
   B Doing work for charity.
   C Following her favourite hobby.
   D Organising the club's social life.

READING 4
Multiple matching

1 Talk to your partner.

What are the qualities of a good friend? Discuss these things:

A friend is someone who

- is interested in the same things as you.
- is loyal and reliable.
- is willing to listen to your problems.
- helps you in a crisis.
- is fun to be with.
- tells you the truth, even if it hurts.
- you've known all your life.
- lives close by and gets on well with your family.

Is your friend hard work?

0	I

Last month my friend Kate's boyfriend finished with her. Tears? She could have flooded rivers. But I'm a good friend, I know there are times in every girl's life when she really needs the firm but gentle shoulder of her best friend.

So I spent a week confined with Kate in her bedroom. I endured hours listening to her misery, making steaming mugs of hot chocolate and watching her eat packet after packet of biscuits.

By Saturday, she was beginning to feel better. Great, I thought. I was more than ready for a night out. Besides, it was just what Kate needed.

1	

And then it happened; I was just getting ready to go out when Kate telephoned. I wouldn't be dancing that night. Kate had twisted her ankle and was in need of more tea and sympathy. The following week Kate failed a maths exam, and left her new coat on the bus. I provided all the support, encouragement and advice I could over these crises. Then, to cheer her up, I lent her my favourite purple velvet jacket … and she splashed it with tomato juice.

2 You are going to read a magazine article about friendship. Choose from the list **A–I** the most suitable heading for each part of the article (**1–7**). There is one extra heading which you do not need to use. There is an example at the beginning (**0**).

A What's in it for me?
B We've been through a lot together
C Some straight talking
D The end of a friendship?
E Further disasters
F A better sort of friendship
G Giving her more space
H I've had enough!
I Doing what a good friend should

2

Kind, patient, caring person that I am, there are limits to my tolerance. I'm not a bad friend, but there has to be more to friendship than being a full-time shoulder to cry on. Right?

3

We've all got a Kate. The friend who turns up in the middle of the night desperate to talk, the one who calls you, in tears, several times a day. She is the Walking Disaster, the friend to whom you can't say NO. Kate is what is known as a High Maintenance Friend. And, although I always think to myself 'poor Kate', I also can't help wondering, could she be playing some part in causing her own disasters? I mean, who else has six crises a day? OK, I'll admit that being the strong one in the friendship makes me feel great in some ways, but Kate's series of dramas also leave me feeling exhausted and resentful. What's more, when I have difficult times, Kate hardly knows about them.

4

When I started seeing more of my other friends, I hoped Kate would get the message and back off a bit. Instead she just got upset and made sulky little comments when I didn't call her back. Sometimes the only thing to do with such friendships is to end them. If you can live with the guilt, you may feel lots of relief in the long run.

5

So why don't I just get rid of this selfish so-called friend? Well, it's just not as easy as that. Kate and I go way back to primary school days. The thought of giving up our shared history is just too much to bear.

Besides, she's fun – sometimes. Life without her is unthinkable. But life with her is hardly a bottomless bowl of Häagen-Dazs either.

6

All I really wanted was to take the pressure off myself, so I decided that Kate and I needed a gentle heart-to-heart. It was risky – I didn't want my old friend to feel totally rejected, so I started out by making it clear how much I value her.

7

Then – deep breath – I explained that she needed more from me than I can give. I suggested that she talk to other friends as well as me when she needs support. The silence and Kate's frozen stare seemed to indicate that this could be the point where our friendship would end. The longer her silence lasted, the more I talked to fill the air, finally convincing myself that I was a really bad friend.

Kate didn't call me for days after that, but when she did phone about a week later, she was the happy, fun Kate I know and love. Sure, I heard about the latest drama in her life, but not for hours. And she actually… asked questions about me!

These days, Kate has a network of new friends, and the balance in our relationship is getting better. Now, when I see Kate, I really enjoy her company – and she's happier too.

No-one is saying that you should only love your friends when they're up, and cross the street to avoid them when they're down. But when you're doing all the giving and your friend is just taking, it's time to weigh it up. Remember you have a right to say NO!

3 Look at this letter that Gemma has written to her pen friend, Kate, and look carefully at each line. Some of the lines are correct, and some have a word which should not be there. If a line is correct, put a tick (✓). If a line has a word which should not be there, write the word in the space on the right.

Dear Kate

I'm sorry if your best friend thinks you're so hard	1 _____
work, but let me give you some of advice.	2 _____
First, back off and give your friend a little more in space.	3 _____
Ask her about it her life, too. Let her know, you're	4 _____
there for when she really needs a sympathetic ear, but	5 _____
avoid rushing to the phone every one time you have	6 _____
a crisis. She doesn't have all this the answers! Then,	7 _____
spend time with other some friends, so she doesn't	8 _____
feel like you're lost without her. Relax yourself and try	9 _____
to have a good laugh sometimes. Life and friendship	10 _____
don't have to be with all problems, you know.	11 _____
Finally, don't worry every time your friend goes out	12 _____
with other people, and not as you. It doesn't mean	13 _____
she hates you! Remember that no-one can be spend	14 _____
all their time with just one person.	15 _____

Lots of love,

Gemma

WRITING 1

A transactional letter

You are interested in spending a holiday at the Fieldside Summer School with a small group of friends. The only information you have is the advertisement shown below. Your friends have given you the task of writing to Fieldside.

Read carefully the advertisement and the notes which have been made below. Then write your letter to the Summer School, covering the points in your notes and adding any relevant information about your group.

Write a letter of 120–180 words in an appropriate style.
Do not write any addresses.

Fieldside Residential Summer School

Fieldside School is situated in beautiful countryside, close to the ancient city of Cotsford where all amenities are available. There is a wide range of afternoon activities, including horse-riding, tennis, water-skiing and parascending, as well as English classes.

how far?
included in price?

- *2 weeks in August possible?*
  Start date?
- *price?*
- *equipment provided?*
- *how to pay?*
- *nearest airport? transfer?*

Talking about photographs

1 Decide who is Student A and who is Student B.

Student A: Look at pictures 1 and 2 and compare and contrast them.

Student B: Listen to your partner and say if you agree.

Pictures 1 and 2 – Think about:
shared tastes
levels of understanding
ways of communicating
possible problems

Student B: Look at pictures 3 and 4. Compare and contrast them.

Student A: Listen to your partner and say if you agree.

Pictures 3 and 4 – Think about
freedom and restrictions
choice of food and drink
topics of conversation
activities

2 Which is more important for you – family or friends? Which of these things would you prefer to do with your family and which with friends? Say why.

a day trip   planning a party
playing board games   buying clothes
learning a new skill   celebrating exam results
eating out

3 What problems could arise in these situations?

working with brothers or sisters
working with a boyfriend/girlfriend, husband/wife
falling in love with someone at work

Blank filling

You will hear part of a radio interview on the topic of office romances. For questions **1–10**, complete the sentences with a word or short phrase.

More than 50% of office romances result in [＿＿＿＿＿＿＿＿] **1**

Lorna Telford manages [＿＿＿＿＿＿＿＿] **2** of the Recruitment Consultants company.

Most office romances begin as [＿＿＿＿＿＿＿＿] **3**.

John thinks it's more difficult to meet people in [＿＿＿＿＿＿＿＿] **4**.

Lorna admits that her husband used to be [＿＿＿＿＿＿＿＿] **5**.

John thinks there may be problems if couples who work together [＿＿＿＿＿＿＿＿] **6**.

Many women with partners at work decide [＿＿＿＿＿＿＿＿] **7**.

Although managers don't like office romances, they usually [＿＿＿＿＿＿＿＿] **8**.

Colleagues felt that [＿＿＿＿＿＿＿＿] **9** as a result of office romances.

Linda feels that people in love [＿＿＿＿＿＿＿＿] **10** on their work.

Uses of do

1 Look at these sentences from the listening text. Compare the use of the words in bold.

1 How **does** it happen?

2 The people having the relationships **don't** realise this

3 … but those who are observing **do**

4 Managers **do** mind

5 They **do not** like relationships at work

2 In each case is the form of *do* used:

- as an auxiliary to form a question or a negative?
- to avoid repeating a longer phrase?
- to add emphasis to what is being said?

3 Listen to the interview again and each time you hear a form of the verb *do*, make a note of which type it is.

4 Rewrite these sentences using a form of *do* to avoid repeating a longer phrase.

1 My brother studies English but my sister doesn't study English.

2 I don't like classical music, but my parents like classical music.

3 I didn't go to Olga's party, but Joanne went to Olga's party.

4 Lorna met her partner through her work, but John didn't meet his partner through his work.

5 Most people don't like filling in questionnaires, but Roy likes it.

5 Add forms of *do* to these sentences to make them more emphatic.

1 People think that the relationship affects their work.

2 What we found was that people try to keep these relationships secret.

3 Rosie finds it difficult to make friends at parties.

4 You may think your mother didn't notice, but she noticed.

5 Pete! How nice to see you. Come and have a cup of coffee.

WRITING 2
An article

You have been asked to write an article of 120–180 words about friendship for a magazine for young people. Choose one of these titles:

1 How to find a good friend.
2 Pets can be better friends than people.
3 My oldest friend and why he/she is important to me.

Remember to prepare a plan before you start to write and to divide your article into paragraphs.

PRONUNCIATION
Contractions

1 Remember that if you don't contract negative forms of auxiliary verbs, you will sound very emphatic.

Listen to these pairs of sentences and practise saying them with your partner.

1 I can't stand jazz music.
I cannot stand jazz music.

2 Please don't be late.
Please do not be late.

3 Mary didn't remember to call me.
Mary did not remember to call me.

4 John won't come to the party.
John will not come to the party.

5 My work hasn't been affected.
My work has not been affected.

2 Listen and repeat these contracted forms.

1 can't	**2** couldn't	**3** couldn't have
4 won't	**5** wouldn't	**6** wouldn't have
7 shan't	**8** shouldn't	**9** shouldn't have
10 oughtn't	**11** oughtn't to have	**12** needn't
13 needn't have	**14** mightn't	**15** mightn't have
16 mustn't	**17** mustn't have	

🔊 LISTENING 6
Multiple matching

You will hear five members of the singing family The Dalton Sisters talking about their careers. For questions **1–5** choose from the list **A–F** what each speaker is talking about. Use the letters only once. There is one extra letter which you do not need to use.

A Making an important decision.

B Pressures from outside the family.

C Arguments between members of the family.

D Changing attitudes to success.

E The problems of being one of a group.

F New types of family problems.

Speaker 1	
Speaker 2	
Speaker 3	
Speaker 4	
Speaker 5	

READING 5
Multiple matching

🔲 1 Talk to your partner

1 What is the difference between *alone* and *lonely*?

2 In which of these situations is it good to be on your own and in which is it not so good?

- reading
- playing computer games
- listening to music
- travelling
- going to the cinema
- going to a party
- doing your homework

3 Describe a time when you really enjoyed being alone, OR describe a time when you felt really lonely.

🔲 2 You are going to read a newspaper article about the problems of young people who live in the country. Choose from the sentences **A–I** the one which fits each gap (**1–7**). There is one extra sentence which you do not need to use. There is an example at the beginning (**0**).

A The car, in fact, enables Jamie's father to do his job as an electrician across North and South Devon.

B He has an old bike, but the country lanes, with their high banks and blind corners, make cycling dangerous. Anyway where would he go?

C But farming is a hard life that demands the involvement of the whole family and most children have their 'jobs' to do before and after school.

D In theory, Jamie enjoys the many advantages of country life: fresh air, freedom from fear, friendly people who always have time to stop and chat.

E Jamie hasn't reached those depths and doesn't want a return to city life – but neither can he face the loneliness of the summer holiday weeks.

F But summer came and the owners needed their home for more profitable holiday lets.

G Every day in term time, he walks to the crossroads outside the village and then travels eight miles by coach along narrow country lanes to the closest school to his home.

H A recent survey of students at one rural school in North Devon found 'being able to meet friends' topped the list of improvements that youngsters wanted in their lives.

I The problem is, Jamie knows that once the holidays start, he is unlikely to see another person his own age until school opens again in September.

A LONG, LONELY SUMMER

1 *Jamie Summers is 13 and hates school holidays. As the end of term approaches he becomes increasingly*
5 *depressed and even the prospect of a school camping holiday fails to raise more than a weak smile.* [0] [I]

He is one of thousands of young
10 people for whom rural isolation means spending long periods alone with parents, seldom venturing beyond the village and having to rely on television and on their own
15 imagination for entertainment.

Home for Jamie is a large farmhouse on the edge of the Exmoor national park. During the summer, if it doesn't rain, he spends most nights
20 in a tent on the hillside behind the farm.

[1] Most of his classmates make similar journeys each day. For Jamie and many like him, school is their
25 only social life. With little chance to meet school friends in the evening, at weekends or during the holidays – and few visits from other family members – his only chance for
30 conversation with people other than his parents is the seven hours a day he spends in school.

He never stays for after-school activities and can only go to school
35 plays and discos with difficulty. Last year he missed collecting a prize because his father did not get home

in time to drive him to the school.

[2] Sometimes he travels 250
40 kilometres a day and worries about how long it will keep going.

The family's story, a cautionary tale for town-dwellers tempted by the idea of rural life, is typical. They
45 came from London to escape noise, pollution, crime and the bullying that Jamie received at school.

The first winter they rented a house in a village where Jamie could walk
50 to school. His mother, Maureen, soon made friends among other parents at the school gate and for a while life was exactly what she and Jamie had hoped for. [3]

55 They moved to another village, from which Jamie began getting the bus to school. Then his father lost his factory maintenance job and they couldn't afford the rent. That
60 was when they found the farmhouse in which they've lived ever since. Their nearest neighbour is the elderly farmer whose cattle graze in the surrounding fields.

65 [4] In practice, he is mostly alone and doesn't know enough about nature to appreciate it. His mother worries if he wanders, because even in the country 'you
70 can't be too careful'.

[5] He is reluctant to visit friends because he can't invite them back. The pretty villages that attract tourists hold little interest for a
75 teenager.

One year, he went back to London to stay with his grandmother for part of the holiday. But she is too old now to cope with a teenager.
80 Anyway, none of the people he started school with remembers or wants to know about him.

It is not only newcomers from London who suffer the problems
85 of isolation. Lonely farmhouses hidden away in folded valleys can be prisons for children.

[6] With few youth clubs or other amenities and virtually no public
90 transport, entertainment is a real difficulty.

Better-off parents establish transport networks for taking children to school and village events, but in the
95 holidays they may still go for days without seeing anyone of their own age except for brothers and sisters.

Parents thinking about a move to the country should think carefully
100 about their children's needs. For Laura, who moved from Sheffield to an isolated Devon cottage when she was fourteen, the contrast was so strong that she attempted
105 suicide and now requires regular counselling.

[7] Which is why, unlike many urban children, he is already looking forward to school starting
110 again.

EXAM PRACTICE 12

1 Read the text below and decide which word **A**, **B**, **C** or **D** best fits each space. There is an example at the beginning (**0**).

Romantic fiction is as old (**0**) _____C_____ love itself and still very (**1**) _____ alive and well. An amazing 41,000 Mills and Boon romantic novels are sold in the UK every day; that (**2**) _____ up to around 15 million copies a year. And (**3**) _____ being popular in the UK, these books have also been (**4**) _____ into 20 other languages and sold in over 100 different countries.

Romantic fiction has changed over the years and Mills and Boon novels continually try to reflect contemporary (**5**) _____ . The company has also tried to give readers greater (**6**) _____ .

Mills and Boon (**7**) _____ over 5000 manuscripts a year from (**8**) _____ writers, but only a few join their list of (**9**) _____ authors. Now, if you've ever (**10**) _____ of writing for Mills and Boon, help is at (**11**) _____ . The company has produced a (**12**) _____ guide, *And Then He Kissed Her…*, which explains how to (**13**) _____ out to write a romantic novel. The booklet contains valuable (**14**) _____ that can be applied to almost any form of creative writing.

So, if you've written a love letter but feel you could write a (**15**) _____ novel, get *And Then He Kissed Her…*. Happy Writing!

0	**A** than	**B** so	**C** as	**D** of
1	**A** than	**B** greatly	**C** much	**D** just
2	**A** adds	**B** makes	**C** comes	**D** gives
3	**A** although	**B** besides	**C** moreover	**D** whereas
4	**A** interpreted	**B** transferred	**C** exchanged	**D** translated
5	**A** attitudes	**B** ways	**C** habits	**D** traditions
6	**A** differences	**B** selection	**C** variety	**D** alternatives
7	**A** receives	**B** registers	**C** remarks	**D** realises
8	**A** beginner	**B** training	**C** hopeful	**D** promised
9	**A** regular	**B** common	**C** correct	**D** routine
10	**A** hoped	**B** wondered	**C** considered	**D** thought
11	**A** work	**B** hand	**C** once	**D** last
12	**A** unique	**B** solitary	**C** single	**D** lone
13	**A** start	**B** take	**C** carry	**D** work
14	**A** directions	**B** proposals	**C** suggestions	**D** indications
15	**A** whole	**B** total	**C** strong	**D** thorough

2 Complete the second sentence so that it has a similar meaning to the first sentence. Use the word given and other words to complete each sentence. You must use between two and five words. Do not change the word given.

Example:
I haven't laughed so much for ages.
since
It's ages _____*since I laughed*_____ so much.

1 Victor started collecting stamps twenty-five years ago.
been
Victor has _____ twenty-five years.

2 Whose wallet is this?
   belong
   Who _____ to?

3 The translation course takes two years.
   a
   It's _____ course.

4 Danny writes more clearly than Karen.
   as
   Karen doesn't _____ Danny.

5 Although she had an injured ankle, Esther still won the tennis match.
   her
   Despite _____ Esther still
   won the tennis match.

6 It's not my fault if the television doesn't work.
   me
   Don't _____ television doesn't work.

7 'Can I have a new pair of football boots?' Robert asked his father.
   for
   Robert asked _____ a new pair of football boots.

8 Chris failed his driving test because he didn't have enough lessons.
   had
   If Chris _____ he'd have
   passed his driving test.

9 It was such a long journey that they were all asleep by the time they arrived.
   so
   The journey _____ that they were
   all asleep by the time they arrived.

10 Louisa has taught her children how to prepare their own meals.
   been
   Louisa's children _____ to prepare their own meals.

3 Read the text below. Use the word given in capitals at the end of each line
to form a word that fits in the space in the same line. There is an example at
the beginning (**0**).

Rows can be good for you

A row is simply expressing your own point of view (**0**) _forcefully_ ,   **FORCE**
and it's (**1**) _____ that people quarrel in different ways. In   **SURPRISE**
some families, rows are tight-lipped affairs, with (**2**) _____   **ANGRY**
covered up by a (**3**) _____ that all is well. In others, it is more   **PRETEND**
(**4**) _____ . My mother threw insults and crockery, while   **DRAMA**
my father ignored the insults, (**5**) _____   **CATCH**
the crockery and produced (**6**) _____ cups of tea   **END**
when they eventually made up.

But rows can lead to greater (**7**) _____ and   **UNDERSTAND**
(**8**) _____ in relationships often indicate development, which   **ARGUE**
is fine as long as the (**9**) _____ is positive. It is only when   **OUT**
there are lots of (**10**) _____ rows with no clear motivation,   **REASON**
or when rows leave you feeling tense, angry and sick that the
alarm bells should start to ring.

4 Read the text below and think of the word which best fits each space. Use only one word in each space. There is an example at the beginning (**0**).

Tom Cruise

At the age of thirty, Tom Cruise had made fifteen films and earned millions (**0**) ___*of*___ dollars. It is interesting that Cruise, (**1**) _____ many other successful and ambitious actors, found stardom only (**2**) _____ a difficult childhood.

Cruise was the third child and the only boy in a (**3**) _____ of four children brought (**4**) _____ by parents who worked hard but (**5**) _____ stayed long in one town – his father, an engineer, went round the USA looking (**6**) _____ work. Cruise had been to half a dozen schools in as (**7**) _____ years. He had to fit (**8**) _____ quickly at each new school and moving about did not help his education, but he was good at sports, which could be carried on from one school to (**9**) _____ .

His parents divorced when he was twelve, and his father died some years later (**10**) _____ seeing any of his son's films. His mother (**11**) _____ charge of the family, and all the children had to find a job after school to help the family (**12**) _____ by.

Now, Cruise has made (**13**) _____ much money that he never (**14**) _____ to work again, but this is not (**15**) _____ option he is likely to consider seriously for many years to come.

CAMBRIDGE
EXAMINATIONS, CERTIFICATES AND DIPLOMAS
ENGLISH AS A FOREIGN LANGUAGE

University of Cambridge
Local Examinations Syndicate
International Examinations

For Supervisor's use only
Shade here if the candidate is ABSENT or has WITHDRAWN

Examination Details	9999/01	99/D99
Examination Title	First Certificate in English	
Centre/Candidate No.	AA999/9999	
Candidate Name	A.N. EXAMPLE	

• Sign here if the details above are correct

• Tell the Supervisor now if the details above are not correct

SAMPLE

Candidate Answer Sheet: FCE Paper 1 Reading

Use a pencil

Mark ONE letter for each question.

For example, if you think **B** is the right answer to the question, mark your answer sheet like this:

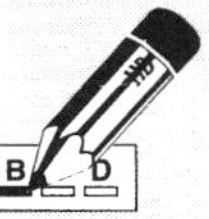

0 A B C D

Change your answer like this:

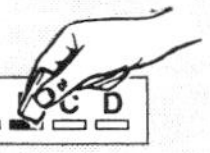

0 A B C D

1	A B C D E F G H I
2	A B C D E F G H I
3	A B C D E F G H I
4	A B C D E F G H I
5	A B C D E F G H I
6	A B C D E F G H I
7	A B C D E F G H I
8	A B C D E F G H I
9	A B C D E F G H I
10	A B C D E F G H I
11	A B C D E F G H I
12	A B C D E F G H I
13	A B C D E F G H I
14	A B C D E F G H I
15	A B C D E F G H I
16	A B C D E F G H I
17	A B C D E F G H I
18	A B C D E F G H I
19	A B C D E F G H I
20	A B C D E F G H I
21	A B C D E F G H I
22	A B C D E F G H I
23	A B C D E F G H I
24	A B C D E F G H I
25	A B C D E F G H I
26	A B C D E F G H I
27	A B C D E F G H I
28	A B C D E F G H I
29	A B C D E F G H I
30	A B C D E F G H I
31	A B C D E F G H I
32	A B C D E F G H I
33	A B C D E F G H I
34	A B C D E F G H I
35	A B C D E F G H I

FCE-1 DP999/99

CAMBRIDGE
EXAMINATIONS, CERTIFICATES AND DIPLOMAS
ENGLISH AS A FOREIGN LANGUAGE

University of Cambridge
Local Examinations Syndicate
International Examinations

For Supervisor's use only
Shade here if the candidate is ABSENT or has WITHDRAWN

Examination Details	9999/03	99/D99
Examination Title	First Certificate in English	
Centre/Candidate No.	AA999/9999	
Candidate Name	A.N. EXAMPLE	

• Sign here if the details above are correct

• Tell the Supervisor now if the details above are not correct

SAMPLE

Candidate Answer Sheet: FCE Paper 3 Use of English

Use a pencil

For **Part 1**: Mark ONE letter for each question.

For example, if you think **C** is the right answer to the question, mark your answer sheet like this:

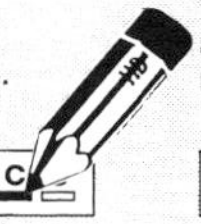

0 A B C D

For **Parts 2, 3, 4** and **5**: Write your answers in the spaces next to the numbers like this:

0 *example*

Part 1	
1	A B C D
2	A B C D
3	A B C D
4	A B C D
5	A B C D
6	A B C D
7	A B C D
8	A B C D
9	A B C D
10	A B C D
11	A B C D
12	A B C D
13	A B C D
14	A B C D
15	A B C D

Part 2		Do not write here
16		16
17		17
18		18
19		19
20		20
21		21
22		22
23		23
24		24
25		25
26		26
27		27
28		28
29		29
30		30

Turn over for Parts 3 - 5 →

FCE-3 DP152/99

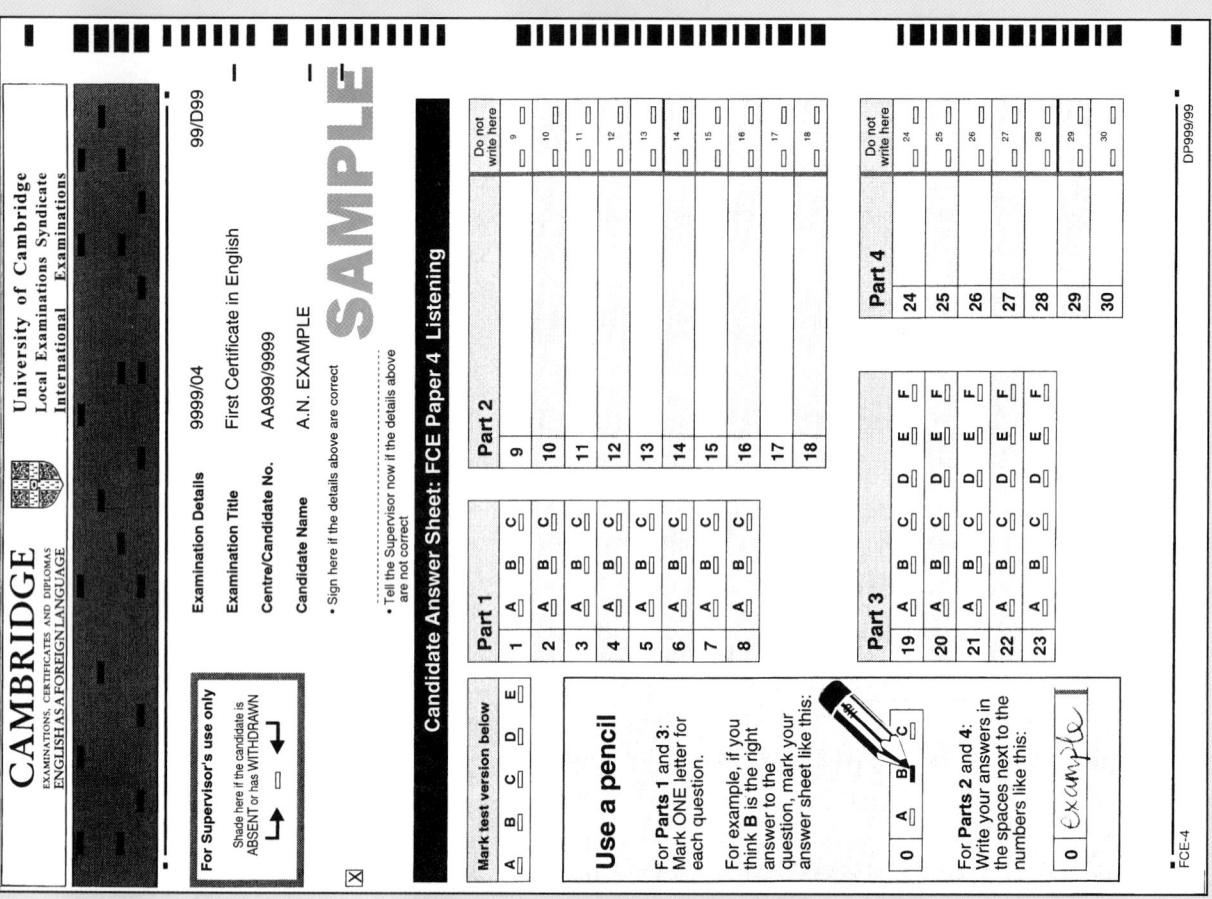

Paper 3 continued

Multi-word verb Review

Unit One

Use the correct form of one of the multi-word verbs in the box to complete each of the sentences.

look through	put on	wear out	show off
grow up	get on with	take off	hold up
~~get up~~	have on	hand in	pull out
make up	come forward	hand over	set up

Example: Louisa usually *gets up* late and studies in the evening.

1 Akemi _____ her make up after having a shower.

2 Lars _____ his pullover because it was too hot.

3 You don't want to have dinner wearing the wet boots you've _____ all day, do you?

4 You should _____ your homework at the end of the lesson.

5 Paul and Marie _____ each other very well.

6 You have to _____ your mind – it's time to decide!

7 Aileen _____ her henna business one year ago.

8 You could _____ that mail order catalogue if you have to choose a new coat.

9 I was born in Greece, but I _____ in New York.

10 I'm afraid my younger brother always _____ terribly in front of visitors.

11 I threw away my old school uniform because it was completely _____ .

12 The police are looking for a woman who _____ a post office in Liverpool today. The woman suddenly _____ a gun and forced the cashier to _____ £10,000. The police are asking anyone who saw the woman to _____ .

Unit Two

Choose one of the prepositions from the box to complete each sentence. You can use some of the prepositions more than once.

out	off	up	through	for	on	of

1 Sandy had to try _____ 9.98 kg of chocolate.

2 Milk goes _____ quickly on a warm day.

3 Sam has given _____ her course to work full time.

4 She's looking _____ part-time work.

5 Carole wrote _____ for an application form.

6 What have you got out _____ your job?

7 Sandy was brought _____ in Essex.

8 Sandy hasn't put _____ weight working with chocolate.

9 We decided to find _____ how you become a model.

10 Sam got _____ to the finals of the competition.

11 Carole learned how to sort _____ people's problems.

12 The desire to eat everything has worn _____ .

Unit Three

Use the correct form of one of the verbs in the box to complete each sentence.

move	take	fill	drop	get
settle	send	set	work	call

1 Seventy young people _____ up places on the course.

2 Some of them _____ out because the course was too hard.

3 Sharon has _____ into her new flat.

4 So how do you _____ about house swapping?

5 You will be asked to _____ in a form.

6 We need to _____ out the solution to certain problems.

7 You don't have to pay now, you can _____ up at the end of your stay.

8 Some families _____ together to organise combined holidays.

9 The wedding present could be _____ on by post.

10 The engagement has been _____ off.

Unit Four

Use the correct form of one of the multi-word verbs in the box to complete each of these sentences.

pick up	carry out	break into	live on
show up	put in	take up	put off
knock down	get away with		

1 The fact the house was near the police station didn't _____ the burglars.

2 Few criminals can_____ the money they make from crime.

3 Your call will _____ on a screen at the police station.

4 Most crime is not _____ by professionals.

5 She may have just gone to _____ the children from school.

6 You might decide to _____ an alarm system.

7 Someone has _____ his car.

8 John was _____ by a mugger who stole his wallet.

9 The gang _____ $20,000 in the bank robbery.

10 Dealing with car theft _____ a lot of police time.

Unit Five

Use the correct form of one of the verbs in the box to complete each of these sentences.

bring	pull	take	come	turn	
put	set	get	pick	run	

1 Lesley's bank manager called her when her money began to _____ out.

2 Other girls _____ on Kelly because she was hard-working.

3 Some of the games here _____ back childhood memories.

4 First they give you a menu, then they _____ back and take your order.

5 Pubs used to _____ on sporting events in the hope of selling more drinks.

6 We arrived, had a coffee, then _____ out to explore the mountainside.

7 When it started to snow, we decided to _____ back immediately.

8 We knew we would never _____ back to the ski lift before it closed.

9 She had never _____ part in a car rally before.

10 The idea of Jenga is to _____ out loose bricks and replace them on top.

Unit Six

Choose one of the prepositions from the box to complete each sentence. You can use some of the prepositions more than once.

up	off	on	in	out	round

1 Polly crossed things _____ her shopping list as she picked them up in the supermarket.

2 They arrived at the airport and checked _____ at the desk.

3 You will have to turn _____ and go back the other way.

4 The plane will take _____ at 15.30.

5 An old friend of mine turned _____ unexpectedly at my house last night.

6 We decided to call _____ Aunt Alice as we were passing her house.

7 They rented _____ their house and went to live in the South of France.

8 I woke _____ in a strange room and wondered where I was.

9 As you listen, fill _____ the missing information.

10 She left _____ her age when completing the form.

Unit Seven

Use the correct form of one of the multi-word verbs in the box to complete each sentence.

build up	cut down	come across
fill up	get out of	take away
set up	get rid of	clear out
go on		

1 He _____ the car with lead-free petrol.

2 You should try to _____ the habit of putting sugar in your coffee.

3 We found these sweets when we were _____ an old cupboard.

4 He has succeeded in _____ the amount of salt he puts in his food.

5 Chantal Coady has _____ a new society.

6 Cholesterol _____ on the walls of the arteries.

7 Once you have lumps in chocolate sauce it's difficult to _____ them.

8 Do you want to eat your meal here or _____ it _____ ?

9 If you _____ eating so much chocolate, you'll put on weight.

10 Harry was breaking up an old sofa when he _____ an ancient sandwich.

Unit Eight

Use the correct form of one of the verbs in the box to complete each sentence.

do	block	pick	turn	switch
go	feed	get	throw	take

1 Fortunately, my CD player didn't _____ up the scratch on the disc.

2 I couldn't _____ without my mobile phone, it's so handy.

3 _____ in touch if you need any help.

4 I was waiting to pay in the shop when suddenly the fire alarm _____ off.

5 I'm _____ up with working in this horrible office.

6 The new Coke recipe _____ out not to be a great success.

7 It's time to _____ away your old address book.

8 I just _____ on the machine and it does all the work for me.

9 The next meeting will _____ place in London in January.

10 She listens to music while studying because it _____ out all other sounds.

Unit Nine

Choose one of the prepositions from the box to complete each sentence. You can use some of the prepositions more than once.

out	after	up	back	over

1 As we walked the wind started to get _____ and a few drops of rain fell.

2 The old man wanted to get _____ at his relations who hadn't been kind to him.

3 I realised there had been an accident when I heard someone calling _____ for help.

4 She has decided to take _____ aerobics as a way of keeping fit.

5 He had hoped his relatives would look _____ him in his old age.

6 Could you pay _____ the money I lent you last week please?

7 I'm afraid I'm going to be a bit late as I've been held _____ in heavy traffic.

8 Mr Taylor isn't here at the moment, could you ring him _____ later?

9 He goes to the gym to work _____ every Thursday evening.

10 It took me a long time to get _____ that cold I had last month.

Unit Ten

Use the correct form of one of the multi-word verbs in the box to complete each sentence. Some of the verbs can be divided by the object. There are two spaces in the sentences where the verb can be divided.

Example: Could you *fill* this form *in* please?

take back	look around	move out
try on	get off	head for
talk into	catch on	get stuck
go about	turn into	

1 Jane likes _____ the shops, though she doesn't often buy anything.

2 My brother _____ me _____ buying a mountain bike so that he could ride it!

3 You are not allowed to _____ the clothes _____ in that shop, but you can _____ them _____ if they don't fit.

4 Gloria's daughter has now _____ of the house and got her own flat.

5 When I go into Marks and Spencer, I always _____ straight _____ the food department.

6 Sometimes people find that their money _____ in vending machines.

7 Gladys _____ the train and realised she'd left her reading glasses at home.

8 Fast food has really _____ among young people in the last few years.

9 At the craft workshop you can talk to the craftsmen and women as they _____ their work.

10 Gloria has _____ her daughter's room _____ a shoe cupboard.

Unit Eleven

Use the correct form of one of the verbs in the box to complete each sentence.

put	drop	go	lose	take
wipe	give	stand	point	run

1 I think that the government should _____ up the tax on petrol.

2 Whole species of wild animals are being _____ out to make fur coats.

3 I would like to _____ out that the college has no recycling policy.

4 Lots of unnecessary handouts are being _____ out every day.

5 Demand for fur coats has really _____ off in the last few years.

6 Local people will _____ out if the beach is turned into a funfair.

7 I think we should _____ ahead with our plans to ban cars from the city centre.

8 Somebody needs to _____ up for our rights to a clean environment.

9 Cathy couldn't wait to _____ off the mask.

10 This car _____ on batteries rather than petrol.

Unit Twelve

Choose one of the prepositions from the box to complete each sentence. You can use some of the prepositions more than once.

up	back	out	off	through

1 Su thinks that parachuting is more fun than washing _____ or cleaning the house.

2 Kate's friend wanted to cheer her _____ .

3 Many office romances end _____ with the couple getting married.

4 Kate phoned again, but her friend didn't call her _____ .

5 Marie had to leave the royal palace when the French revolution broke _____ .

6 I was put _____ my dinner when I saw a huge spider sitting in a corner of the kitchen.

7 She looked _____ the photographs in order to seem polite.

8 I looked _____ her number in the phone book.

9 Research has shown _____ the problems caused by office romances.

10 If you pass your driving test, you'll want to dash _____ and buy a car.

Grammar Reference

Unit One

Present simple

This tense is used to describe habits, states and routines – that is, things which usually or always happen or which are usually or always true. In many languages, this tense is also used to describe what is happening now. Notice that this is not the case in English.

Uses:

a to talk about things which are always true:

*Water **boils** at 100° centigrade.*
*He **has** blue eyes.*

b to talk about habits and routines:

*I **walk** to school (usually).*

Present continuous

This tense is used to describe what is happening now:

*He **is studying** French.*

NB When describing a photograph or picture, we usually use the Present continuous – we talk about it as if it were happening now:

*The man in the picture **is crossing** the road.*

Order of adjectives

The following order is often used, but there are many exceptions.

Opinion	size	shape	colour	material	+ noun
horrible	small	square	blue	nylon	head scarf
wonderful	big	round	yellow	cotton	teddy bear

NB It is unusual to use more than two or three adjectives before a noun.

In case

In case is used when we want to be prepared for something that may happen. *In case* is followed by the Present simple tense but refers to future or present time.

*Take an anorak **in case it rains**.*

In case can also be used with the Past tense:

*I took an overcoat **in case it was cold**.*

Unit Two

To be used to + -ing + noun

This form is used to indicate how a person feels about something or about doing something. It expresses how comfortable or familiar a thing or action is to them.

*Pablo **is used to eating** later in the evening.*
*I am **used to the cold**.*

To get used to

This shows a change in how we feel about something:

*I **can't get used to** this weather .*
(I'm not able to change my feelings.)

*I am **getting used to eating** later.*
(My feelings about it are changing with experience.)

*I've **got used to drinking** this strange water.*
(My feelings have now changed as a result of experience.)

Present perfect

This tense is formed by: *Have* + the past participle of the verb.

Uses:

a to talk about past experiences in your life:

*I've **been** to Egypt three times.*

b to talk about things which have happened in unfinished periods of time:

*I've **drunk** too much coffee today.*
*I've **learnt** how to use a PC.*

c to talk about things which have recently happened:

*She's **just written** a letter to him.*

Present perfect vs Past simple

If you need to decide which tense to use, ask yourself the question *When?*

*I've **never been** to Italy, but I **went** to Greece last summer.*

*I've **never been** to Italy.*
When? In my life (Present perfect).

*I **went** to Greece last summer.*
When? Last summer (Past simple).

The Past simple is used to talk about things which happened in periods which have finished.

Comparison of adjectives

One-syllable adjectives	two-syllable adjectives	three or more syllable adjectives
calm → calmer	tidy → tidier	enthusiastic → more enthusiastic
old → older	dirty → dirtier	responsible → more responsible
hot → hotter	helpful → more helpful	
wet → wetter	handsome → more handsome	

Exceptions: good → better
bad → worse

far → further/farther (*further*, but not *farther*, can mean 'more' or 'in addition'):

Tell me if you need any **further** *information.*

One-syllable adjectives form the comparative by adding *er*. Single consonants at the end of the word double before adding *er*.

Two-syllable adjectives ending in *y* form the comparative by changing *y* to *i* and adding *er*.

Two-syllable adjectives ending in other letters and all adjectives of three or more syllables form the comparative by adding *more*.

Positive comparisons are made with *than*:
*John is old***er than** *Mary.*

Comparisons of equality are made with *as ... as*:
John is **as tall as** *Mary.*

The same + noun + *as*:
Jim is **the same height as** *Sue.*

Negative comparisons are made with *not as ... as*:
This baby is **not as young as** *that one.*

Less is used where the adjective takes *more* in the positive:
John is **less enthusiastic than** *Mary.*

NB *Not as ... as* is possible with all adjectives.
Less than is usually found in more formal language.

Superlatives

The superlative is formed by adding *est* to one-syllable adjectives, *iest* to two-syllable adjectives ending in *y* and *most* before longer adjectives:

It's **the oldest building** *in the city.*
It was **the prettiest village** *I had ever visited.*
He is **the most enthusiastic student** *in the class.*

Unit Three

Causative *have*

This form exists in a variety of tenses and in each case it is the verb 'to have' which indicates the tense. The verb indicating the action is always the past participle.

I'm **having my car repaired**.
(This means that someone is repairing my car.)

Compare with

I'm **repairing my car**.
(This means I am repairing it myself.)

Causative *have* is formed by:
The subject = Sharon
The verb to have = is having
The object = her central heating
The past participle of the main verb = serviced.

→ *Sharon is having her central heating serviced.*

Genitive *'s*

The genitive *'s* is mainly used to indicate possession of things by people, and family relationships. Add *'s* to singular nouns.

*Sally***'s** *dog.*
*Sally and Peter***'s** *dog.*
*Nick***'s** *brother.*

Add *'* only to plural nouns ending in *s:*

*The girls***'** *books.*
*My grandparents***'** *house.*

Plural nouns not ending in *s* are an exception:

*The children***'s** *books.*

Animals, days and cities sometimes take the genitive. Most other objects do not:

The **dog's** *basket.*
Monday's *lesson.*
London's *theatres.*

but

The leg of the table or *The chair leg.*

Grammar Reference

Needs doing

This form is used to indicate that a certain job should be done, but we do not know, or do not want to know, who is going to do the job:

*The windows **need cleaning.***
(They are dirty.)
*The tape recorder **needs mending.***
(It is broken.)

For/Since

For and *since* are used with perfect tenses to indicate length of time.
Since can also be used with the Past simple.
Since refers to a date in the past and is used to talk about things happening between then and now.
For refers to the period of time that has passed between a point of time in the past and now.

*I've known Mary **since March.***
*I've known Mary **for three months.***
(It is now June.)

Since can also be used in the middle of sentences which begin with a time period:

***It's a long time since** I've seen you.*
(I haven't seen you for a long time).

Since + Past simple:

***It's two years since** I left the army.*
(I left the army two years ago – finished action in the past.)

Unit Four

Past simple/Past continuous

The Past simple is used:

a to talk about events in the past:
I went** to the cinema **last night.

b to talk about events that happened one after another:
***I finished** my homework and **sat down** to watch TV.*

The Past continuous is used to talk about events which had begun but hadn't finished at a specific time in the past:
***I was watching TV at 9:00** yesterday evening.*

The Past simple and continuous are used together:

a when one action is interrupted by another:
*I **was watching** TV when the lights **went out.***

b when one action takes place during a longer one:
***When/While I was shopping** in Oxford Street I **saw** a car accident.*

Deductions

Modal verbs are used to say how sure or unsure we are about things:

*This **must be** Louisa's diary, it's got her name inside.*
(I'm sure it's hers.)
*This **can't be** his mother, she's not old enough.*
(I'm sure it isn't his mother.)

*He **could be** a teacher.*
*It **might be** her birthday today.*
*This **may be** Jane's pen.*
(It's possible but I'm not sure.)

In the past, these verbs are formed with *have*:

*It **must have been** his house.*
*That **can't have been** his mother.*
*It **might have been** the butler who killed her.*

Relative pronouns

Relative pronouns agree with nouns:

*The house **where** I live.*
*The lady **whose** house was burgled.*
*The man **who** was arrested.*
*The books **which/that** are on the table.*

Relative pronouns are used to combine two ideas about one subject:

There is a man outside.
  +
He is selling ice cream.
There is a man outside who is selling ice cream.

Unit Five

Linking words

1 *After/After that*

After is generally followed by a noun, gerund or phrase:

***After coffee** we went home.*
***After drinking** our coffee we went home.*
***After we had drunk our coffee** we went home.*

When *after* is used at the beginning of a sentence, we are saying that the events happened in the order which they are mentioned.
After + first event + second event.

2 *After that/Afterwards*

These refer to something already mentioned.

First event + *afterwards* + second event:
*We had coffee. **After that** we went home.*
***Afterwards** we went home.*

Grammar Reference

3 *Before*

Before follows the same rules as *after* when it is at the beginning of a sentence. It can be followed by a noun, gerund or phrase.

When *before* is used at the beginning of a sentence it indicates that two events which are mentioned are in reverse order:

Before + second event + first event:
Before I **paid** the bill I **checked** the total to make sure it was correct.

However, when *before* is used between two events the order is:

First event + *before* + second event:
I checked my change **before** *I left the shop.*

4 *Although/Despite*

These are used to indicate contrast.

Although is followed by a subject and verb:
Although *there was very little snow, the skiing resort was crowded.*

Despite is followed by a noun, a noun phrase or gerund + subject + verb:
Despite the fact that *it was cold, the central heating was turned off.*
Despite the cold weather, *we decided to climb the mountain.*
Despite feeling *cold, we decided to climb the mountain.*

NB We can also say *even though (although)*
in spite of (despite)

Used to + infinitive

This tells us about things that happened in the past but which don't happen now. These are things which happened regularly over a long period of time.

He **used to play football** *when he was a child.*
Does he play football now? (no)
Did he play football often? (yes)

NB *Used to* does not exist in the present. The present equivalent of *used to* is *usually*.

Past perfect

When we tell a story, we set a time in the past in which the narrative takes place. When we refer to actions and periods before that, the Past perfect is used:

When we got back to the house, **he had removed** *the furniture.*
(First he removed the furniture, then we got back.)
When we got back to the house, **he removed** *the furniture.*
(First we got back, then he removed the furniture.)

Unit Six

Time and money expressions as adjectives

It's a **four-hour flight** *from Birmingham to Athens.*
        Adj   + noun
(The flight from Birmingham to Athens takes four hours).

He had to pay a **ten-pound parking fine**.
                Adj   + noun
(He had to pay a fine of ten pounds.)

NB When the price or the time are used as adjectives, they have no plural form.

Compound adjectives

These are formed when a noun and adjective, or verb and adjective, are combined with a hyphen to form an adjectival phrase:

A girl with blue eyes = A *blue-eyed girl.*
A woman who looks friendly = A *friendly-looking woman.*

To avoid sentences becoming lists of adjectives, it is good style to use compound adjectives before the main noun, especially when further adjectives follow:

A **tall grey-haired man** *with green eyes and a moustache.*

Future time

a The Present simple is used when we talk about time-tables and things which happen at fixed times and so cannot be changed:

The flight **lands at 16:00.**

The important question to ask yourself is:
Can I change it – is it my decision?

b The Present continuous is used to talk about plans which we have already made with somebody else:

I'm meeting *the Manager* **at 2:30**.

The important questions to ask yourself are:
Have I already decided?
Have I made an arrangement with someone else?
If the answer is 'yes', then use the Present continuous to describe your plans.

c *Going to* + infinitive is used for future plans and intentions that involve only ourselves, or where no definite arrangement has been made.

I'm going to *learn Russian* **next year**.

Compare:
My Russian classes **start** *next week.*
(It doesn't depend on me.)
I'm starting *Russian classes next week.*
(I've decided and I've arranged to join the class.)

So/Such

So is used with adjectives to make them stronger:
*This sport is **so** dangerous.*

And to link them to resulting actions:
*It was **so** cold that I wore two pairs of socks.*

Such can be used in a similar way with adjective and noun groups:
*It is **such** a dangerous sport.*
(countable).
*It is **such** cold weather.*
(uncountable).
*It was **such** cold weather that I wore two pairs of socks.*

So can be used with quantifiers:
*There were **so many** people that I could not breathe.*
(countable).
*There were **so few** people at the disco that we came home early.*
(countable).
*There was **so much** rice that we couldn't eat it all.*
(uncountable).
*There was **so little** wind that we couldn't go sailing.*
(uncountable).

Such can only be used with quantifiers that have an indefinite article:
*There were **such a lot** of people that...*
*There was **such a lack** of water that...*

Unit Seven

-ing form/infinitive

Some verbs are followed either by the *-ing* form or by an infinitive:
*I want **to go**.*
*I enjoy **going**.*

The commonest verbs which are followed by the *-ing* form are:

admit, appreciate, avoid, consider, delay, deny, detest, dislike, endure, enjoy, escape, excuse, face, feel, like, finish, forgive, give up, can't help, imagine, involve, mention, mind, miss, postpone, practise, put off, resent, resist, risk, can't stand, suggest, understand.

The commonest verbs which are followed directly by an infinitive are:

afford, agree, appear, arrange, ask, attempt, bear, begin, care, choose, consent, dare, decide, determine, expect, fail, forget, happen, hate, help, hesitate, hope, intend, learn, like, love, manage, mean, neglect, offer, prefer, prepare, pretend, promise, propose, refuse, regret, remember, seem, start, trouble, try, want, wish.

Some of these verbs can also be followed by the *-ing* form, often with a different meaning:
*Remember **to close** the door (in the future)*
*I remember **closing** the door (in the past)*

Too/Enough

Too and *enough* are opposite concepts used to talk about quantity and degree:
*This house is **too small** = This house **is not large enough**.*

Too is used before adjectives *(too **hot**)*.
Enough is used after adjectives *(**cold** enough)*.

Too is used before quantifiers and nouns:
*Too **many/few people***
(countable noun).
*Too **much/little water***
(uncountable noun).

Enough is used directly with countable and uncountable nouns:
*There **are not enough** plates.*
*There **is not enough** rice.*

Conditional 0/1

The zero conditional uses *if* or *when* to say what always or usually happens in a given situation:
*When you **press** this button, a bell **rings**.*

The first conditional is used to predict what will happen given certain other facts. We use it for things that will probably happen in the real future and for predictions:
*If I **see** her, **I'll give** her a message.*
*If it **rains, there'll be** a lot of traffic.*

If is followed by the present tense, and the subject of the main clause by the future, even when the order is changed:
*I'll give her a message **if I see** her.*

Prefer/Rather

a *I prefer* is used to refer to a general situation:
*I **prefer eating** Greek food to French food.* (always/usually)

b *I'd prefer* is used to refer to a specific situation:
*I'd **prefer to go** to a restaurant.*
(now/on this occasion)

NB *I'd rather* + infinitive without 'to' can be used in place of *I'd prefer*.

Unless/If

If refers to a positive condition:
*If I **win** I'll be happy.*

Unless refers to a negative condition and can be used instead of *if not* when we refer to exceptional circumstances which would change a situation:
*Unless I **win**/If I **don't win** I **won't be** happy.*

Future time (*will* + infinitive)

This form is used when we make decisions, offers and promises at the time of speaking:
*What **shall I** have? Let's see .....Oh yes, **I'll have** a salad.*
(I'm deciding now.)

A: Have a lovely holiday!
*B: Thanks. **I'll send** you a card.* (I promise.)

A: Oh no, I've left my bag in the car.
*B: **I'll go** back and get it for you.* (I offer.)

Looks/Seems/Appears

These phrases are useful for describing photographs:

It looks as if they + verb.
They look + adjective.
It looks like + (a) noun.

She seems to be + adjective.
She seems to be + verb + *-ing*.
He appears to be + adjective.
He appears to be + verb + *-ing*.

I get the impression that he is...
Maybe they're...
Perhaps they're...

Relative Clauses

Relative Clauses can be 'defining' or 'non-defining'. They begin with a relative pronoun – *who* or *that* used for people, and *which* or *that* in other cases.

Defining relative clauses identify nouns – they tell us which person, thing etc. the speaker means:
*The girl **who** sits next to me is Japanese.*
(no punctuation surrounding this type of clause).

The relative pronoun can be omitted if it is the object of the clause:
*The girl **(that) I spoke to** was Japanese.*

Non-defining relative clauses give extra information about a person or thing:
*Mr Brown, **who is an electrician,** mended our kitchen light.*
(This extra information is enclosed by commas.)

Whose is used to indicate possession:
*My brother, **whose house** was burgled last week, has been asked to help with police investigations.*

You can't use 'that' or omit the relative pronoun in non-defining relative clauses.

Unit Eight

The Passive

The passive voice is formed by making the object of the active phrase into the subject of a new phrase:
Active – *I **wash** my car every week.*
Passive – *My car **is washed** every week.*

Passive voice equivalents exist for all major active tenses.

The passive is used in three main ways:

a To describe a process.

b When the action is more important than who does it:
*The photocopier **was repaired** in two hours.*

c When we do not know, or do not want to say, who does the action:
*A window **has been broken**.*

NB The agent (*by....*) is only used when it includes important information:
*America **was discovered** by Columbus in 1492.*

Never add 'by someone' to a passive phrase.

Will/Going to (Predictions)

When making predictions we can use *will* or *going to*.
Will is used more to express the speaker's own opinion:
*I think **it'll be** a good party.*

Going to is used when there is evidence of the future event:
*She's **going to have** a baby.*

Conditional 2

Formed with *If* + past tense, subject + *would*.
This is used to predict what would happen given an improbable or hypothetical situation.
*If I **were** a fish, I **would live** in the sea.* (But I'm not!)

Compare:

a *If it **rains, I'll take** an umbrella.*
(I think it is probably going to rain – first conditional.)

b *If I **went, I wouldn't speak** to him.*
(I'm probably not going.)

So/Nor

So is used with modal and auxiliary verbs to agree with positive statements:
*I like pizza. – **So** do I.*
*I can swim. – **So** can she.*

Nor is used to agree with negative statements.
*I don't like cabbage. – **Nor** do I.*
*I haven't done my homework. – **Nor** has Marion.*

So/Nor cannot be used to disagree with statements:
I'm not going to the party. – Really? I am.

Unit Nine

Present perfect continuous

The Present perfect continuous is used for activities:

a which take place over an extended period of time, or which are repeated often in an extended period of time:
I've been playing *tennis for five years* (regularly).
I've been playing *tennis all morning* (continuously).

b which began in the past and either continue or have finished in the present time period specified:
I've been writing *letters today.*
(Today has not finished.)
I've been reading *in English this morning.*
(I have not had lunch yet.)
NB I am not necessarily reading or writing now.

c which are general rather than specific or counted:
I've been listening *to a lot of classical music lately.*

Regrets (*I wish/If only*)

Past regrets can be expressed by using *I wish/If only* + Past perfect:

I went for a picnic. It rained. (When? – in the past).
I feel sad. (Why? – because it spoilt the picnic) =
I wish/If only it hadn't rained.
In this phrase we are expressing the fact that we would like to change what happened but it is impossible, and so we feel sad.

I wish/If only I hadn't argued *with my father.*
(But I did and I can't change it now; I'm sorry about it – I regret it.)

I regret is followed by *-ing*, and is normally used for events which are in our control. It is a more formal way of expressing our feelings than *I wish/If only*.

Conditional 3

This tense is formed with Past perfect, *would* + *have* + past participle. It refers to past time – to things that cannot now be changed:

If it ***had rained,*** (Did it rain? – No)
I ***would have taken*** *an umbrella.*
(Did I take an umbrella? – No. Why? – because it didn't rain.)
If it ***hadn't been*** *sunny,* (Was it sunny? – Yes)
I ***wouldn't have got sunburnt.*** (Did I get sunburnt? – Yes.)

Notice that in speech the third conditional is nearly always contracted:
If ***I'd seen*** *him,* ***I'd have ('ve) said*** *hello.*

In writing we often contract *had* and *would* but not *have* in third conditional sentences.

Unit Ten

Modal verbs – Obligation

The meaning of the various verbs can be summarised as follows:

Positive:

You must go *You have to go*	It's obligatory, you have no choice.
You need to go *You should go*	It's very advisable, but you choose.
You ought to go	I advise you to go, but you choose.
You can go	If you want, you choose.
You may go	You have my permission to go.

Negative:

You mustn't go *You can't go*	It's forbidden, you have no choice.
You shouldn't go *You oughtn't to go*	I advise you not to go, but you choose.
You don't have to go *You don't need to go*	It's not obligatory, you choose.
You needn't go	It's not necessary, you choose.

Make, let, allow

Make + infinitive is used to express obligation.
They ***make*** *you* ***wear*** *a uniform at my school.* (active)
You ***are made to wear*** *a uniform at my school.* (passive)

Let + infinitive is used to express permission in the active:
They ***let*** *you park here on Saturdays.*

Allow + infinitive with *to* is used to express permission in the passive:
You ***are allowed*** *to park here on Saturdays.*

Wishes

a *To wish* can be used as a simple verb:
I ***wish*** *you a Merry Christmas.*

b *Wish* + Past perfect is used to express past regrets.

c *Wish* + *was/were/had* is used to express wishes about states:
I ***wish*** *I* ***had*** *blue eyes* (but I haven't).
I ***wish*** *he* ***was/were*** *rich* (but he isn't).

d *Wish* + *could* is used to express wishes about actions:
I ***wish*** *I* ***could*** *drive* (but I'm not able to).
I ***wish*** *you* ***could*** *dance* (but you are not able to).

e *Wish* + *would* is used to express annoyance at the habits of others:
I ***wish*** *you* ***wouldn't*** *sing in the bath.*
(I would like you to stop, but you won't.)
He ***wishes*** *it* ***would*** *stop raining.*
(He'd like it to stop raining, but he can't change it.)

Unit Eleven

Reported Statements

Most tenses in direct speech change in reported speech:

Present simple → Past simple
Present perfect → Past perfect
Present perfect continuous → Past perfect continuous
Present continuous → Past continuous
Past simple → Past perfect
Past continuous → Past perfect continuous

NB The Past perfect remains the same in reported speech.

Other similar forms change in similar ways:

am going to → **was** going to
am used to doing → **was** used to doing
have to → **had** to
am able → **was** able
have something done → **had** something done.

There are occasions where you needn't change the tense:

a where facts are still true:
My name is Paul – He said his name is Paul.

b Past simple to Past perfect depends on time references:
'Peter left when I arrived'– She said Peter left when she arrived.
(Time references are clear – no need to change.)

*'I was sick'.– She said she **had been** sick* (Here the Past simple (*she was*) could be misinterpreted as representing the Present simple ie *she is sick now*.)

Modal verbs can be divided into those that change and those that do not.

These can change:	These stay the same:
can → could	should
may → might	could
will → would	would
must → had to	ought
shall → should	might

NB *Would* does not change to *would have* in reported speech.

Time Indicators

Main changes:

today → that day
now → then
this → that
here → there
ago → before/previously
tomorrow → the next day/the following day
yesterday → the day before/the previous day
last night → the night before/the previous night
next week → the following week/the week after (that)

Reported questions

a *Wh* questions:
*What time **is** it, Jenny? – Nick asked Jenny what time it **was**.*
Do not forget to change the word order and omit the question mark, because in reported speech these are not questions any more.

b *Yes/No* questions:
*'**Are you coming** to the cinema, Jenny?' – Nick asked Jenny **whether/if** she **was coming** to the cinema.*

c Requests:
*'**Would** you **pass** the salt please, Sid?'*
This type of question can be reported in full:
*Tom asked Sid **if** he **would pass** him the salt.*
or with an infinitive, which summarises the action:
*Tom asked Sid **to pass** him the salt.*

d Orders: usually an imperative:
*'**Go** to your room!' – Sarah's mother told her **to go** to her room.*

Impersonal passive

This form is used with certain verbs when we are sure about the truth of the information:
*He is **said to be** living in the USA.*
(Some people say he is living in the USA, but it may not be true).

Other useful verbs are: *reported to be, believed to be, thought to be, understood to be.*

Reporting verbs

Often the meaning of a sentence in direct speech is summarised by a verb in reported speech.
*'Would you like to go to the cinema, Jane?' **said** Eric.*
*Eric **invited** Jane to the cinema.*

There are three main types:

Type A: Verb + person + infinitive with 'to'.
*He **told me to sit** down.*

Type B: Verb + infinitive with 'to'.
*She **agreed to give** him a reference.*

Type C: Verb + -*ing*.
*She **regretted leaving** her job.*

NB *He **apologised for losing** the report.*

It's (high) time + subjunctive

This form is used when something needs doing urgently:
It's (high) time we went. (subjunctive)
(Adding 'high' makes this form stronger.)
This means we should have already gone – it is stronger than *It's time to go.*

NB The subjunctive is formed in the same way as the past tense.

Unit Twelve

Question tags

A question tag is a short interrogative phrase to a statement.
It's cold (statement)
isn't it? (tag).

Negative tags are added to positive statements and positive tags to negative statements.
It's not *cold,* ***is it?***

The question tag repeats the auxiliary verb or modal auxiliary verb from the statement, and the subject pronoun. If there is no auxiliary verb in the statement, *do* is used:
You **like** *oranges,* **don't** *you?*

There are exceptions, for example, imperatives:
Sit down, will you?
Please help, won't you?

Future in the past

These forms are used when we take a point in the past and talk about what happened after that.

When he was six, everyone knew **he was going to be** *a footballer.*
He **went on to** *play in the school team.*
He **was to** *appear in a total of thirty-four international matches before he retired.*

Uses of *do*

Do is an auxiliary verb that is used to form questions and negatives.

Do you know *the time?*
I'm sorry I **don't know** *the time.*

Do can also be used to avoid repeating a longer phrase.
I don't like ice-cream, but my sister **does***.*

Do is also used in positive statements to give emphasis to the verb.
Oh, I **do** *like your new dress.* (Really, I'm not just being polite!)
I **do** *work hard at school.* (I know you think I don't.)

Irregular verbs

The verbs marked * can be either regular or irregular, eg burn – burnt or burned.

infinitive	past simple	past participle
arise	arose	arisen
be	was, were	been
bear	bore	borne
beat	beat	beaten
become	became	become
begin	began	begun
bend	bent	bent
bind	bound	bound
bite	bit	bitten
bleed	bled	bled
blow	blew	blown
break	broke	broken
bring	brought	brought
build	built	built
burn*	burnt	burnt
burst	burst	burst
buy	bought	bought
catch	caught	caught
choose	chose	chosen
come	came	come
cost	cost	cost
creep	crept	crept
cut	cut	cut
deal	dealt	dealt
dig	dug	dug
do	did	done
draw	drew	drawn
dream*	dreamt	dreamt
drink	drank	drunk
drive	drove	driven
eat	ate	eaten
fall	fell	fallen
feed	fed	fed
feel	felt	felt
fight	fought	fought
find	found	found
fly	flew	flown
forbid	forbade	forbidden
forget	forgot	forgotten
forgive	forgave	forgiven
freeze	froze	frozen
get	got	got

infinitive	past simple	past participle
give	gave	given
go	went	gone, been
grind	ground	ground
grow	grew	grown
hang	hung	hung
have	had	had
hear	heard	heard
hide	hid	hidden
hit	hit	hit
hold	held	held
hurt	hurt	hurt
keep	kept	kept
kneel	knelt	knelt
know	knew	known
lay	laid	laid
lead	led	led
lean*	leant	leant
learn*	learnt	learnt
leave	left	left
lend	lent	lent
let	let	let
light	lit	lit
lose	lost	lost
make	made	made
mean	meant	meant
meet	met	met
pay	paid	paid
put	put	put
read	read	read
ride	rode	ridden
ring	rang	rung
rise	rose	risen
run	ran	run
say	said	said
see	saw	seen
sell	sold	sold
send	sent	sent
set	set	set
shake	shook	shaken
shine	shone	shone
shoot	shot	shot
show	showed	shown

infinitive	past simple	past participle
shrink	shrank	shrunk
shut	shut	shut
sing	sang	sung
sink	sank	sunk
sit	sat	sat
sleep	slept	slept
slide	slid	slid
smell*	smelt	smelt
sow	sowed	sown
speak	spoke	spoken
speed	sped	sped
spell*	spelt	spelt
spend	spent	spent
spill*	spilt	spilt
spin	spun, span	spun
spit	spat	spat
split	split	split
spoil*	spoilt	spoilt
spread	spread	spread
spring	sprang	sprung
stand	stood	stood
steal	stole	stolen
stick	stuck	stuck
sting	stung	stung
strike	struck	struck
swear	swore	sworn
sweep	swept	swept
swim	swam	swum
swing	swung	swung
take	took	taken
teach	taught	taught
tear	tore	torn
tell	told	told
think	thought	thought
throw	threw	thrown
wake	woke	woken
wear	wore	worn
weep	wept	wept
win	won	won
wind	wound	wound
write	wrote	written

Wordlist

Unit One

amusing /əˈmjuːzɪŋ/
analyst /ˈænəlɪst/
anorak /ˈænəræk/
appreciation /əpriːsɪˈeɪʃn/
artistic /ɑːˈtɪstɪk/
associated /əˈsəʊsɪeɪtɪd/
attitude /ˈætɪtʃuːd/
beige /ˈbeɪʒ/
boring /ˈbɔːrɪŋ/
bossy /ˈbɒsɪ/
characteristics /kærəktəˈrɪstɪks/
charming /ˈtʃɑːmɪŋ/
checked /ˈtʃekt/
clothing /ˈkləʊðɪŋ/
coast /kəʊst/
compulsory /kəmˈpʌlsrɪ/
cosmetics /kɒzˈmetɪks/
cotton /ˈkɒtn/
creative /kriːˈeɪtɪv/
curly /ˈkɜːlɪ/
daily /ˈdeɪlɪ/
department /dɪˈpɑːtmənt/
description /dɪˈskrɪpʃn/
efficient /ɪˈfɪʃnt/
enthusiasm /ɪnˈθjuːzɪæzm/
environmental /ɪnvaɪrənˈmentl/
equipment /ɪˈkwɪpmənt/
eyebrows /ˈaɪbraʊz/
fingerprints /ˈfɪŋgəprɪnts/
flexible /ˈfleksɪbl/
friendliness /ˈfrendlɪnəs/
fussy /ˈfʌsɪ/
heel /hiːl/
honest /ˈɒnɪst/
ice /aɪs/
identical /aɪˈdentɪkl/
identity /aɪˈdentɪtɪ/
indicate /ˈɪndɪkeɪt/
interview /ˈɪntəvjuː/
lazy /ˈleɪzɪ/
leather /ˈleðə(r)/
lipstick /ˈlɪpstɪk/
lively /ˈlaɪvlɪ/
luggage /ˈlʌgɪdʒ/
majority /məˈdʒɒrətɪ/
marketing /ˈmɑːkətɪŋ/
nasty /ˈnɑːstɪ/
needle /ˈniːdl/
noticeable /ˈnəʊtɪsəbl/
observant /əbˈzɜːvənt/
patient /ˈpeɪʃnt/
pattern /ˈpætn/
pen-friend /ˈpenfrend/
personality /pɜːsəˈnælətɪ/
pessimistic /pesɪˈmɪstɪk/

plaster /ˈplɑːstə(r)/
polish /ˈpɒlɪʃ/
popular /ˈpɒpjələ(r)/
practical /ˈpræktɪkl/
rectangular /rekˈtæŋgjələ(r)/
reliable /rɪˈlaɪəbl/
respond /rɪˈspɒnd/
risk (v) /rɪsk/
rucksack /ˈrʌksæk/
sandals /ˈsændlz/
scheme /skiːm/
selfish /ˈselfɪʃ/
sensible /ˈsensəbl/
sensitive /ˈsensətɪv/
shyness /ˈʃaɪnəs/
spare /speə(r)/
spoil /spɔɪl/
striped /straɪpt/
successful /səkˈsesfl/
tablet /ˈtæblət/
tend /tend/
tent /tent/
thirsty /ˈθɜːstɪ/
torch /tɔːtʃ/
traditional /trəˈdɪʃnəl/
trainee /treɪˈniː/
trustworthy /ˈtrʌstwɜːðɪ/
underline /ʌndəˈlaɪn/
unique /juːˈniːk/
waterproof /ˈwɔːtəpruːf/
weight /weɪt/
woollen /ˈwʊlən/

Unit Two

ability /əˈbɪlətɪ/
absence /ˈæbsəns/
accommodation /əkɒməˈdeɪʃn/
advances /ədˈvɑːnsɪz/
agency /ˈeɪdʒənsɪ/
airy /ˈeərɪ/
ambition /æmˈbɪʃn/
applicant /ˈæplɪkənt/
appointment /əˈpɔɪntmənt/
available /əˈveɪləbl/
babysitter /ˈbeɪbɪsɪtə(r)/
beauty /ˈbjuːtɪ/
book /bʊk/
calm /kɑːm/
career /kəˈrɪə(r)/
caring /ˈkeərɪŋ/
casual /ˈkæʒʊəl/
century /ˈsentʃərɪ/
challenge /ˈtʃæləndʒ/
chaotic /keɪˈɒtɪk/
chocolates /ˈtʃɒkləts/
conference /ˈkɒnfrəns/

constantly /ˈkɒnstəntlɪ/
contract /ˈkɒntrækt/
cope /kəʊp/
crisis /ˈkraɪsɪs/
dealing /ˈdiːlɪŋ/
dedicated /ˈdedɪkeɪtɪd/
degree /dɪˈgriː/
desirable /dɪˈzaɪrəbl/
develop /dɪˈveləp/
driving licence /ˈdraɪvɪŋ ˈlaɪsəns/
earn /ɜːn/
Easter /ˈiːstə/
emotionally /ɪˈməʊʃnəlɪ/
encourage /ɪŋˈkʌrɪdʒ/
enquire /ɪŋˈkwaɪə(r)/
enthusiastic /ɪnθjuːzɪˈæstɪk/
entire /ɪnˈtaɪə(r)/
exotic /ɪgˈzɒtɪk/
experience /ɪkˈspɪərɪəns/
fate /feɪt/
financial /fɪˈnænʃl/
gradually /ˈgrædʒuːəlɪ/
graphics /ˈgræfɪks/
height /haɪt/
hindrance /ˈhɪndrəns/
immune /ɪˈmjuːn/
impress /ɪmˈpres/
intelligent /ɪnˈtelɪdʒənt/
interpersonal /ɪntəˈpɜːsnəl/
keen /kiːn/
managerial /mænəˈdʒɪərɪəl/
model /ˈmɒdl/
modelling /ˈmɒdlɪŋ/
nervous /ˈnɜːvəs/
overweight /əʊvəˈweɪt/
overwhelming /əʊvəˈwelmɪŋ/
personnel /pɜːsəˈnel/
persuade /pəˈsweɪd/
physically /ˈfɪzɪklɪ/
polite /pəˈlaɪt/
postpone /pəʊsˈpəʊn/
potential /pəˈtenʃl/
product /ˈprɒdʌkt/
punctual /ˈpʌŋktʃuəl/
qualifications /kwɒlɪfɪˈkeɪʃnz/
qualities /ˈkwɒlətɪz/
queue /kjuː/
quick-thinking /kwɪk ˈθɪŋkɪŋ/
range /reɪndʒ/
reserved /rɪˈzɜːvd/
responsibility /rɪspɒnsɪˈbɪlɪtɪ/
responsible /rɪˈspɒnsəbl/
retailing /ˈriːteɪlɪŋ/
reward /rɪˈwɔːd/
role /rəʊl/
sample /ˈsɑːmpl/
screen /skriːn/
sensible /ˈsensɪbl/
shock /ʃɒk/
skills /skɪlz/
skinny /ˈskɪnɪ/
smart /smɑːt/

smoothly /ˈsmuːðlɪ/
sociable /ˈsəʊʃəbl/
spot /spɒt/
stand /stænd/
swallow /ˈswɒləʊ/
sweater /ˈswetə(r)/
talkative /ˈtɔːkətɪv/
team /tiːm/
temptation /tempˈteɪʃn/
tidy /ˈtaɪdɪ/
training /ˈtreɪnɪŋ/
twice /twaɪs/
type /taɪp/
typing /ˈtaɪpɪŋ/
unconsciously /ʌnˈkɒnʃəslɪ/
uniform /ˈjuːnɪfɔːm/
vegetarian /vedʒɪˈteərɪən/
weird /wɪəd/
well-built /wel ˈbɪlt/
well-organised /wel ˈɔːgənaɪzd/
willing /ˈwɪlɪŋ/
win /wɪn/

Unit Three

advice /ədˈvaɪs/
angry /ˈæŋgrɪ/
annoying /əˈnɔɪɪŋ/
arrangement /əˈreɪndʒmənt/
balcony /ˈbælkənɪ/
behave /bɪˈheɪv/
behaviour /bɪˈheɪvjə(r)/
belongings /bɪˈlɒŋɪŋz/
birthday /ˈbɜːθdeɪ/
block /blɒk/
bone /bəʊn/
bride /braɪd/
bungalow /ˈbʌŋgələʊ/
burglar /ˈbɜːglə(r)/
carpentry /ˈkɑːpəntrɪ/
client /ˈklaɪənt/
combined /kəmˈbaɪnd/
community /kəˈmjuːnətɪ/
contact /ˈkɒntækt/
cottage /ˈkɒtɪdʒ/
critical /ˈkrɪtɪkəl/
custom /ˈkʌstəm/
damage /ˈdæmɪdʒ/
decorating /ˈdekəreɪtɪŋ/
delicacy /ˈdelɪkəsɪ/
delightful /dɪˈlaɪtfl/
deliver /dɪˈlɪvə/
designer /dɪˈzaɪnə(r)/
destination /destɪˈneɪʃn/
detached /dɪˈtætʃt/
detail /ˈdiːteɪl/
directory /daɪˈrektrɪ/
disappointed /dɪsəˈpɔɪntɪd/
discipline /ˈdɪsəplɪn/
disgusting /dɪsˈgʌstɪŋ/
effort /ˈefət/
emergency /ɪˈmɜːdʒənsɪ/

escape /ɪˈskeɪp/
exchange /ɪksˈtʃeɪndʒ/
excursion /ɪksˈkɜːʃn/
expenses /ɪkˈspensɪz/
expert /ˈekspɜːt/
fantastic /fænˈtæstɪk/
fee /fiː/
feed /fiːd/
firm /fɜːm/
force /fɔːs/
form /fɔːm/
fortnight /ˈfɔːtnaɪt/
freedom /ˈfriːdəm/
furniture /ˈfɜːnɪtʃə(r)/
garage /ˈɡærɑːʒ/
genuine /ˈdʒenjuːɪn/
genuinely /ˈdʒenjuːɪnlɪ/
gift /ɡɪft/
grandparent /ˈɡrænpeərənt/
groom /ɡruːm/
guest /ɡest/
heating /ˈhiːtɪŋ/
host /həʊst/
indiscreet /ɪndɪˈskriːt/
individual /ɪndɪˈvɪdʒʊəl/
insurance /ɪnˈʃʊərəns/
intention /ɪnˈtenʃn/
interest /ˈɪntrəst/
invitation /ɪnvɪˈteɪʃn/
jump /dʒʌmp/
jumper /ˈdʒʌmpə(r)/
light bulb /ˈlaɪt bʌlb/
likely /ˈlaɪklɪ/
location /ləʊˈkeɪʃn/
loo paper /ˈluː peɪpə(r)/
luxury /ˈlʌkʃərɪ/
manners /ˈmænəz/
mature /məˈtʃʊə(r)/
mend /mend/
minimum /ˈmɪnɪməm/
mixture /ˈmɪkstʃə(r)/
motorway /ˈməʊtəweɪ/
neighbour /ˈneɪbə(r)/
object(n) /ˈɒbdʒekt/
occupied /ˈɒkjəpaɪd/
offend /əˈfend/
owner /ˈəʊnə/
pack (n) /pæk/
package /ˈpækɪdʒ/
patio /ˈpætɪəʊ/
persist /pəˈsɪst/
pet /pet/
petrol /ˈpetrəl/
plants /plɑːnts/
pleasantly /ˈplezəntlɪ/
pleasure /ˈpleʒə/
porter /ˈpɔːtə(r)/
portion /ˈpɔːʃn/
possession /pəˈzeʃn/
postcard /ˈpəʊskɑːd/
practise /ˈpræktɪs/
present (n) /ˈprezənt/

privacy /ˈprɪvəsɪ/
prize /praɪz/
rare /reə(r)/
rarely /ˈreəlɪ/
rebuild /riːˈbɪld/
refuse (n) /ˈrefjuːs/
relationship /rɪˈleɪʃnʃɪp/
remind /rɪˈmaɪnd/
rent /rent/
repair /rɪˈpeə(r)/
respect /rɪˈspekt/
rules /ruːlz/
semi-detached /semɪ dɪˈtætʃt/
serve /sɜːv/
service /ˈsɜːvɪs/
shower /ˈʃaʊə(r)/
shy /ʃaɪ/
specialist /ˈspeʃəlɪst/
stamp /stæmp/
starving /ˈstɑːvɪŋ/
stress /stres/
strict /strɪkt/
struggle /ˈstrʌɡl/
stubborn /ˈstʌbən/
subject(n) /ˈsʌbdʒɪkt/
suburb /ˈsʌbɜːb/
suitable /ˈsuːtəbl/
suspicious /səˈspɪʃəs/
swap /swɒp/
tank /tæŋk/
tense /tens/
terraced /ˈterəst/
thin /θɪn/
thoroughly /ˈθʌrəlɪ/
tourist /ˈtʊərɪst/
toy /tɔɪ/
tradition /trəˈdɪʃn/
traffic /ˈtræfɪk/
travel /ˈtrævl/
treasures /ˈtreʒəz/
trip /trɪp/
vacuum cleaner /ˈvækjʊm kliːnə(r)/
vandals /ˈvændlz/
view /vjuː/
vital /ˈvaɪtl/
watch (n) /wɒtʃ/
wedding /ˈwedɪŋ/
wool /wʊl/
worth /wɜːθ/

Unit Four

adolescent /ædəˈlesənt/
alibi /ˈælɪbaɪ/
amateur /ˈæmətə/
approximately /əˈprɒksəmətlɪ/
assault /əˈsɒlt/
attack /əˈtæk/
aware /əˈweə(r)/
banknotes /ˈbæŋknəʊts/
black market /blæk ˈmɑːkɪt/
bother /ˈbɒðə(r)/

burglar alarm /ˈbɜːglər əlɑːm/
burglary /ˈbɜːglərɪ/
carelessness /ˈkeələsnəs/
carpet /ˈkɑːpɪt/
china /ˈtʃaɪnə/
committed /kəˈmɪtɪd/
crime /kraɪm/
criminal /ˈkrɪmɪnəl/
decrease(n) /ˈdiːkriːs/
delicate /ˈdelɪkət/
destroy /dɪˈstrɔɪ/
detect /dɪˈtekt/
detergent /dɪˈtɜːdʒənt/
diver /ˈdaɪvə(r)/
domestic /dəˈmestɪk/
double /ˈdʌbl/
drill /drɪl/
drunk /drʌŋk/
dust /dʌst/
elegant /ˈelɪgənt/
estimate(n) /ˈestɪmət/
evidence /ˈevɪdəns/
false /fɒls/
fog /fɒg/
force /fɔːs/
forgery /ˈfɔːdʒərɪ/
grab /græb/
guard /gɑːd/
halve /hɑːv/
identify /aɪˈdentɪfaɪ/
illegal /ɪˈliːgl/
increase (n) /ˈɪŋkriːs/
inherit /ɪnˈherɪt/
install /ɪnˈstɔːl/
insurance /ɪnˈʃuərəns/
invention /ɪnˈvenʃn/
jealousy /ˈdʒeləsɪ/
jewellery /ˈdʒuːəlrɪ/
joke /dʒəʊk/
kidnap /ˈkɪdnæp/
mess /mes/
mugging /ˈmʌgɪŋ/
murder /ˈmɜːdə(r)/
nasty /ˈnɑːstɪ/
nest /nest/
offence /əˈfens/
opportunity /ɒpəˈtʃuːnətɪ/
policy /ˈpɒləsɪ/
portable /ˈpɔːtəbl/
possessions /pəˈzeʃənz/
powerless /ˈpaʊələs/
precautions /prɪˈkɔːʃnz/
prevent /prɪˈvent/
prevention /prɪˈvenʃn/
protect /prəˈtekt/
quarrel /ˈkwɒrəl/
raids /reɪdz/
receipt /rɪˈsiːt/
recommendation /rekəmenˈdeɪʃn/
revenge /rɪˈvendʒ/
reverse /rɪˈvɜːs/
risk (n) /rɪsk/

screen /skriːn/
shoplift /ˈʃɒplɪft/
shotgun /ˈʃɒtgʌn/
snow /snəʊ/
speeding /ˈspiːdɪŋ/
stable /ˈsteɪbl/
stealing /ˈstiːlɪŋ/
survey(n) /ˈsɜːveɪ/
suspect(v) /səˈspekt/
target /ˈtɑːgɪt/
technique /tekˈniːk/
technology /tekˈnɒlədʒɪ/
theft /θeft/
thief /θiːf/
trend /trend/
vulnerable /ˈvʌlnərəbl/

Unit Five

accident /ˈæksɪdənt/
accompanied /əˈkʌmpənɪd/
aches /eɪks/
ahead /əˈhed/
aim /eɪm/
alone /əˈləʊn/
alternative /ɔːlˈtɜːnətɪv/
although /ɔːlˈðəʊ/
ancient /ˈeɪnʃnt/
army /ˈɑːmɪ/
baker /ˈbeɪkə(r)/
billiards /ˈbɪljədz/
board games /ˈbɔːd geɪmz/
borrow /ˈbɒrəʊ/
bricks /brɪks/
brilliant /ˈbrɪljənt/
carvings /ˈkɑːvɪŋz/
casualty /ˈkæʒʊəltɪ/
chess /tʃes/
childhood /ˈtʃaɪldhʊd/
compact disc /kɒmpæk ˈdɪsk/
competition /kɒmpəˈtɪʃn/
crash /kræʃ/
deal /diːl/
debt /det/
despite /dɪˈspaɪt/
documents /ˈdɒkjəmənts/
draughts /drɑːfts/
dreadful /ˈdredfl/
drums /drʌmz/
enthusiasts /ɪnˈθjuːzɪæsts/
event /ɪˈvent/
eventually /ɪˈventʃəlɪ/
export (n) /ˈekspɔːt/
fair /feə(r)/
fashionable /ˈfæʃnəbl/
favourite /ˈfeɪvrət/
fitness /ˈfɪtnəs/
flags /flægz/
fold /fəʊld/
gear /gɪə(r)/
guarantee /gærənˈtiː/
gym /dʒɪm/

heap /hi:p/
heart /hɑ:t/
highly /ˈhaɪlɪ/
hockey /ˈhɒkɪ/
huge /hju:dʒ/
hunting /ˈhʌntɪŋ/
imported /ɪmˈpɔ:tɪd/
incredibly /ɪŋˈkredəblɪ/
innocence /ˈɪnəsəns/
invent /ɪnˈvent/
invention /ɪnˈvenʃn/
inventor /ɪnˈventə(r)/
investment /ɪnˈvesmənt/
keen /ki:n/
knock over /nɒk ˈəʊvə(r)/
label /ˈleɪbl/
landmark /ˈlænmɑ:k/
leisure /ˈleʒə(r)/
leisure industry /ˈleʒə(r) ɪndʌstrɪ/
loan /ləʊn/
loose /lu:s/
lungs /lʌnz/
match /mætʃ/
medal /ˈmedl/
melt /melt/
memories /ˈmemrɪz/
metal /ˈmetl/
mugged /mʌgd/
obsession /əbˈseʃn/
origins /ˈɒrɪdʒɪnz/
overtake /əʊvəˈteɪk/
pains /peɪnz/
path /pɑ:θ/
players /ˈpleɪəz/
preparation /prepəˈreɪʃn/
provincial /prəˈvɪnʃl/
quiz /kwɪz/
racquet /ˈrækɪt/
rally /ˈrælɪ/
ravine /rəˈvi:n/
referee /refəˈri:/
regular /ˈregjələ(r)/
regularly /ˈregjələlɪ/
relax /rɪˈlæks/
replace /rɪˈpleɪs/
representative /reprəˈzentətɪv/
rivalry /ˈraɪvəlrɪ/
rollerskating /ˈrəʊləskeɪtɪŋ/
rugby /ˈrʌgbɪ/
safety /ˈseɪftɪ/
score /skɔ:(r)/
screaming /ˈskri:mɪŋ/
season /ˈsi:zn/
shout /ʃaʊt/
silence /ˈsaɪləns/
similar /ˈsɪmələ(r)/
single /ˈsɪŋgl/
slope /sləʊp/
spine /spaɪn/
squash /skwɒʃ/
stadium /ˈsteɪdɪəm/
stamina /ˈstæmɪnə/

storage /ˈstɔ:rɪdʒ/
straight /streɪt/
strength /streŋθ/
supply /səˈplaɪ/
take off /teɪk ˈɒf/
terminus /ˈtɜ:mɪnəs/
tiles /taɪlz/
tin /tɪn/
tomb /tu:m/
tracksuit /ˈtræksu:t/
truth /tru:θ/
valuables /ˈvæljəblz/
wooden /ˈwʊdn/
workshop /ˈwɜ:kʃɒp/
wrapping /ˈræpɪŋ/

Unit Six

abandon /əˈbændən/
addition /əˈdɪʃn/
afford /əˈfɔ:d/
ambition /æmˈbɪʃn/
ambulance /ˈæmbjələns/
anger /ˈæŋgə(r)/
anticipation /æntɪsɪˈpeɪʃn/
attic /ˈætɪk/
balloon /bəˈlu:n/
basket /ˈbɑ:skɪt/
beach /bi:tʃ/
beg /beg/
bite /baɪt/
booklet /ˈbʊklət/
boots /bu:ts/
bowl /bəʊl/
bucket /ˈbʌkɪt/
canal /kəˈnæl/
capital /ˈkæpɪtl/
categories /ˈkætəgrɪz/
caution /ˈkɔ:ʃn/
change /tʃeɪndʒ/
charter /ˈtʃɑ:tə(r)/
choice /tʃɔɪs/
coach /kəʊtʃ/
columns /ˈkɒləmz/
constraints /kənˈstreɪnts/
contribution /kɒntrɪˈbju:ʃn/
countryside /ˈkʌntrɪsaɪd/
crease /kri:s/
crossroads /ˈkrɒsrəʊdz/
cruise /kru:z/
cry /kraɪ/
currency /ˈkʌrənsɪ/
delay /dɪˈleɪ/
delayed /dɪˈleɪd/
desolate /ˈdesələt/
diary /ˈdaɪərɪ/
disposable /dɪˈspəʊzəbl/
draw /drɔ:/
enclosed /ɪŋˈkləʊzd/
environment /ɪnˈvaɪərənmənt/
essential /ɪˈsenʃl/
extreme /ɪkˈstri:m/

facilities /fə'sɪlɪtɪz/
familiar /fə'mɪljə(r)/
fare /feə(r)/
ferry /'ferɪ/
festival /'festɪvl/
fever /'fi:və(r)/
flames /fleɪmz/
flavour /'fleɪvə(r)/
flight /flaɪt/
former /'fɔ:mə(r)/
frog /frɒg/
frustrated /frə'streɪtɪd/
fulfil /fʊl'fɪl/
furious /'fjʊərɪəs/
generous /'dʒenrəs/
globe /gləʊb/
helicopter /'helɪkɒptə(r)/
homesickness /'həʊmsɪknəs/
honeymoon /'hʌnɪmu:n/
hovercraft /'hɒvəkrɑ:ft/
hungry /'hʌŋgrɪ/
independent /ɪndɪ'pendənt/
inhabitants /ɪn'hæbɪtənts/
inoculate /ɪn'ɒkjəleɪt/
intensity /ɪn'tensɪtɪ/
jeep /dʒi:p/
journey /'dʒ3:nɪ/
knot /nɒt/
landing /'lændɪŋ/
latter /'lætə(r)/
lift /lɪft/
luggage /'lʌgɪdʒ/
memorable /'memrəbl/
memory /'memrɪ/
motel /məʊ'tel/
movement /'mu:vmənt/
network /'netw3:k/
once /wʌns/
overcoat /'əʊvəkəʊt/
overland /'əʊvəlænd/
pack (v) /pæk/
package /'pækɪdʒ/
panic /'pænɪk/
passenger /'pæsɪndʒə(r)/
policy /'pɒləsɪ/
pond /pɒnd/
portion /'pɔ:ʃn/
position /pə'zɪʃn/
regional /'ri:dʒənl/
reply /rɪ'plaɪ/
representative /reprə'zentətɪv/
reservation /rezə'veɪʃn/
resident /'rezɪdənt/
route /ru:t/
sand /sænd/
scheduled /'ʃedʒu:ld/
sense /sens/
shallow /'ʃæləʊ/
shapes /ʃeɪps/
solution /sə'lu:ʃn/
specialise /'speʃəlaɪz/
sting /stɪŋ/

stone /stəʊn/
suitable /'su:təbl/
sunglasses /'sʌnglɑ:sɪz/
theory /'θɪərɪ/
thumb /θʌm/
tour /tʊə/
traffic lights /'træfɪk laɪts/
triangle /'traɪæŋgl/
turning /'t3:nɪŋ/
unit /'ju:nɪt/
unpack /ʌn'pæk/
unpredictable /ʌnprə'dɪktəbl/
van /væn/
vending machine /'vendɪŋ məʃi:n/
wallet /'wɒlɪt/
weight /weɪt/
widely /'waɪdlɪ/
winner /'wɪnə(r)/

Unit Seven

accessories /æk'sesərɪz/
addiction /ə'dɪkʃn/
anniversary /ænə'v3:sərɪ/
atmosphere /'ætməsfɪə/
authentic /ɔ:'θentɪk/
blood /blʌd/
build up /bɪld 'ʌp/
calories /'kælərɪz/
cereals /'sɪərɪəlz/
chilled /tʃɪld/
commercial /kə'm3:ʃl/
complex /'kɒmpleks/
container /kən'teɪnə(r)/
cool /ku:l/
debate /dɪ'beɪt/
dessert /dɪ'z3:t/
diet /'daɪət/
directions /dɪ'rekʃnz/
discount /'dɪskaʊnt/
disease /dɪ'zi:z/
display /dɪ'spleɪ/
distribution /dɪstrɪ'bju:ʃn/
fattening /'fætnɪŋ/
fibre /'faɪbə(r)/
flavouring /'fleɪvrɪŋ/
freezer /'fri:zə(r)/
frozen /'frəʊzn/
grilled /grɪld/
grip /grɪp/
habit /'hæbɪt/
harmless /'hɑ:mləs/
headache /'hedeɪk/
herbs /h3:bz/
leaflet /'li:flət/
measure /'meʒə(r)/
multiply /'mʌltɪplaɪ/
newsletter /'nju:zletə(r)/
nut /nʌt/
nutrition /nju:'trɪʃn/
outdoor /'aʊtdɔ:(r)/
overweight /əʊvə'weɪt/

pour /pɔː(r)/
proportion /prə'pɔːʃn/
pulses /'pʌlsɪz/
rapidly /'ræpədlɪ/
recipes /'resəpɪz/
refrigerators /rɪ'frɪdʒəreɪtəz/
research /'riːsɜːtʃ/
sofa /'səʊfə/
specialities /speʃɪ'ælətɪz/
spices /'spaɪsɪz/
square /skweə(r)/
stale /steɪl/
stomach-ache /'stʌmək eɪk/
takeaway /'teɪkəweɪ/
tend /tend/
thermometer /θə'mɒmətə(r)/
traditional /trə'dɪʃnl/
undercooked /ʌndə'kʊkt/
whereas /weə'ræz/
while /waɪl/

Unit Eight

accept /ək'sept/
access /'ækses/
account /ə'kaʊnt/
accuracy /'ækjʊərəsɪ/
accurately /'ækjʊərətlɪ/
admit /əd'mɪt/
aerosol /'eərəsɒl/
angle /'æŋgl/
balance /'bæləns/
ballet /'bæleɪ/
ban /bæn/
benefit /'benəfɪt/
bent /bent/
boiler /'bɔɪlə(r)/
bookings /'bʊkɪŋz/
breakdown /'breɪkdaʊn/
briefly /'briːflɪ/
cable /'keɪbl/
calculation /kælkjə'leɪʃn/
computerisation /kəmpjuːtəraɪ'zeɪʃn/
confidential /kɒnfɪ'denʃl/
confiscate /'kɒnfɪskeɪt/
consequence /'kɒnsɪkwəns/
consistently /kən'sɪstəntlɪ/
constant /'kɒnstənt/
continuous /kən'tɪnjʊəs/
conventional /kən'venʃnəl/
convincing /kən'vɪnsɪŋ/
cope /kəʊp/
currently /'kʌrəntlɪ/
decade /'dekeɪd/
defect /'diːfekt/
defence /dɪ'fens/
disaster /dɪ'zɑːstə(r)/
discover /dɪ'skʌvə(r)/
discovery /dɪ'skʌvrɪ/
distraction /dɪ'strækʃn/
disturbance /dɪ'stɜːbəns/
drawback /'drɔːbæk/

drought /draʊt/
efficient /ɪ'fɪʃnt/
expression /ɪk'spreʃn/
faculty /'fækəltɪ/
fax /fæks/
flooding /'flʌdɪŋ/
forecast /'fɔːkɑːst/
fresh /freʃ/
fundamental /fʌndə'mentl/
generation /dʒenə'reɪʃn/
growth /grəʊθ/
handwriting /'hændraɪtɪŋ/
hassle /'hæsl/
healthy /'helθɪ/
heatwave /'hiːtweɪv/
heavy /'hevɪ/
household /'haʊshəʊld/
impact /'ɪmpækt/
imperfection /ɪmpə'fekʃn/
increase (v) /ɪŋ'kriːs/
increase (n) /'ɪŋkriːs/
industrial /ɪn'dʌstrɪəl/
invasion /ɪn'veɪʒn/
invent /ɪn'vent/
issues /'ɪʃuːz/
lens /lenz/
limit /'lɪmɪt/
memo /'meməʊ/
misbehave /mɪsbɪ'heɪv/
necessity /nɪ'sesətɪ/
nuclear /'njuːklɪə/
operator /'ɒpəreɪtə(r)/
opinion /ə'pɪnjən/
overseas /əʊvə'siːz/
pastime /'pɑːstaɪm/
population /pɒpjə'leɪʃn/
powerful /'paʊəfl/
predict /prɪ'dɪkt/
predictable /prɪ'dɪktəbl/
prediction /prɪ'dɪkʃn/
pressure /'preʃə(r)/
prestigious /prɪ'stɪdʒəs/
printer /'prɪntə(r)/
process /'prəʊses/
prospect /'prɒspekt/
publicity /pʌb'lɪsətɪ/
realistic /rɪə'lɪstɪk/
reception /rɪ'sepʃn/
regions /'riːdʒnz/
replacement /rɪ'pleɪsmənt/
reputation /repjə'teɪʃn/
responsible /rɪ'spɒnsɪbl/
result /rɪ'zʌlt/
retirement /rɪ'taɪəmənt/
revolution /revə'luːʃn/
risky /'rɪskɪ/
salary /'sælrɪ/
satellite /'sætəlaɪt/
scholarship /'skɒləʃɪp/
scratch /skrætʃ/
severe /sə'vɪə/
significant /sɪg'nɪfɪkənt/

single /ˈsɪŋgl/
software /ˈsɒftweə(r)/
surface /ˈsɜːfɪs/
syrup /ˈsɪrəp/
tap /tæp/
tendency /ˈtendənsɪ/
thirst /θɜːst/
tiny /ˈtaɪnɪ/
tooth /tuːθ/
trademark /ˈtreɪdmɑːk/
transactions /trænˈzækʃnz/
underneath /ˌʌndəˈniːθ/
value /ˈvæljuː/
variation /ˌveərɪˈeɪʃn/
wire /ˈwaɪə(r)/
workforce /ˈwɜːkfɔːs/
workload /ˈwɜːkləʊd/

Unit Nine

afterwards /ˈɑːftəwədz/
allergy /ˈælədʒɪ/
ankle /ˈæŋkl/
apology /əˈpɒlədʒɪ/
athletes /ˈæθliːts/
bandage /ˈbændɪdʒ/
bargain /ˈbɑːgən/
bleed /bliːd/
boundary /ˈbaʊndrɪ/
cancer /ˈkænsə/
champion /ˈtʃæmpɪən/
championship /ˈtʃæmpɪənʃɪp/
childhood /ˈtʃaɪldhʊd/
commentary /ˈkɒməntrɪ/
compulsory /kəmˈpʌlsrɪ/
concentrate /ˈkɒnsəntreɪt/
copy /ˈkɒpɪ/
cure /kjʊə/
damaging /ˈdæmədʒɪŋ/
decrease (n) /ˈdiːkriːs/
deter /dɪˈtɜː/
disinfectant /ˌdɪsɪnˈfektənt/
disruption /dɪsˈrʌpʃn/
dose /dəʊs/
doubt /daʊt/
efficiency /ɪˈfɪʃnsɪ/
enemy /ˈenəmɪ/
energy /ˈenədʒɪ/
enraged /ɪnˈreɪdʒd/
evident /ˈevɪdənt/
existence /ɪgˈzɪstəns/
expose /ɪkˈspəʊz/
fit /fɪt/
fitness /ˈfɪtnəs/
fortune /ˈfɔːtʃuːn/
frequently /ˈfriːkwəntlɪ/
fright /fraɪt/
garlic /ˈgɑːlɪk/
giggle /ˈgɪgl/
gradually /ˈgrædʒəlɪ/
historic /hɪsˈtɒrɪk/
ignore /ɪgˈnɔː(r)/

imagination /ɪˌmædʒɪˈneɪʃn/
inactive /ɪnˈæktɪv/
inadequately /ɪnˈædɪkwətlɪ/
incredible /ɪŋˈkredɪbl/
inexpensive /ˌɪnɪkˈspensɪv/
ingredients /ɪŋˈgriːdɪənts/
instructions /ɪnˈstrʌkʃnz/
interval /ˈɪntəvl/
irony /ˈaɪərənɪ/
irritate /ˈɪrɪteɪt/
jogging /ˈdʒɒgɪŋ/
joyous /ˈdʒɔɪəs/
legend /ˈledʒənd/
lengthened /ˈleŋθənd/
lifestyle /ˈlaɪfstaɪl/
lightweight /ˈlaɪtweɪt/
limbs /lɪmz/
limp /lɪmp/
marathon /ˈmærəθən/
medicine /ˈmedsn/
midday /ˌmɪdˈdeɪ/
monitor /ˈmɒnɪtə(r)/
motivated /ˈməʊtɪveɪtɪd/
nerves /nɜːvz/
notable /ˈnəʊtəbl/
outdoor /ˌaʊtˈdɔː(r)/
painful /ˈpeɪnfl/
pension /ˈpenʃn/
plains /pleɪnz/
pointless /ˈpɔɪntləs/
popularity /ˌpɒpjəˈlærətɪ/
proof /pruːf/
protection /prəˈtekʃn/
punish /ˈpʌnɪʃ/
range /reɪndʒ/
regret /rɪˈgret/
regular /ˈregjələ(r)/
relative /ˈrelətɪv/
remedy /ˈremədɪ/
revival /rɪˈvaɪvl/
rocky /ˈrɒkɪ/
roof /ruːf/
rough /rʌf/
routine /ruːˈtiːn/
seed /siːd/
sensitive /ˈsensətɪv/
skin /skɪn/
slippery /ˈslɪprɪ/
sneeze /sniːz/
sniff /snɪf/
socket /ˈsɒkɪt/
sore /sɔː(r)/
spectators /spekˈteɪtəz/
speculation /ˌspekjəˈleɪʃn/
spoil /spɔɪl/
spread /spred/
steam /stiːm/
stereotype /ˈsterɪəʊtaɪp/
stimulate /ˈstɪmjəleɪt/
strength /streŋθ/
sunburnt /ˈsʌnbɜːnt/
sunshine /ˈsʌnʃaɪn/

swollen /ˈswəʊlən/
symptoms /ˈsɪmptəmz/
teenagers /ˈtiːneɪdʒəz/
temptation /tempˈteɪʃn/
thirsty /ˈθɜːstɪ/
throughout /θruːˈaʊt/
toe /təʊ/
treatment /ˈtriːtmənt/
unfriendly /ʌnˈfrendlɪ/
unhurt /ʌnˈhɜːt/
vast /vɑːst/
victory /ˈvɪktrɪ/
waistline /ˈweɪslaɪn/
warmth /wɔːmθ/
waterproof /ˈwɔːtəpruːf/

Unit Ten

acceptable /əkˈseptəbl/
agreement /əˈɡriːmənt/
announcement /əˈnaʊnsmənt/
annoy /əˈnɔɪ/
assistant /əˈsɪstənt/
attract /əˈtrækt/
bill /bɪl/
blame /bleɪm/
bracelets /ˈbreɪsləts/
branch /brɑːntʃ/
brochure /ˈbrəʊʃʊə/
candles /ˈkændlz/
carve /kɑːv/
cashier /kæˈʃɪə/
challenge /ˈtʃælɪndʒ/
chat /tʃæt/
checkout /ˈtʃekaʊt/
chest /tʃest/
coins /kɔɪnz/
commission /kəˈmɪʃn/
compare /kəmˈpeə(r)/
congratulate /kənˈɡrætʃəleɪt/
convenient /kənˈviːnɪənt/
crafts /krɑːfts/
cupboard /ˈkʌbəd/
customer /ˈkʌstəmə(r)/
cutlery /ˈkʌtlərɪ/
direct /daɪˈrekt/
exclusive /ɪkˈskluːsɪv/
executive /ɪɡˈzekjətɪv/
fondness /ˈfɒndnəs/
footware /ˈfʊtweə(r)/
helpful /ˈhelpfʊl/
indoors /ɪnˈdɔːz/
innovative /ˈɪnəvətɪv/
interrupt /ˌɪntəˈrʌpt/
invention /ɪnˈvenʃn/
lightweight /ˈlaɪtweɪt/
luxury /ˈlʌkʃərɪ/
mail-order /ˈmeɪlɔːdə(r)/
make-up /ˈmeɪkʌp/
marble /ˈmɑːbl/
massive /ˈmæsɪv/
misleading /mɪsˈliːdɪŋ/

old-fashioned /əʊldˈfæʃnd/
outfit /ˈaʊtfɪt/
passer-by /pɑːsəˈbaɪ/
passion /ˈpæʃn/
patience /ˈpeɪʃns/
persuasive /pəˈsweɪsɪv/
precious /ˈpreʃəs/
purchase /ˈpɜːtʃəs/
pushy /ˈpʊʃɪ/
reality /rɪˈælətɪ/
recital /rɪˈsaɪtl/
retail /ˈriːteɪl/
rings /rɪŋz/
rude /ruːd/
scenario /səˈnɑːrɪəʊ/
shame /ʃeɪm/
socks /sɒks/
souvenir /suːvəˈnɪə/
store /stɔː(r)/
substitute /ˈsʌbstɪtʃuːt/
suit /suːt/
tasteful /ˈteɪsfl/
treat /triːt/
trolley /ˈtrɒlɪ/
unhelpful /ʌnˈhelpfl/
utensils /juːˈtenslz/
wallet /ˈwɒlɪt/
warmly /ˈwɔːmlɪ/

Unit Eleven

abroad /əˈbrɔːd/
ambitious /æmˈbɪʃəs/
aristocrat /ˈærɪstəkræt/
bankrupt /ˈbæŋkrʌpt/
battery /ˈbætrɪ/
breathe /briːð/
bury /ˈberɪ/
celebrity /səˈlebrətɪ/
ceremony /ˈserəmənɪ/
climate /ˈklaɪmət/
concern /kənˈsɜːn/
confidence /ˈkɒnfɪdəns/
create /kriːˈeɪt/
crops /krɒps/
cyclist /ˈsaɪklɪst/
demand /dɪˈmɑːnd/
destruction /dɪˈstrʌkʃn/
earthquake /ˈɜːθkweɪk/
eruption /ɪˈrʌpʃn/
exceed /ɪkˈsiːd/
explosion /ɪkˈspləʊʒn/
extinct /ɪkˈstɪŋkt/
failure /ˈfeɪljə/
famine /ˈfæmɪn/
fault /fɔːlt/
forest /ˈfɒrɪst/
fumes /fjuːmz/
fur /fɜː/
gift /ɡɪft/
guidelines /ˈɡaɪdlaɪnz/
handouts /ˈhændaʊts/

harvest /'hɑːvɪst/
hurricane /'hʌrɪkən/
improve /ɪm'pruːv/
invisible /ɪn'vɪzɪbl/
length /leŋθ/
litter /'lɪtə(r)/
mask /mɑːsk/
mud /mʌd/
pedestrian /pə'destrɪən/
planet /'plænət/
pollution /pə'luːʃn/
preference /'prefrəns/
priority /praɪ'ɒrətɪ/
profitable /'prɒfɪtəbl/
proposal /prə'pəʊzl/
publish /'pʌblɪʃ/
recycling /riː'saɪklɪŋ/
riot /'raɪət/
short-sighted /ʃɔːt'saɪtɪd/
shortage /'ʃɔːtɪdʒ/
smog /smɒg/
solution /sə'luːʃn/
subsequent /'sʌbsɪkwənt/
supporter /sə'pɔːtə(r)/
survive /sə'vaɪv/
tax /tæks/
temporarily /'temprəlɪ/
terrorist /'terərɪst/
timber /'tɪmbə(r)/
unaware /ʌnə'weə(r)/
underground /'ʌndəgraʊnd/
unsure /ʌn'ʃʊə(r)/
volcanos /vɒl'keɪnəʊz/
zip /zɪp/

Unit Twelve

aggressive /ə'gresɪv/
amenities /ə'miːnətɪz/
anger /'æŋgə(r)/
assassination /əsæsɪ'neɪʃn/
battered /'bætəd/
battle /'bætl/
birth /bɜːθ/
bizarre /bɪ'zɑː(r)/
bullying /'bʊlɪŋ/
cage /keɪdʒ/
cattle /'kætl/
cautious /'kɔːʃəs/
contemporary /kən'temprɪ/
cope /kəʊp/
copies /'kɒpɪz/
counselling /'kaʊnslɪŋ/
creative /kriː'eɪtɪv/
crockery /'krɒkərɪ/
desire /dɪ'zaɪə(r)/
desperate /'despərət/
exhausted /ɪg'zɔːstɪd/
exhilarating /ɪg'zɪləreɪtɪŋ/
fiction /'fɪkʃn/
forceful /'fɔːsfl/
funeral /'fjuːnrəl/

gentle /'dʒentl/
hesitant /'hezɪtənt/
horoscope /'hɒrəskəʊp/
hospitable /hɒ'spɪtəbl/
hurt /hɜːt/
insults /'ɪnsʌlts/
irritable /'ɪrɪtəbl/
isolation /aɪsə'leɪʃn/
loneliness /'ləʊnlɪnəs/
lonely /'ləʊnlɪ/
misery /'mɪzərɪ/
motivation /məʊtɪ'veɪʃn/
mug /mʌg/
neglect /nɪ'glekt/
novel /'nɒvl/
occupation /ɒkjə'peɪʃn/
option /'ɒpʃn/
outcome /'aʊtkʌm/
parachute /'pærəʃuːt/
passionate /'pæʃnət/
precaution /prɪ'kɔːʃn/
proper /'prɒpə(r)/
quarrel /'kwɒrəl/
reptile /'reptaɪl/
resentful /rɪ'zentfl/
romance /rə'mæns/
rural /'rʊərəl/
sadness /'sædnəs/
satisfy /'sætɪsfaɪ/
scheme /skiːm/
seldom /'seldəm/
shoulder /'ʃəʊldə(r)/
snake /sneɪk/
stardom /'stɑːdəm/
stare /steə(r)/
status /'steɪtəs/
suicide /'suːɪsaɪd/
sympathetic /sɪmpə'θetɪk/
sympathy /'sɪmpəθɪ/
synthetic /sɪn'θetɪk/
tear /tɪə(r)/
term /tɜːm/
texture /'tekstʃə(r)/
thick /θɪk/
threat /θret/
tolerance /'tɒlərəns/
transform /træns'fɔːm/
typical /'tɪpɪkl/
unreasonable /ʌn'riːznəbl/
upset /ʌp'set/
urban /'ɜːbən/
velvet /'velvət/
vet /vet/
wax /wæks/
weep /wiːp/
wretched /'retʃɪd/